WORLD SERIES:

THE GAMES AND THE PLAYERS

Robert Smith

WORLD SERIES:

THE GAMES AND THE PLAYERS

Garden City, New York

DOUBLEDAY & COMPANY, INC.

1967

FOR MY LOVING DAUGHTER
NORA

LIBRARY OF CONGRESS CATALOG CARD NUMBER 67–19130
COPYRIGHT © 1967 BY ROBERT SMITH
ALL RIGHTS RESERVED
PRINTED IN THE UNITED STATES OF AMERICA
FIRST EDITION

Illustrations

Muddy Ruel scores the winning run for Washington in the 1924 series

Baseball greats mourn the death of Christy Mathewson, 1925

Joe DiMaggio scores in 1939 series after Keller bowls over Cincinnati catcher Lombardi

Ducky Medwick slides into third and starts a riot, 1934

Connie Mack's last great team, the Athletics of 1931

Mickey Cochrane voices comments in 1934 series as Pepper Martin scores

Dizzy Dean with Will Rogers during the 1934 series

Joe DiMaggio singles against the Giants, 1937

Satchel Paige makes the World Series, 1948

Enos Slaughter of the Cardinals scores series-winning run against Red Sox, 1946

The call that possibly cost Cleveland a World Series victory in 1948

Mickey Owen loses the last-out strike and the dam bursts

Bob Turley and Elston Howard celebrate victory over Braves in Milwaukee, 1958

Milwaukee fan catches Mathews homer in 1957 series

Leo Durocher shows vast relief after Giants escape Cleveland's bases-loaded situation in 1954

Carl Erskine pitching for Brooklyn against the Yankees, 1953

Don Larsen escorted by Yogi Berra after perfect game against the Dodgers, 1956

The umpire misses a call in the 1952 series

Homer by Dodgers' Charlie Neal causes anguish to White Sox's Al Smith, 1959

Miracle catch by Willie Mays of Vic Wertz's drive in Giant-Indian game, 1954

Stengel and Durocher during 1951 series

Whitey Ford pitching for the Yankees against the Braves, 1957

Warren Spahn in action against the Yankees, 1957

Joe Black, Dodgers, tags out Yogi Berra in desperation play, 1952

Mickey Mantle carried from field in 1951 series

Fans try to snatch the caps of victorious Yankees, 1956

FOLLOWING PAGE 264

Joe Pepitone loses the throw as the Dodgers win out in 1963

Bill Mazeroski homers against the Yankees to win the series for Pittsburgh, 1960

Cincinnati's Elio Chacon scores against Yankees' Elston Howard, 1961

Cardinal catcher, Tim McCarver, protests call in 1964 series against Yankees

Cincinnati's Frank Robinson and Elio Chacon out of action on Berra's pop fly, 1961

Sandy Koufax, hero of Dodgers' four-straight series victory over Yanks in 1963

Willie Davis of the Dodgers roars his disagreement with call in game against Baltimore Orioles, 1966

Everyone, including Dodgers' Tommy Davis, hopes to catch homer by Frank Robinson of Orioles, 1966

1903

BOSTON A.L. vs. PITTSBURGH N.L.

WON BY BOSTON, 5 GAMES TO 3

Game Scores:

Pittsburgh 7	Boston 3	October 1 at Boston
Boston 3	Pittsburgh 0	October 2 at Boston
Pittsburgh 4	Boston 2	October 3 at Boston
Pittsburgh 5	Boston 4	October 6 at Pittsburgh
Boston 11	Pittsburgh 2	October 7 at Pittsburgh
Boston 6	Pittsburgh 3	October 8 at Pittsburgh
Boston 7	Pittsburgh 3	October 10 at Pittsburgh
Boston 3	Pittsburgh 0	October 13 at Boston

The first World's Championship Series between the American and National Leagues was a best-five-out-of-nine series which had no official sanction. The Boston Puritans, also called Somersets, and Pilgrims, were just a bush-league team to the National League folk and to many of the fans. The Pittsburgh team, with the great Hans Wagner at short, was the class of the country.

But Roxbury, Massachusetts, a part of Boston, was full of wild-eyed Irishmen who thought Jimmy Collins' Boston boys could lick any nine men in the world at baseball, foot-racing, rassling, or rough-and-tumble, and for either money or marbles. The players wanted to make sure it was for money, however,

9

and threatened a strike unless they were assured a divvy of the gate.

The winning player's share for the eight games was $1200. The losers got more because big-hearted Barney Dreyfuss, the Pittsburgh owner, turned his entire cut of the pot over to his players.

The hero of the series, by all that seems just, should have been the man who lost it—Deacon Phillippe, the great Pirate pitcher, who pitched five full games in the series and won three of them. He probably would have won four if the crowd roped off in the outfield in the seventh game had not necessitated a ground rule, making a fair hit that fell in the crowd good for three bases. The Boston team got five of these pop-fly triples.

Phillippe, a lanky right-hander from Rural Retreat, Virginia, was forced to carry an extra burden in this series because Pittsburgh was short of pitchers. The great Sam Leever had a sore arm and Edward Doheny, one of the regular staff, who had left the team at the end of the season, was, even while this World Series was going on, being committed to the insane asylum at Danvers, Massachusetts, after he had beaten over the head with a poker a number of men his fevered mind took for detectives.

Phillippe's task was eased a little by the fact that the eight games were spread through two weeks, because of the weather and because the Pittsburgh management was careful to postpone one game to make it fall on a Saturday. The Pittsburgh fans were wild about the Deacon. After he had won the fourth game (the first one played in Pittsburgh) the crowd carried him to the clubhouse, where he had to stand for thirty minutes and shake all the hands that were thrust upon him. Possibly this exercise took some of the gimp out of his arm, for he did not win another game. Before the seventh game, Phillippe received a diamond pin from his admirers.

Hans Wagner, the greatest shortstop in baseball, was expected to star in the series. He turned in some spectacular running stops and throws in the first two contests but he seemed far off his game as the series dragged through thirteen wet and chilly October days. His series batting average was only .214. And he made the final out in the last game when he went down swinging at the sharp-breaking curve of Big Bill Dinneen of Boston.

Dinneen was Boston's particular hero, although every one of this fast, scrappy, but light-hitting Boston team was carried around in triumph when the series was over. Dinneen, who became a famous umpire, did his best work in the second game when, with his frightening speed, he turned back the famous Pittsburgh sluggers (including Honus Wagner, Manager Fred Clarke, Tommy Leach, Jimmy Sebring, and Ginger Beaumont) with only three hits, struck out eleven, and gave his outfield but two chances. He did nearly as well in the final game, when he shut out the Pirates with four hits and struck out seven.

Lou Criger, the Boston catcher, turned in one of the cleverest plays of the series when he choked off a Pittsburgh rally in the fourth inning of the final game. Wagner, after singling, broke for second with Tommy Leach on third. Criger faked a throw to second and almost in the same motion snapped the ball down to Manager Jimmy Collins at third base to catch Leach flat-footed. To the Boston fans, this more than made up for Criger's poor play in the first game of the series. Apparently suffering from "stage fright," the great catcher in that game made two errors which helped account for four Pittsburgh runs. His tenseness was undoubtedly increased by one fact which did not come to light until years later: he had just turned down a $12,000 bribe to throw the series to the Pirates.

This first series between the American and National League champions proved two things: that the American League was really a major league; and that ball parks were too small to hold the crowds that a real championship series would draw. (There were other National-American League "city series" at the time but they hardly drew flies.)

The helmeted policemen at the third game in Boston had all they could do to keep the milling mob from crowding right on to the infield. To try to stop men and boys from climbing the low fences into the park was hopeless. The packed fans in the outfield pushed and swayed and shifted so that the size of the playing field altered from inning to inning.

After Boston lost the first game, the home fans must have decided that the wiseacres were right and that the Somerset-Pilgrims-Puritans (they were not yet called the Red Sox) did not belong on the same field as the great Pittsburgh club, for the second-game attendance was diminished. Once having tasted victory, however, the fans came howling back for more. More than a hundred made the journey to Pittsburgh to watch their boys drag triumph from sure defeat, and to swap taunts with Pittsburgh fans, players, and police.

Leading hitters:

BOSTON RED SOX
Stahl: .309

PITTSBURGH PIRATES
Sebring: .366

Winning pitchers:

BOSTON RED SOX
Young: won 2, lost 1
Dinneen: won 3, lost 1

PITTSBURGH PIRATES
Phillippe: won 3, lost 2

1904

NO WORLD SERIES

There was no World Series in 1904 because John McGraw said, "No." McGraw, manager of the New York Giants, champions of the National League, announced that he would pay no attention to the challenge from the Boston Americans, who had won again.

"They're just a bunch of —— bush leaguers," he said. But McGraw took that stand because owner John T. Brush of the Giants felt the same way, only double. To Brush, this whole American League was a gang of contract jumpers, malcontents, radicals, agitators, and plain semi-pros. Had McGraw alone been the one to decide, the series probably would have been played.

The Boston team just barely won the championship that year. But for one pitch, the team to challenge the Giants would have been the New York Highlanders (their home park was on the "highlands" where the Columbia-Presbyterian Medical Center now stands). Had the Highlanders won and Brush refused to meet *them* in a series, New York fans might have torn the park down, for the rivalry between the two teams was as fierce as that between New York and Brooklyn in a later day. But Brush would certainly have refused. He hated the very thought of that team up on the hill, which had "sneaked" into New York despite all the efforts of the Giants' owners to grab up or shut off any piece of ground big enough to play ball on.

The goat of the American League pennant race that year was pitcher Jack Chesbro, of North Adams, Massachusetts, star of the New York Highlanders. Chesbro was called "Algernon" for the same reason that a fat boy is called "Skinny," and called "Happy" because he usually was. It was his wild pitch in the ninth inning of the first game of a double-header with Boston that allowed the Boston team to put itself two games ahead, and out of reach, of New York. There were those who insisted that it was not a wild pitch at all but a passed ball—an error by the catcher —and that Chesbro's shame was undeserved. Happy Jack's widow tried for many years to have the records altered to "clear her husband's name." But teammates of Chesbro seemed to agree that the ball went "a mile over Catcher Jack Kleinow's head."

Jack Chesbro had done enough hard work that year to be forgiven for this late-season lapse. The game was played in New York on October 10, late enough for a World Series, before a regular World Series crowd—28,000, including a large contingent of Boston's Royal Rooters, who had brought along their band to play "Tessie," the Boston victory song. Chesbro had won forty-one games for New York that year, using his famous spitball, the trick pitch invented years before by Bobby Matthews, and recently reintroduced by Elmer Stricklett of the Chicago White Sox. And he seemed to be about to clinch the pennant for New York when that spitter got away from him and slow-footed Lou Criger came in to score.

The Boston pitchers had had a great season too. Cy Young, who even then was considered old enough to retire, pitched a perfect game against the Philadelphia Athletics that season, not a man reaching first. Jesse Tannehill of Boston had pitched a no-hitter too, with only two men reaching. And Bill Dinneen was as strong as ever, so the Boston fans and sportswriters were convinced that their boys could lick any team in the nation. They roared with rage when McGraw scorned the challenge. The place to decide whether their team was the equal of New York's was on the ball field, they felt, not in newspaper columns or in offhand conversation at a race track.

There was no denying that the Giants were a great team that year. Iron Man McGinnity, Christy Mathewson, and Dummy Taylor were all at the top of their form. They had the strongest infield in the league. And late in the season, they added to their outfield a brash, scrappy, hard-hitting, red-necked lad called Turkey Mike Donlin, who soon became the favorite of the fans.

McGraw himself played in only three games that year but he made himself felt in every game with his aggressive coaching, his rows with umpires, his public arguments with his bitter rival, Barney Dreyfuss of Pittsburgh, and his amazing swagger both off the field and on. To many people—and perhaps to himself— he must have seemed the biggest man in New York. He walked, talked, and dressed like a man on top of the world. No umpire, no ballplayer, no sportswriter, not even the president of the National League could prevail against him. He strutted from one triumph to another. And when the season was over he strutted at race tracks and cabarets in the company of the most famous figures of the day.

The Boston infield was also one of the best of all time. Jimmy Collins, at third base, was still exhibiting his specialty, the running bare-handed scoop and throw of a base-line bunt. Candy LaChance was the classiest first baseman in the world, to most fans' eyes. Hobe Ferris at second, and Freddy Parent at short, thanks to Manager Jimmy Collins' careful teaching, had turned into two of the cleverest men in the game. To the Boston Royal Rooters they looked every bit as strong as Tenney, Lowe, and Long, the great men who had played at Jimmy Collins' side on the old Boston Beaneaters (the National League entry).

They were still not a great hitting team. But they had Buck Freeman, who had led the league in home runs the year before, and Kip Selbach, considered by some the best lead-off man in the game.

The Boston team this year belonged to playboy John I. Taylor, son of General Charles Taylor, who owned the Boston *Globe*. General Taylor had bought the team and given it to his boy for a present, "to keep his mind occupied." They managed to keep his mind filled right to the brim as they scrambled, stumbled, and fought their way through a season that saw Boston, Chicago, and New York swap the league lead back and forth half a dozen times, right down to the season's end.

15

1905

NEW YORK N.L. vs. PHILADELPHIA A.L.

WON BY NEW YORK, 4 GAMES TO 1

Game Scores:

New York 3	Philadelphia 0	October 9 at Philadelphia
Philadelphia 3	New York 0	October 10 at New York
New York 9	Philadelphia 0	October 12 at Philadelphia
New York 1	Philadelphia 0	October 13 at New York
New York 2	Philadelphia 0	October 14 at New York

This was the shut-out series. And naturally the men to see, when the Giants played the Athletics in 1905, were the pitchers, all of whom still live in fame: Christy Mathewson, Chief Bender, Eddie Plank, Joe McGinnity, and Andy Coakley. All of them were at their best in the series and every one of them pitched each of his games well enough to win. In the only game where more than three runs were scored, Coakley's 9 to 0 defeat, only one run was earned. There were five errors behind Andy, three by the third baseman. There were five stolen bases.

The hero of this series was Christy Mathewson, the husky football star from Bucknell, the man who believed in percentages, who put the pressure on only when he needed to, who worked calmly, almost lazily, with perfect control, his tousled hair falling from under his cap, and his blue eyes cold as ice. Mathewson's

16

strange "fadeaway," which he had learned from a washed-up minor league pitcher, stood the Athletics on their ears. The fade-away was a slow reverse curve, given a great deal of spin by tight finger pressure, so that it seemed to be coming faster than it was and faded or lost momentum before the batter expected it to. It resembled the modern "screwball."

Mathewson pitched and won three full games, twenty-seven scoreless innings, in which he struck out eighteen, allowed but one walk, and gave up fourteen hits.

But young Charles Albert Bender, Philadelphia's handsome, smiling Indian, might have been the hero himself, had the breaks gone his way. Bender pitched two full games, eighteen innings, in which he allowed only two runs, one more than the Giants needed to win the deciding game for Mathewson.

Iron Man McGinnity pitched two games and won one. Using his looping, underhanded "Old Sal," he drove the Philadelphia batters crazy as they told each other the guy had nothing on the ball but his hand. Again and again McGinnity threw up balls that seemed as large as grapefruit, rising apparently right off the rubber to a point about even with the batter's chest. Again and again Philadelphia batters hauled off on these pitches only to see the ball go popping off their bats high into the air or squirting feebly to the ground. And some of them, despite the apparent fatness of Joe's pitches, could not meet the ball at all.

Eddie Plank of Philadelphia, who had won twenty-six games in the regular season, pitched two games in this series, in which he struck out eleven men. He allowed three runs in one game and one in another and each time he gave the Giants enough to win.

Missing from the series was a pitcher as famous as any of those who worked and better than any of them when he was right. He was George Edward "Rube" Waddell, Connie Mack's big, loose-jointed, bent-nosed, eccentric left-hander, who led the American League that year with twenty-six wins and eleven defeats. There were wise guys in Philadelphia and New York who told others, behind their hands, that some gambler had got next to Rube and paid him to stay out of the series. But not even a squad of police could have kept Rube out of the games if he had not had a sore arm, injured in a joking scuffle with Andy Coakley near the end of the season. Even with the big Rube ready to swagger out to the mound and blaze in his fast ball it is doubtful if the Athletics could have ever beaten Mathewson. In those days, as in this, a team had to have runs to win. And no one was getting any runs from The Big Six, as Mathewson was named in the sports columns. (The Big Six was a famed fire company in New York.)

There was, obviously, a minimum of hitting in this series. Only two players, both Giants, earned a batting average over .300. Turkey Mike Donlin had .316 and Roger Bresnahan, the catcher, had .313. The heaviest hitter of the Athletics was Topsy Hartsel, with an average of .294. There hadn't been a .300 hitter on the Athletics during the regular season either. Top man at the bat for Connie Mack that year was first baseman Harry Davis, who rated .284.

A good many of the fans came out to see the games in this series feeling sure that there would be hell to pay if tough John McGraw, who had scandalized the press of the nation by his "rowdyism," went to work on Connie Mack, the lean, soft-spoken manager of the Athletics. Why, that very season, in Pittsburgh (where he was always spoiling for a fight), McGraw had thrown a baseball at umpire Bob Emslie, whom McGraw always called "Blind Bob." And he had one day offered to fight every man in the Cincinnati ball park.

But in the World Series this year, little John was better behaved than he had ever been in his life before. As gracious in victory as he was intractable in defeat, he charmed everyone he met. The umpires, Hank O'Day (called Tank O'Day by the players because of his taste for beer) and John Sheridan, had no more trouble than if they'd been calling a set of college games.

The goat of the series, if there could be any in such a tight group of games, was perhaps Lave Cross, Philadelphia third baseman, who flubbed an easy chance with two out in the final inning of the third game to allow men to score from second and third. The very next day, with Plank hurling a four-hit game, Lave let a grounder go through his legs in the fourth inning and gave the Giants the single run they needed to win.

18

The 1905 World Series was the first officially sanctioned championship series between the winners of the pennants in the National and American Leagues. It was run under rules set up by baseball's National Commission and was shortened to a "four-out-of-seven" series, to give the clubs a chance to complete it before weather and waiting had tired out players and spectators.

Leading hitters:

NEW YORK GIANTS
Donlin: .316

PHILADELPHIA ATHLETICS
Hartsel: .294

Winning pitchers:

NEW YORK GIANTS
Mathewson: won 3, lost 0
McGinnity: won 1, lost 1

PHILADELPHIA ATHLETICS
Bender: won 1, lost 1

19

1906

CHICAGO A.L. vs. CHICAGO N.L.

WON BY WHITE SOX, 4 GAMES TO 2

Game Scores:

White Sox 2	Cubs 1	October 9 at West Side Park
Cubs 7	White Sox 1	October 10 at Comiskey Park
White Sox 3	Cubs 0	October 11 at West Side Park
Cubs 1	White Sox 0	October 12 at Comiskey Park
White Sox 8	Cubs 6	October 13 at West Side Park
White Sox 8	Cubs 3	October 14 at Comiskey Park

The most notable thing about the 1906 World Series to many fans who tried to attend it was the fact that, after it became clear that a real fight was in progress, there was not a park in Chicago big enough to hold everyone who wanted to get in to the games. Even bitter cold and threats of snow could not keep the crowds away. When the fifth game was played, with perfect weather at last, long lines extended in every direction from the old West Side ball park, and when the gates were thrown open many a ticket holder was lost in the crush. Late arrivals, with or without tickets, were lucky to get as far as the sidewalk near the park. Many an old-timer will never forget the milling, angry mobs outside the parks, the rows and rows of hackney cabs, the whinnying horses, the struggling cops.

This series finished forever the grumblings of the few old mossbacks who had maintained right along that the country could never support two major leagues.

The names of the heroes of the 1906 series still live in baseball history: Wildfire Schulte, the Cubs' deer-footed right fielder; Three-Finger Mordecai Brown, the Cubs' pitching wizard; Nick Altrock of the White Sox, then a truly great pitcher, and now better remembered as baseball's first great clown; Ed Walsh, the Big Moose, who took over Stricklett's spitball for his own specialty; fielder Jones, crafty leader of the White Sox; Johnny Kling of the Cubs, the best catcher in the game; and, of course, the Cubs' immortal trio: Joe Tinker, John Evers, and Frank Chance.

Yet perhaps the one outstanding performer, because his success was so unexpected and counted for so much, was a man hardly anyone had heard of before the series, and few people remember now: George Rohe of the White Sox, a substitute third baseman who found his name in the lineup only because George Davis, the regular shortstop, had been injured, and Lee Tannehill, the regular third baseman, had been moved over to short.

Rohe ruined Mordecai Brown's four-hitter in the first game and won the game for Nick Altrock (who also gave four hits) by slamming a triple in the fourth inning, then cantering home safely on a bad throw by Brown. In the third game, Rohe cinched victory for his team by driving in all the runs at once. He cleaned the bases in the sixth inning when he drove the first ball pitched to him far into left field for another triple. In the fifth game, a comedy of feeble pitching and high school fielding (the White Sox made six errors), Rohe went to bat four times to get a double and two singles, which helped his team pull out ahead. He earned a batting average of .333 for the series.

The White Sox that year were the Hitless Wonders, with a season team batting average of .228! They were not given a chance against the hard-hitting Cubs, even though they had won nineteen straight in their own league to grab the pennant after being hopelessly out of the race. Out-of-town papers did not even bother to send writers to cover the series. The Cubs were three-to-one favorites in Chicago the day before the first game

21

and few fans dared bet on the White Sox. The Cubs had the hitting, with Schulte, Steinfeldt, Hofman, Sheckard, and Chance. They had the greatest pitchers of the day: Brown, Orval Overall, and the tireless Eddie Reulbach. And they had the best-known double-play combination in history: Tinker to Evers to Chance.

But the Hitless Wonders outhit them—they turned up four .300 hitters in the series (Rohe, Donahue, Isbell, and Davis) while only Hofman of the Cubs made that grade. The White Sox pitchers outpitched them—though Eddie Reulbach pitched a great one-hitter and Mordecai Brown turned in a two-hit performance to win the fourth game. And the White Sox fielders outfielded them—in the one game where they fell apart to the tune of six errors, they still managed to come out with the runs needed to win. And of course it was an error that lost the first game for the Cubs.

Ed Walsh, the man who always seemed to be posing for his picture, threw a two-hitter of his own at the Cubs in winning the third game.

And in the fourth game the Cubs were themselves reduced to the status of hitless wonders, when they built a victory out of seven hits and at least five sacrifices—Joe Tinker taking the suicide route three times.

As the series moved along from game to game, with the weather becoming better and the chances of the underdog White Sox brighter and brighter, the whole city of Chicago seemed to go insane. There would be shouting and singing and argument and celebration night after night, hours after the game was over. And when the series had come to its unlooked-for end, the White Sox followers simply ran wild. They set out to grab every member of their team that they could lay their hands on —apparently to divide him up into small pieces for souvenirs. The tall-helmeted cops had to battle a pathway through the crowds to get the players to safety. Then the fans gathered before the grandstand and screamed for speeches until President Murphy of the Cubs came out and owned that his club had been licked by a better team, and a great team.

In this series too, overflow crowds had forced the adoption

of ground rules which made for a number of cheap doubles in some of the games and kept the police busy pushing the crowd back to make room enough to play. But not all the police maintained the judicial calm expected of them. In the first inning of the final game, after a hit by Davis of the White Sox had dropped into the edge of the crowd for a double, Wildfire Schulte, who had been waiting there for the ball, pointed his finger into a policeman's face and let out a howl of rage.

"He shoved me!" he screamed.

But all his protests were in vain.

Leading hitters:

CHICAGO WHITE SOX
Rohe and Donahue: .333

CHICAGO CUBS
Hofman: .304

Winning pitchers:

CHICAGO WHITE SOX
Altrock: won 1, lost 1
White: won 1, lost 1
Walsh: won 2, lost 0

CHICAGO CUBS
Brown: won 1, lost 2
Reulbach: won 1, lost 0

1907

CHICAGO N.L. vs. DETROIT A.L.

WON BY CHICAGO, 4 GAMES TO 0. ONE TIE GAME.

Game Scores:

Chicago 3	Detroit 3	October 8 at Chicago
(12 innings)		
Chicago 3	Detroit 1	October 9 at Chicago
Chicago 5	Detroit 1	October 10 at Chicago
Chicago 6	Detroit 1	October 11 at Detroit
Chicago 2	Detroit 0	October 12 at Detroit

When the Chicago Cubs won the National League pennant again in 1907, leading Pittsburgh home by 17 games, Frank Chance, now called the Peerless Leader, took no chances on blowing the World Series. As soon as it became apparent that Detroit was going to win the American League pennant, Chance set his Cubs to working out against Detroit weaknesses and strength. He made every player learn the hitting, fielding, and base-running habits of the men they were going to meet, drilled them in the "moves" of the Detroit pitchers, and hitched up all the loose ends in their own play. When the series began, the Cubs, not overconfident this time, but well-conditioned and thoroughly trained, were straining at the leash.

The feature of the series was the nerve-cracking first game, which lasted twelve innings, until darkness shut down with no decision reached. This was the closest the Detroit Tigers came to winning a game, and it was very close indeed. For Wild Bill Donovan of Detroit, who went the whole distance, had struck out in the ninth inning the man who should have been the final batter, for one of his twelve strikeouts of the game, when catcher Butch Schmidt, yielding at last to the strain, let the ball get away from him and Harry Steinfeldt scurried home with the run that tied it up for keeps.

The man who had been expected to star in the classic was Tyrus Cobb of Detroit, the fast fresh rookie who, in his second full season, had led the American League with a batting average of .350. As so often seems to happen, however, the stars of the regular season were dimmed in the series. Cobb was a flop at bat as was his slugging partner, Sam Crawford, called "Wahoo" because he came from Wahoo, Nebraska. Cobb received a diamond and gold medal when the series opened but he hit for a mere .200 in the five games. He was held tight to the bases by the well-drilled Cubs pitchers and by rifle-armed catcher Johnny Kling, now better than ever.

The goat of the series was of course Detroit catcher Butch Schmidt, who not only let that first game trickle away, but saw fourteen of the fleet-footed Cubs steal bases ahead of his futile throws. The Cubs, however, seemed to know something that Manager Hughey Jennings (who was christened "Hughey" and not "Hugh") apparently did not yet appreciate: that the man to steal bases on was not the catcher but the pitcher, whose task it was to keep the runners from getting that dangerous lead and fatal start. When Jennings thought to end the wholesale theft by bringing in substitute catcher Jimmy Archer, who snapped the ball off his ear, from a flat-footed stance, Archer looked useless too. Yet before two years had passed the Cubs got Archer for their own and made him into at least a temporary equal of the great Johnny Kling.

How far the Tigers were behind the parade in this series was perhaps well symbolized by their lumbering pitcher, Wild Bill Donovan, who in one game hit a clean line drive to right field, and was thrown out at first by right fielder Schulte!

Crowds at this series were larger than ever before, then suddenly thinned out when the series shifted to Detroit. The weather in the last two games was miserable; and when the teams moved to Detroit the hometown fans seemed to have lost their courage. Some seven thousand fans came out to see the final game, which was the fourth straight victory for the Cubs—an unheard-of, unpredicted, and unbelievable triumph.

The weather may have had a little to do with the Tigers' humiliation. In the fourth game, Donovan, holding a one-run lead, had allowed only two singles in the first four innings. Then a cold rain came down with Wildfire Schulte at the plate and the game was delayed for fifteen minutes. Donovan's arm grew cold, he failed to rewarm it properly, and could not find the plate. Schulte walked. That made two on base, for Evers had reached on a bad throw. Joe Tinker sacrificed, putting men on second and third, and Overall's single scored two runs. The Cubs never gave up that lead. In the seventh they added three more runs on three bunts, a sacrifice, some sleepy infield play, and a delayed steal.

Hughey Jennings had little chance to let out his famous war cry "Eee-yah!" He was thoroughly outsmarted by the alert and determined Frank Chance. And when Chance broke a finger and had to stay out of the final game, old Mordecai Brown put on a show of pitching generalship, control, and bearing down in the clutch that old-timers long talked about. He scattered seven hits, had four strikeouts (two of them on Cobb), and walked only one man. The final score was 2 to 0.

The Detroit team probably had its own hero in Germany Schaefer, their pock-marked second baseman, a famous cut-up on the diamond and off. What Germany did was ask the National Commission, before the series began, if the players were going to share in the gate receipts of a possible tie game. The National Commission rules did not cover this contingency, so they immediately went into session and decreed that the players would share in the receipts of any such game. Then, lo and behold, the very first game was tied—the first World Series tie and one of the few in history. All the players were mighty glad Germany had spoken up.

There might have been a scandal about this tie game, too. Some writers and fans, and a few of the magnates, were convinced that it was a put-up job—that the players were deliberately trying to stretch the series. Else why would they have brought the matter up beforehand? But the players choked that scandal in the throats of its originators by finishing the series in four more games.

The magnates weren't quite ready for *that*. The games were supposed to return to Chicago for a Sunday contest, and the park was already sold out. By acting with such honesty and dispatch, those Cubs had sent thousands of dollars right down the drain.

Owner Murphy of the Cubs immediately decided on an "exhibition" game to fill the park on that Sunday. He would bring both teams back anyway and, naturally, the fans would crowd in to see them. They were the same teams, weren't they?

But the sting had gone out of the rivalry. The Cubs were the champs, the Tigers were in the dumps—and very few people wanted to see the subject reopened. The "exhibition" was offered to a half-empty house.

The taste of defeat was sweetened somewhat for the Detroit players when open-handed owner Bill Yawkey of the Detroit club (uncle and foster-father of the present Red Sox owner) threw an extra $15,000 into the players' pool. Owner Murphy of Chicago, not wanting to see the losers get more than the winners, as they had in 1903, made a contribution to the Cub players' pool too. But he had his generosity under pretty good control and put in only $10,000.

Leading hitters:

CHICAGO CUBS
Steinfeldt: .471

DETROIT TIGERS
Rossman: .400

Winning pitchers:

CHICAGO CUBS
Overall: won 1, lost 0
Reulbach: won 1, lost 0
Pfeister: won 1, lost 0
Brown: won 1, lost 0

1908

CHICAGO N.L. vs. DETROIT A.L.

WON BY CHICAGO, 4 GAMES TO 1

Game Scores:

Chicago 10	Detroit 6	October 10 at Detroit
Chicago 6	Detroit 1	October 11 at Chicago
Detroit 8	Chicago 3	October 12 at Chicago
Chicago 3	Detroit 0	October 13 at Detroit
Chicago 2	Detroit 0	October 14 at Detroit

The 1908 World Series lives in fame more for the ruckus that preceded it than for the series games themselves. This was the year of the famous "Merkle Boner" by which, according to John McGraw, the New York Giants were "euchred out of the Championship." For as long as men lived who had played in or watched that game there was disagreement over it. But nowadays the problem that started the row would never arise. It is just taken for granted today that a man who fails, as Merkle did, to run down from first to second on a ground ball, can be forced out at second base, even if the winning run is crossing the plate.

In that day, Merkle was not the only man who had jogged to the clubhouse while the winning run crossed the plate in the last of the ninth, without bothering to "run out" the hit. But Merkle knew, as soon as he heard the argument behind him, that he was wrong and he wished, he said, for a hole to hide in. What went on behind him was not baseball. There was a wild scramble for the ball. Spectators and non-playing ballplayers were all over the field, interfering with the umpires' vision. One New York player seized the ball and tried to heave it out of the park. But a Chicago man got another ball and made the "play" that tied the pennant race, forced a playoff, and lost the flag for the Giants.

The series itself was the 1907 series all over again, except that this time the Tigers won a game and young Ty Cobb showed the skill and power that had earned him the league batting championship. The first game, played in the rain, was a thriller. The Cubs blew a 5 to 1 lead in the seventh and eighth innings and the final inning began with the Cubs behind by 6 to 5. But six consecutive hits off pitcher Eddie Summers gave the Cubs five runs in the ninth and a victory.

In the second game, the pitchers starred. Detroit's Wild Bill Donovan, who usually had fine control, threw one wild pitch but pitched scoreless and nearly hitless ball for seven innings, and Orvie Overall of the Cubs kept the Tigers away from the plate for eight full innings. In the home eighth inning, the game being played in Chicago, Solly Hofman got a scratch hit off Donovan, and Joe Tinker, whose bat never frightened any pitcher, belted a high fly that the wind turned into a home run. After that, Wild Bill came apart and the Cubs racked up six runs altogether. In the ninth the Tigers got their only run off Overall, who gave them just four hits in the game.

The third game, played in Chicago on Columbus Day, saw the Detroit sluggers rise up and smite Chicago pitching for eleven hits, including a two-bagger and three singles by Ty Cobb, who also stole two bases. George Mullin of Detroit should have had a shutout in this game. He gave up seven hits but the Chicago scores came after errors by the Detroit infielders, which allowed all three Cub runs.

Back in Detroit for the fourth game, the pitchers once more took charge, and Detroit never scored again. Mordecai Three-Finger Brown, whose natural sinker ball would drive a saint to sin, gave the Tigers only four hits, two of them by Wahoo Sam

30

Crawford and none by Cobb. Meanwhile the Cubs, with Wildfire Schulte and Frank Chance leading the way, scored three times. Schulte got two hits, scored one of the three runs, and stole two bases. Frank Chance, who led the club in batting for the series, got two hits and scored a run. The other run was scored by little Johnny Evers.

In the final game, Orvie Overall, who had not had one of his best years, completely hypnotized the Tigers. He allowed them three hits, two singles and a double, and struck out ten. Donovan pitched a strong game too, without a wild pitch (Overall made one). He kept the ten Chicago hits well scattered and allowed only two runs, one by Johnny Evers and one by John Kling, the catcher who had changed his name from Klein. Three of the ten hits were by big Frank (Husk) Chance, whose series average was .421. Johnny Evers hit .350 and Wildfire Schulte .389. By the time the game was played, the Detroit fans had practically conceded the championship to the crafty Cubs. Only 6210 paid their way into the park, the poorest crowd since the American and National Leagues had first played for the World's Championship.

Frank Chance's careful drilling of his batteries to keep the fast Tigers from running wild on the bases did not entirely choke off Ty Cobb this time. The fresh kid from Georgia managed to steal two bases. But the Cubs, notably Schulte, Evers, and Chance, stole thirteen bases altogether, and Chance took four of them.

The series was not allowed to conclude without one bitter aftertaste of the Merkle Boner. Bill Klem, the great umpire, who umpired the series, accused the Giants' team physician of trying to bribe him before the replay of the Merkle game. There was a hearing and the physician, who had no other accuser nor any other witness against him, was barred from ball parks for life.

Leading hitters:

CHICAGO CUBS
Chance: .421

DETROIT TIGERS
Cobb: .368

Winning pitchers:

CHICAGO CUBS
    Overall: won 2, lost 0
    Brown: won 2, lost 0

DETROIT TIGERS
    Mullin: won 1, lost 0

1909

PITTSBURGH N.L. vs. DETROIT A.L.

WON BY PITTSBURGH, 4 GAMES TO 3

Game Scores:

Pittsburgh 4	Detroit 1	October 8 at Pittsburgh
Detroit 7	Pittsburgh 2	October 9 at Pittsburgh
Pittsburgh 8	Detroit 6	October 11 at Detroit
Detroit 5	Pittsburgh 0	October 12 at Detroit
Pittsburgh 8	Detroit 4	October 13 at Pittsburgh
Detroit 5	Pittsburgh 4	October 14 at Detroit
Pittsburgh 8	Detroit 0	October 16 at Detroit

The World Series of 1909 was the best, the wildest, the most evenly contested to date and the first one to go the full distance agreed on—seven games. (The 1903 series went eight games but there could have been nine, under the agreement.) It was also the first and only time the two "greatest baseball players alive," Ty Cobb and Honus Wagner, ever met head-to-head in a series. It was the last World Series for Ty Cobb; the only series in which Detroit's Wild Bill Donovan, who had tried for two previous series, won a victory; and probably the only series that ended with the firing of a baseball player (Pittsburgh's Bill Abstein, first baseman) for striking out ten times in the seven games. It marked the completion of a miraculous season for Pittsburgh, who had just moved into their brand new ball park, Forbes Field. They won the National League pennant with 110 victories, six more than the runner-up Cubs. And they won the series with the help of an almost unheard-of rookie named Babe Adams, who won only twelve games in the season. Babe won three games in the World Series, while the Pittsburgh aces, Camnitz, Willis, and Leifield, could not spin a thread.

The attendance at the 1909 series, at the end of what had been the most prosperous season baseball had known (a season marred nonetheless by the suicide of Harry Pulliam, the National League president), was the greatest yet and the return to the clubs and to the players the richest.

The first game, played at Pittsburgh, drew 29,264 paid customers, an enormous crowd for that day. And Pittsburgh, which was destined to win all the odd-numbered games, while Detroit took the even-numbered ones, gladdened its fans at once by winning behind the six-hit pitching of young Babe Adams. Ty Cobb went hitless in this game but stole a base. And from that time forth he played in the shadow of bowlegged Honus Wagner. Veteran Honus (he had been in the major leagues for thirteen years and was then thirty-five years old) led his team at bat with a .333 average and stole six bases. And he responded to the challenge of young Ty Cobb (twenty-two years old then and playing his fifth year in the majors) with calm determination. At one point in the series, Ty, who was notorious for his manner of clearing baselines with the help of sharpened spikes, shouted down to Wagner, playing shortstop: "Hey, Kraut-head! I'm coming down on the next pitch." Ty came down and Wagner took the throw and waited for him. The sharp spikes flashed as Cobb roared into the base. But Wagner held his ground and laid the hard ball right on Cobb's face. "He split my lip for me," said Cobb afterward, in rueful admiration. Altogether Ty stole only two bases in the seven games.

The second game, also played in Pittsburgh, was won by Wild Bill Donovan before an even larger crowd, 30,915. Donovan struck out seven Pirates and gave up only five hits, four singles and a double. The Tigers landed on Camnitz for six hits and five runs in the first three innings and held the lead from then on.

In the third game, nearly everybody hit, but the Pirates hit harder. Even the luckless Abstein got a two-bagger off Ed Summers as the Pirates packed away five runs in the first at-bat. Jim Delahanty, Detroit second baseman, one of five famous ballplaying brothers, got two doubles in this game. He was the hitting star of the series for Detroit.

Game number four, being even-numbered, belonged to Detroit. George Mullin, their twenty-nine-game winner, struck out ten Pirates, gave up five hits, and allowed no runs. This game saw the return to action of veteran Deacon Phillippe, hero of the first World Series. The old Deacon relieved Leifield in the fifth and allowed but one hit the rest of the way. Leifield was completely off the beam that day. In the first four innings he allowed seven hits and five runs and hit two batters.

Back in Pittsburgh for the fifth game, the Pirates rallied behind young Babe Adams again and outscored the Tigers, despite home runs by Wahoo Sam Crawford and the Detroit left fielder Kangaroo Davey Jones. Manager Fred Clarke of the Pirates hit a home run on his own and Honus Wagner stole two bases. Babe Adams struck out eight and allowed six hits.

Detroit won game number six, despite the efforts of Pittsburgh's twenty-five- and twenty-two-game winners, Howard Camnitz and Vic Willis, assisted by old man Phillippe, who pitched two innings and allowed one hit. The Tiger sluggers hit hard, with Cobb, Crawford, and Delahanty each racking up a two-bagger—a very solid hit indeed in those days before the cork-centered ball.

The final game was Babe Adams' best, a six-hit shutout, and it was the Detroit pitchers' worst. Not only did the National League base runners continue to roam the baselines as if someone had lost the baseball (they stole eighteen bases in the series), but Manager Fred Clarke of Pittsburgh received four walks, stole two bases, and scored two runs without an official time-at-bat.

Ty Cobb's only headline in this series was awarded him after the second game, in which he stole home during the third inning.

When Babe Adams came home to Pittsburgh a thousand fans soon gathered in the front yard of his home, nearly half of them girls intent on kissing him. Babe, after a quick survey of the mob, sneaked out the back door and did not come back until the girls were gone.

Leading hitters:

PITTSBURGH PIRATES
Wagner: .333

DETROIT TIGERS
Delahanty: .346

Winning pitchers:

PITTSBURGH PIRATES
Adams: won 3, lost 0
Maddox: won 1, lost 0

DETROIT TIGERS
Mullin: won 2, lost 1
Donovan: won 1, lost 1

1910

PHILADELPHIA A.L. vs. CHICAGO N.L.

WON BY PHILADELPHIA, 4 GAMES TO 1

Game Scores:

Philadelphia 4	Chicago 1	October 17 at Philadelphia
Philadelphia 9	Chicago 3	October 18 at Philadelphia
Philadelphia 12	Chicago 5	October 20 at Chicago
Chicago 4	Philadelphia 3	October 22 at Chicago
(10 innings)		
Philadelphia 7	Chicago 2	October 23 at Chicago

None of the wiseacres of baseball, outside of Philadelphia, gave Connie Mack's Athletics half a chance to win the World Series of 1910 against the veteran Chicago Cubs. The Athletics were mostly kids, some of them college boys, who were, it was generally acknowledged, a rather sissified breed unlikely to stand up against a crew as wily and tough as Frank Chance's pennant winners. But the Athletics simply ran wild over the Cubs, beating them three straight, and clubbing their veteran pitchers from one end of town to the other. They could have won four straight, Connie Mack always insisted, if only he had had sense enough to follow a hunch and use a pinch-hitter in the ninth for his weak-hitting catcher, Ira Thomas. But Ira, nearing thirty, was one of the few old-timers on the club and Connie did not have the heart to lift him with victory so near. So the Cubs carried the game into ten innings and made off with it.

Another good reason why the Athletics were not supposed to beat the Cubs was the loss of their great outfielder Rube Oldring, who had batted .308 during the season and was counted on to cover most of the outfield. Rube broke his leg just before the series began and young Amos Strunk, just twenty-one, who had played in only sixteen games that year, had to fill in at center field. Then too the mighty Eddie Plank, in his tenth season as a pitching stalwart for Connie Mack, was lame in the arm when October came and was not going to be able to pitch.

But the Cubs had a little hard luck too. Their spark plug, second baseman Johnny Evers, had also broken a leg before the series and he had been replaced by Heinie Zimmerman. Heinie filled in well; but not so well as deer-footed Amos Strunk, who collected five hits in four games, including a double and a triple. As for pitchers, Connie needed only two. Chief Albert Bender, always Connie's favorite, won the first game and Jack Coombs, one of those college boys from Colby, won the other three. During the season, in which the Athletics won 102 games (high mark to that date for an American League team), Jack Coombs had won thirty-one games and the Chief had won twenty-three.

Actually the series was a breeze for the Philadelphia pitchers, the hitting of the youngsters was so formidable. Eddie Collins, another college boy, from Columbia, playing second base alongside Jack Barry from Holy Cross, batted .429 in the series to lead both clubs. Third baseman Frank Baker, not yet called "Home Run," batted .409. Even pitcher Jack Coombs, with five hits in thirteen at-bats, posted an average of .385 to contribute to the highest team batting average ever posted in a World Series, .317, a mark that stood for fifty years.

Chief Bender won the first game, in Philadelphia, allowing only three hits and striking out eight. The single Cub run came in the ninth. Philadelphia bats were relatively silent in this game. After they collected six hits in three innings from Orvie Overall,

38

they managed only one hit in the remaining five at-bats off Harry McIntire. But that's all they needed.

In the second game, the young monsters of the Philadelphia infield broke loose. Eddie Collins got two doubles and a single off Mordecai Brown; Harry Davis, first baseman, hit for a single and a double; and Jack Barry came up with a single. Amos Strunk, having gone hitless in the first game, contributed a double and a single. In all, the A's made fourteen hits, five of them for extra bases.

In Chicago for the third game, the Philadelphia sluggers turned on the juice again. This time right fielder Danny Murphy, one of the real ancients on the club (he was thirty-four), drove out a home run, the only one of the series. Barry and Davis got three hits each, and so did pitcher Jack Coombs. Frank Baker got two and everyone else on the club except Ira Thomas got one. In the fourth inning Philadelphia was leading 8 to 3 and Coombs coasted in with a fat lead.

The fourth game is the one that Connie Mack brooded about for years. With the A's leading 3 to 2 in the eighth inning, Ira Thomas was coming up with the bases full and only one out. Connie's first notion was to send up Topsy Hartsel to bring in those runs. Topsy was nearing the end of his string but he could still drive a ball into the deep outfield, which was more than old Ira had been doing. But Connie's heart won out over his head. Ira went up, hit into a double play, and gave the Cubs a chance to tie it up and win.

Hartsel replaced Strunk in the outfield for the final game and Topsy stole two bases and scored two of the seven Philadelphia runs. A five-run eighth inning saved this game for Jack Coombs. Eddie Collins made three of the A's nine hits.

This series, although it went only five games, paid out the best for the players of any series up to that time. Because attendance at the fourth game, played on a Saturday, was a disappointing 19,150 (others had all been over 24,000) the players were allowed to substitute the fifth-game receipts for the fourth game and as a result the winners took home over $2000 each. The final game drew more than 27,000.

Leading hitters:

PHILADELPHIA ATHLETICS
Collins: .429

CHICAGO CUBS
Schulte and Chance: .353

Winning pitchers:

PHILADELPHIA ATHLETICS
Bender: won 1, lost 1
Coombs: won 3, lost 0

CHICAGO CUBS
Brown: won 1, lost 2

1911

PHILADELPHIA A.L. vs. NEW YORK N.L.

WON BY PHILADELPHIA, 4 GAMES TO 2

Game Scores:

New York 2	Philadelphia 1	October 14 at New York
Philadelphia 3	New York 1	October 16 at Philadelphia
Philadelphia 3 (11 innings)	New York 2	October 17 at New York
Philadelphia 4 (10 innings)	New York 2	October 24 at Philadelphia
New York 4	Philadelphia 3	October 25 at New York
Philadelphia 13	New York 2	October 26 at Philadelphia

The 1911 World Series developed special excitement because of the sharp rivalry between John McGraw and Connie Mack, the two greatest managers in the game. McGraw had once labeled the Philadelphia franchise a "white elephant" in the league, because he felt sure they would never win ball games enough to pay the rent. The Athletics took up the White Elephant as their symbol and the Philadelphia fans were intent in forcing John McGraw to eat his words.

The crowd that turned out to see the first game at the Polo Grounds in New York was the largest ever to attend a World Series up to that date: 38,281. Fans lined up outside the fence hours before the game began and hundreds gathered in a nearby auditorium to see the game "re-enacted" on a board. A hundred telegraphers with their "keys" were stationed in an area behind home plate to send details of the doings to the world.

Several of the men who had met each other in the shutout series of 1905 were still in the opposing lineups, notably the great pitchers, Mathewson, Bender, Plank, and Ames. Danny Murphy, Philadelphia second baseman in 1905, was an outfielder now. Davis still played first base for Mack. And Briscoe Lord, a rookie outfielder in 1905, had been out to Cleveland for two seasons and was back now in Philadelphia, where he had just recorded the best season batting average of his life (.310). Only the pitchers remained of McGraw's 1905 lineup. But New York had an Indian to match Connie Mack's Albert Bender. He was John (Chief) Meyers, from California, a hard-hitting catcher.

It was in this series that Frank Baker, Philadelphia third baseman, earned the name of "Home Run Baker"—not because he hit so many home runs (he hit two) but because he timed them so well. His first home run came in the sixth inning of the second game and drove in two runs, enough to beat Rube Marquard 3 to 1. He hit another in the ninth inning of the third game, when Mathewson was leading 1 to 0. Baker's homer tied the score and gave the A's the chance they needed to win.

For sheer moment-to-moment tension, this was the greatest series yet. All the games except the final one hung in the balance until the end and could have been won by either side with a timely hit. There were two overtime games, some freakish breaks, and a six-day hiatus on account of rain.

The first game brought Mathewson and Bender together and they struggled to a near-standoff. The big Indian struck out 11 New Yorkers while Mathewson fanned only four of the A's. The hits were five for New York and six for Philadelphia. But the New Yorkers got more runs.

Game number two, won by Baker's home run, was played on Monday in Philadelphia, it being against the law to play baseball on Sunday in the East. Eddie Plank, who was supposed to have developed his pitching skill by knocking birds off fences with stones, knocked off eight Giants by strikeout and gave them five hits. Philadelphia got only four, but they added up to more bases. The Giant leadoff man, Josh Devore, struck out four times in a row. He did not get fired, however, as poor Abstein had in 1909.

The third game kept all the chilled spectators on the edges of their seats. Played in New York, it drew almost as many spectators as the first game had, and it lasted until nearly dark. When Baker homered in the ninth, he made it 1 to 1. It stayed this way until the eleventh, when Philadelphia got two runs and the Giants could make only one. It would have been a shame for Jack Coombs to have lost this game, for he gave up only three hits in eleven innings.

Between the third game and the fourth game it rained and rained. When the clubs were able to meet again, on October 24, Mathewson was ready to go once more and so was Bender. The A's hit Mathewson fairly well this time. Baker hit no home runs but he made two doubles while Danny Murphy and Jack Barry also got two apiece.

The fifth game went ten innings, but according to umpire Bill Klem, who did not say so until afterward, it should have kept on going even further, perhaps until darkness ended it. In the last of the tenth, with Laughing Larry Doyle, the Giants' second baseman, on third base, Fred Merkle lifted a sacrifice fly up into the twilight shadows and after the catch, Larry, prancing and shouting, galloped down the baseline, over the plate, and into the arms of his joyous teammates. What no one but Klem, the plate umpire, noticed was that Larry had not touched the plate on the way in. If the A's had made a play on him, he'd have called Larry out and the series might have been ended in the next inning. But Larry scored, the A's packed up, and the series continued.

The last game played in Philadelphia, before a diminished but still frantic crowd of some 20,000 fans, was a laugher. Neither Red Ames nor Hooks Wiltse nor Rube Marquard could restrain the Philadelphia youngsters. Danny Murphy got four hits. Briscoe Lord got three and Frank Baker got two. Chief

Bender meanwhile doled out only four to the Giants and tucked the series safely away.

One of the oddities of the series, and one aspect that popped the eyes of New York fans, was the way the A's' catchers choked off the Giants on the baselines. The Giants had stolen 347 bases that season, they were always ready to run, and National League base runners had *always* run wild against American League pitching. But the Giants managed only four steals during the series, two each by Herzog and Doyle. Apparently the American League had finally discovered that it was up to the pitcher to keep the runners close to the bag.

After the series a group of the more volatile Giant fans, burning because the New York cleanup batter, John Joseph (Red) Murray, had failed to make a hit in the six games, put a rope around the neck of a dummy, called it Red Murray, and hung it to a lamppost near the Polo Grounds. (Red hit .291 in the season but went 0 for 21 in the series.)

Leading hitters:

PHILADELPHIA ATHLETICS
Baker: .375

NEW YORK GIANTS
Doyle: .304

Winning pitchers:

PHILADELPHIA ATHLETICS
Bender: won 2, lost 1
Plank: won 1, lost 1
Coombs: won 1, lost 0

NEW YORK GIANTS
Mathewson: won 1, lost 2
Crandall: won 1, lost 0

1912

BOSTON A.L. vs. NEW YORK N.L.

WON BY BOSTON, 4 GAMES TO 3 (1 TIE)

Game Scores:

Boston 4	New York 3	October 8 at New York
New York 6	Boston 6	October 9 at Boston
New York 2	Boston 1	October 10 at Boston
Boston 3	New York 1	October 11 at New York
Boston 2	New York 1	October 12 at Boston
New York 5	Boston 2	October 14 at New York
New York 11	Boston 4	October 15 at Boston
Boston 3	New York 2	October 16 at Boston

The 1912 series was the only one since 1903 that required eight games for a decision. That is because the second game ended in a tie after eleven innings, when darkness made further play impossible. This was another nip-and-tuck series, with the favorite becoming the underdog and fighting back from a three-two deficit to bring matters all even again—only to blow the prize with a brace of errors that would have enraged a high school coach.

The mighty New York Giants, having spread-eagled the field in the National League with 103 victories and a ten-game lead, were heavily favored to demolish the upstart Red Sox in straight

45

sets. The Red Sox had a thirty-four-game winner in Smoky Joe Wood. But the Giants had the greatest pitcher in the business, Christy Mathewson, who won twenty-three games in the regular season (his thirteenth with the Giants). And they had Rube Marquard, who had just tied Tim Keefe's record of nineteen wins in a row. Rube had won twenty-six that year. Red Ames, another veteran, had won only eleven but he had worked in thirty-three. Ancient Hooks Wiltse (he was thirty-two) was also available for service. And rookie Jeff Tesreau had won seventeen games in this, his first season with the McGraw club, and had led the league in earned-run average, thanks to frequent use of a spitball. Anyway, McGraw didn't think much of Joe Wood. He'd have been more afraid of a curve-ball pitcher like Bender, he said, but he felt the Giants could hit Wood's fast ball, smoke or not.

The Giants did hit it too but just not often enough or far enough. And some overeagerness in the field, when both Fred Snodgrass and little Josh Devore tried for a long fly by Tris Speaker that turned into a triple, helped the Red Sox make the most of their six hits in the first game. The misplays in this game —a missed double play by second baseman Larry Doyle was the other one—did not count as errors. But they were an indication of things to come.

In the second game the Giants made five errors, three by shortstop Art Fletcher and a crucial one by second-string catcher Art Wilson, that allowed Tris Speaker to make it all the way home on an inside-the-park drive with the run that tied the score.

The third game was a sort of ghost victory for the Red Sox, for many fans went home thinking the Sox had won with three runs in the last of the ninth. Actually, while three runners did cross the plate, the blow that sent the latter two in was caught on the fly by Josh Devore in a desperation fingertip grab, deep in the autumn haze that covered right field. Devore, without missing a stride, kept on sprinting for the clubhouse and a few thousand went home before finding out who won, only to find the bitter truth staring at them from atop their evening paper: That had been the third out and the Giants had won.

Joe Wood, by winning game number four, changed McGraw's mind about this particular fast-ball pitcher. And catcher Bill Carrigan, by knocking off two of McGraw's "running-wild" base runners in the eleventh inning of the tie game, had already convinced McGraw that there were other major leaguers besides Tris Speaker on this young club. The real star of game number four, however, was Heinie Wagner of the Red Sox, who looked like his great namesake that afternoon when he ranged right and left to grab base hits away from the New York sluggers.

The fifth game, in Boston on Columbus Day, was a complete sellout, as the New York games had been. Thousands were turned away from the gates and all thirty-five thousand seats were gone by twelve noon. The hero of this game was a rookie Red Sox pitcher, twenty-two-year-old Hugh Bedient, who outpitched Christy Mathewson, granting only three hits and a single run. The Boston scoring came on two three-base hits in succession in the third inning. After that, Mathewson allowed not another man to reach base and Bedient just had to be better to win it.

The loss of the sixth game was blamed by Boston players on the club president, Jim McAleer, who talked Jake Stahl (soon to be known as Jake the Giant-Killer) into pitching Bucky O'Brien instead of Joe Wood. O'Brien, after allowing a run on a balk (a feint to first base, sandlot style), seemed to disintegrate, and the Giants piled up five runs before the Red Sox could warm up a relief pitcher. Bitter over the defeat, Joe Wood's brother Paul punched O'Brien in the eye before the club left for Boston. Some players growled that he should have punched McAleer.

The seventh game in Boston saw more hard feelings, more foul-ups, and more excitement. A whole section of the seats had been sold twice over, leaving Boston's volunteer cheering section, the Royal Rooters, with no place to sit. The Rooters thereupon paraded angrily around the field, with their band playing, until mounted police drove them behind the rails. The long delay in getting the game started seemed to chill Joe Wood's pitching arm and he took his worst beating of the year—six runs in the first inning. Thanks to the high wind, there were two home runs in this game (they were still a series rarity), with each side getting one. It was a sad day for the Red Sox, brightened only by a spectacular unassisted double play by, of all people, the Red Sox center fielder, Tris Speaker, who always played the shortest center field in the game. This time he grabbed a short fly by Art Fletcher and continued at top speed right across second base to double up Art Wilson before Art could figure where Speaker had come from.

The eighth game was lost by two incredible errors by two able New York ballplayers, center fielder Fred Snodgrass and catcher John (Chief) Meyers. And such is the way of baseball fans that these errors lived on in legend when most of the rest of the series had been forgotten. The Royal Rooters stayed home from the game, but the ballplayers fought for the victory like quarrelsome cats. The game went ten innings, with Bedient pitching seven and Joe Wood pitching three—and getting the victory. Harry Hooper, Boston right fielder, made an "illegal" catch of a home run ball (he fell into the stands and caught it while lying atop the fans). Then Fred Snodgrass, after moving just a few feet to catch a routine fly ball, let the ball trickle through his glove for the famous "Snodgrass muff" that allowed the tying run to get on base. Soon afterward Chief Meyers and first baseman Fred Merkle allowed an easy foul fly to fall between them, giving Tris Speaker an extra chance—all he needed —to drive in the tying run.

Leading hitters:

BOSTON RED SOX
Speaker: .300

NEW YORK GIANTS
Herzog: .400

Early Days

1. When Bill Dinneen shut out the Pirates on the final day of the 1903 Series, the Boston Royal Rooters sang their team song "Tessie" to the accompaniment of their own band. *Boston Public Library, Rare Book Department.*

2. The Pirate bench at the first World Series in Boston, 1903. Just beyond the post is Honus Wagner. Manager Fred Clarke peers around the corner. *Boston Public Library, Rare Book Department.*

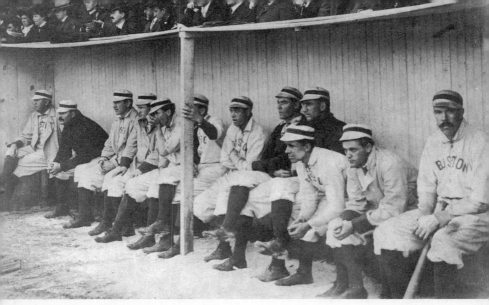

3. The 1903 Red Sox on the bench at the World Series. At the far left is big Cy Young, already a veteran. Third from the right, with elbows on his knees, is little Hugh Duffy, who held then and still holds, the top major league season batting average (.438). *Boston Library, Rare Book Department.*

4. Scenting victory in New York in 1904, the Royal Rooters from Boston whoop it up in the stands, while tough Bill Dinneen exchanges words with a tough New York cop. *Boston Public Library, Rare Book Department.*

5. The Philadelphia Athletics, American League Champions in 1905. Connie Mack in center, with the great Rube Waddell kneeling at his right hand. Rube could not pitch in the series because he injured his left shoulder wrestling on the train with Pitcher Andy Coakley, who is sitting cross-legged on the ground on the right of the first row. Chief Albert Bender stands at Connie Mack's right shoulder. *Boston Public Library, Rare Book Department.*

6. Isbell of the White Sox (sliding) and Frank Chance, Peerless Leader of the Chicago Cubs (rear to camera), posed for this scene at 1906 World Series. *Boston Public Library, Rare Book Department.*

7. A rookie star of the 1908 World Series was a Georgia youngster named Ty Cobb, who did not have much of a throwing arm. As it turned out, he didn't need one, for he had everything else. *Culver Pictures, Inc.*

The Teens

8. Miracle worker Johnny Evers, left, who captained the Boston Braves of 1914, greets Eddie Plank of the Athletics, before the series begins. This was probably the only friendly interclub gesture of the entire series. *Culver Pictures, Inc.*

Winning pitchers:

BOSTON RED SOX

Wood:	won 3,	lost 1
Bedient:	won 1,	lost 0

NEW YORK GIANTS

Tesreau:	won 1,	lost 2
Marquard:	won 2,	lost 0

1913

PHILADELPHIA A.L. vs. NEW YORK N.L.

WON BY PHILADELPHIA, 4 GAMES TO 1

Game Scores:

Philadelphia 6	New York 4	October 7 at New York
New York 3	Philadelphia 0	October 8 at Philadelphia
Philadelphia 8	New York 2	October 9 at New York
Philadelphia 6	New York 5	October 10 at Philadelphia
Philadelphia 3	New York 1	October 11 at New York

When Connie Mack led his team to their third World's Championship in 1913 he became the first manager to accomplish that feat. And this time he did it easily, for the Giants never had a look-in. Fred Snodgrass, the man who made the 1912 muff, but a fine ballplayer all the same and vital to the health of the New York club, had come up lame this year and could play only briefly in the series. (His lameness actually led to the lifelong enmity between McGraw and Wilbert Robinson, with each blaming the other for ordering Fred to steal a base in the regular season.) The Giants' other "goat," Fred Merkle, also suffered from a leg injury. He played, but his speed and his range were far below normal. And Chief Meyers, who shared the blame with Merkle for avoiding Speaker's foul fly in the 1912 series, broke his finger in the first game.

Still the Giants managed to put up a valiant struggle, and

even to win a game, despite the fact that Hooks Wiltse had to fill in for Merkle at first base. Substitute Giant catcher Larry McLean actually led all the batters with a .500 average for the series.

The first game was won by Chief Bender, despite eleven New York hits. Led by their murderous $100,000 infield, the Athletics also got eleven hits. But they hit longer, with Stuffy McInnis and Barry each getting a two-bagger while second baseman Collins and catcher Wally Schang hit triples. Home Run Baker, the top Athletic slugger, justified his nickname with a home run.

It took the Giants ten innings to win the second game, for Eddie Plank stayed even with Christy Mathewson through nine innings, with neither side scoring. In the tenth inning, Eddie weakened and the Giants made three quick runs which the A's could not match. Hooks Wiltse had saved the game in the ninth with rifle throws to the plate that each time cut off the winning run.

In the third game, Connie Mack started his sensational youngster, Bullet Joe Bush, whose real name was Leslie Ambrose Bush. Joe was not yet twenty-one at series time but he faced down the veteran Giants for four innings before he yielded a run. The A's had presented him with a five-run lead in the first two innings, to ease the strain a little. First baseman McInnis went hitless in this game but the rest of the gold-plated infield got six hits among them, including a triple by Eddie Collins. Wally Schang hit a home run.

In game number four Al Bender faced Rube Marquard again, and again Connie Mack's big Indian came in first, even though he staggered some at the end. Bender coasted along with a 6 to 0 lead until the seventh and eighth, when the Giants, thanks to a triple by Art Shafer, an infielder playing in the outfield, and a home run by gimpy Fred Merkle, piled up five runs. Luckily the Chief was able to choke off pinch-hitters Moose McCormick and Eddie Grant in the ninth to save his victory, the sixth World Series victory for Bender, who never won another. (He tried just once more, in the 1914 series, and lasted less than six innings.)

The final game was a triumph for Eddie Plank, who this time outpitched and outlasted Christy Mathewson. He gave up just two hits, while big Christy allowed six. This was Mathewson's last World Series effort. Before the Giants won another pennant, Christy had been traded to Cincinnati to bring back Buck Herzog.

Thrifty Connie Mack used only twelve players in this series, seven regulars, two catchers, and three pitchers. He never had to relieve a pitcher nor was he ever tempted to use a pinch-hitter. McGraw used five pinch-runners and six pinch-hitters. But only one of his pinch-hitters produced for him. Moose McCormick, batting for Marquard in the first game, singled and scored a run.

One of the notable details of this series was the fact that it was played on five successive days, starting on a Tuesday and ending on a Saturday. There were no "traveling" days between New York and Philadelphia in that era. Only Sundays, heavy rain, snow, or darkness stayed the ballplayers of that day from the completion of their toils.

The series was starting earlier in the season now, with Mc-Graw no longer insisting on waiting for Columbus Day, so fans were able to sit in the stands without risking frostbite. The Polo Grounds was overflowing for the first game and yet a few hundred more fans jammed in when the clubs came back to play game number three. The baseball moguls had not yet hit upon the happy scheme of making a fan buy tickets in "strips"—one for each game—so there was often fluctuation in attendance as the fortunes of the home club grew dark or bright. But in this series, tightly played and hard fought, every Polo Grounds seat was occupied for the three games played there.

Leading hitters:

PHILADELPHIA ATHLETICS
Baker: .450

NEW YORK GIANTS
McLean: .500

Winning pitchers:

PHILADELPHIA ATHLETICS
Bender: won 2, lost 0
Plank: won 1, lost 1
Bush: won 1, lost 0

NEW YORK GIANTS
Mathewson: won 1, lost 1

1914

BOSTON N.L. vs. PHILADELPHIA A.L.

WON BY BOSTON, 4 GAMES TO 0

Game Scores:

Boston 7	Philadelphia 1	October 9 at Philadelphia
Boston 1	Philadelphia 0	October 10 at Philadelphia
Boston 5 (12 innings)	Philadelphia 4	October 12 at Boston
Boston 3	Philadelphia 1	October 13 at Boston

The 1914 series marked the ultimate triumph of the "miracle" Braves of Boston, who had been in the National League cellar as late as July 18 and who then beat the heavily favored Athletics four games in a row, and became the first club ever to make a clean sweep of the World Series. Although they have lived in baseball history as the Cinderella team who won a pennant and a series by means of some sort of magic incantation, they were really not so bad as the standings at mid-year made them look.

The Braves played in hard luck at the start of the season when Johnnie Evers (pronounced Eevers by Johnnie but Ehvers by the Boston fans), the aggressive second baseman who had been fired from the managership of the Chicago Cubs, took sick. And Rabbit Maranville, the shortstop whose vest pocket catch kept Boston fans howling in glee, got a sore throat and took to bed. But once that combination was back on the field and the

54

trio of mighty pitchers—Dick Rudolph, Bill James, and Lefty George Tyler—rid themselves of assorted jinxes, the Braves roared to the top and stayed there.

The Athletics had wobbled some during their own season, to the point where Manager Connie Mack himself was disgusted. But he decided, he said, "to win the pennant" and so began to place his outfielders "so the fly balls would drop into their hands." Win they did, but his team was riven with dissension, prompted largely by the efforts of the new Federal League to win his stars away by offers of larger salaries. And when they ran into the snarling, hungry Boston club, they could not stand up to them.

George Stallings, the "Miracle Man" who managed the Braves, was a gentle, convivial soul off the field. But on the bench he was sarcastic, profane, loud, and bitterly combative. He flung threats of heavy fines at his players and freely insulted the opposition, even offering to assault gentle Connie Mack physically. He schooled his players to show nothing but anger toward the opponents, one or two of whom were really upset when the Braves would not even speak a polite word to them on the field. The field captain of the Braves was Johnnie Evers, another Jekyll-and-Hyde type who was the soul of courtesy away from the ball field but as mean as an injured wildcat when the game was on.

But the hero of the series was a quiet, good-natured fellow that no one could dislike—Hank Gowdy, the Boston catcher. Hank hit only .243 during the regular season but in the World Series he outdid all of Connie Mack's $100,000 infield. Eddie Collins, Jack Barry, and Frank Baker all added together could not match Gowdy's .545 batting average. Hank hit a home run, a triple, three doubles, and a single.

The Athletics were doubly favored to win the first game of the series, after the Braves' third baseman, a hard-hitting redhead named J. Carlisle Smith, broke his leg in the next-to-the-last game of the regular season. The series was scheduled to begin in the A's home park and the mighty Chief Bender had been selected to pacify the tribe from Boston. Stallings, however, pretended a total lack of concern. He didn't care who pitched for the A's. His club would win in four straight. (No one knows if he really believed that or if it was part of his psychological warfare tactics.) Chief Bender, making his last appearance in an Athletics' uniform (he had already signed with the Federal League) was a very peaceful Indian indeed, whatever the reason. The Braves took eleven hits away from him, including a double and a triple by Hank Gowdy, who went three for three. Bald Dick Rudolph gave the A's only five.

The next day, the A's best left-hander, Eddie Plank (who also had signed to play in the Federal League), choked off the Braves with only seven hits and did not give up a run until the ninth. But Big Bill James yielded only two hits and no runs at all.

The next game was the first Braves World Series game ever staged in Boston and three hundred fans stood in line all night to see it. Stallings had continued his psychological warfare by bringing all his road equipment home and announcing that his club would not have to return to Philadelphia. There was no National League park in Boston then and the Braves filled Fenway Park as full as the Red Sox had ever done, with more than 35,000 fans on hand. The Braves nearly blew this one. They committed a number of inept plays that did not show in the score, the worst being Evers' hanging on to a badly played ground ball in the tenth inning, while he expressed his feelings —and while the runner kept right on going to score. But thanks to the mighty bat of Hank Gowdy, who hit two doubles and a home run, the Braves pulled the game out. The A's led 4 to 2 in the tenth inning, when Gowdy hit his home run. A walk, a hit by Evers, and a sacrifice fly tied the game. Then Gowdy hit a double in the twelfth and his pinch-runner scored when Joe Bush, the A's pitcher, threw a bunted ball into left field.

Stallings had already given up hope of winning it in four. Now he knew he was bound to. He canceled the club's train reservations to Philadelphia and announced that the Braves could not lose now. Naturally, he was right. Connie Mack would not pitch either of his top men (did he know they had planned to desert him?) but started a twenty-three-year-old named James Robert Shawkey, who had won sixteen games in the season. He used another young man, a left-hander named Herbert Pennock, just twenty, to finish up the game. Shawkey gave up only four hits and Pennock gave up two. Dick Rudolph, of the Braves, yielded seven. But the Braves got their hits close together and turned them into three runs. The A's scored only one, and that one was driven in by Bob Shawkey himself.

This series marked the end of the A's $100,000 infield. Home Run Baker stayed home all next season and was sold to the Yankees. Eddie Collins was sold to the White Sox. And Jack Barry, after starting the next season in Philadelphia, went to the Red Sox before the season was over. Chief Bender, after a poor season in the Federal League, came back to Philadelphia to pitch for the Phillies but never had a good year again. Eddie Plank had a great year with St. Louis in the Federal League, then stayed there with the St. Louis Browns.

Leading hitters:

BOSTON BRAVES
    Gowdy: .545

PHILADELPHIA ATHLETICS
    Baker: .250

Winning pitchers:

BOSTON BRAVES
    Rudolph: won 2, lost 0
    James: won 2, lost 0

1915

BOSTON A.L. vs. PHILADELPHIA N.L.

WON BY BOSTON, 4 GAMES TO 1

Game Scores:

Philadelphia 3	Boston 1	October 8 at Philadelphia
Boston 2	Philadelphia 1	October 9 at Philadelphia
Boston 2	Philadelphia 1	October 11 at Boston
Boston 2	Philadelphia 1	October 12 at Boston
Boston 5	Philadelphia 4	October 13 at Philadelphia

In 1915, Boston again won four straight World Series games from Philadelphia. This time it was the Red Sox who took them from the Phillies. And the Phillies won the first game so the feat did not count. But the Red Sox did manage to set a new attendance figure for the World Series. The Miracle Braves had built themselves a beautiful new ball park on Commonwealth Avenue, bigger in many ways than anyone needed, and then never got a chance to fill it up. Instead the Red Sox did, packing in about 42,000 paid customers for each of the two games played in Boston.

The hero of this series was the President of the United States, Woodrow Wilson, who came to Philadelphia for the second game and threw out the first ball, the first time a President had ever attended the series. Next to President Wilson in national fame and perhaps ahead of him as a drawing card was the

58

country's greatest pitcher, Grover Cleveland Alexander, named after the previous Democratic President, but called Pete by himself and friends. Alexander had done most of the work in winning the pennant for the Phillies. He had won thirty-one games in the season, twelve of them shutouts, and had lost only ten. Fans also turned out to see history's greatest home-run hitter: Gavvy Cravath, who had collected twenty-four home runs that year for the Phillies—a record that seemed sure to last a century. (There was a kid pitcher named Ruth on the Red Sox squad who had no thought of equaling it. He just kept wishing he could *pitch*.)

But the true heroes, once Alexander had taken the first game by outpitching Ernie Shore—and getting that kid Ruth to ground out as a pinch-hitter in the ninth—were the Boston pitchers and two outfielders, the incomparable Duffy Lewis and Harry Hooper. Hooper made two home runs among his seven hits, both of them in the last game. Cravath collected only a double and a triple in sixteen at-bats. Duffy Lewis, Boston's left fielder, hit .444. George Foster pitched and won two games for the Red Sox and made four hits in eight times at bat. Dutch Leonard had to throw a three-hitter to beat Alexander. The other game was won by Ernie Shore, who lost the first one. Babe Ruth, who had won more games than any of them in the season, spent the series on the bench, except for that brief appearance in the first game.

The first game was a tight one, with Shore almost matching Alexander, and actually allowing fewer hits. But Alex could come up with a strikeout when he needed it and he posted six.

George Foster, in the second game, gave the slugging Phillies only three hits and struck out eight. The Philadelphia shortstop, called "Beauty" Bancroft because he had a habit of calling "beauty!" whenever a good pitch got by him, must have identified himself a dozen times or more in this game. He got one of the hits. Cravath and first baseman Fred Luderus got the others.

Game number three, which set the attendance mark in Boston, was almost a duplicate of the second, with the Phillies again getting only three hits and Dutch Leonard striking out six. The Phillies fought hard for this one and lost it in the ninth when their carefully worked out strategy went wrong. Duffy Lewis came to bat in the Boston ninth with Harry Hooper on third, Speaker on second, and first base open. Duffy Lewis had been a pest all day. He had scampered far out into deep, deep left field (deeper then than any outfielder had a right to be) to haul in a four-hundred-foot drive by Gavvy Cravath that would have been an easy home run in Philadelphia. He had already made two hits off Alexander. Manager Pat Moran discussed with Alexander and his catcher the notion of putting Duffy on base. But they decided he had had all the hits he was entitled to and Alex pitched to him. Duffy promptly drove hit number three into center field and Hooper came home with the winning run.

In the fourth game, the Red Sox again made it 2 to 1 but this time needed no ninth inning to do it in. Duffy Lewis starred again in the county-wide outfield with startling catches of two blows by Gavvy Cravath, both of which would have been home runs in Gavvy's home park—or in Fenway Park for that matter, which is where the Red Sox ordinarily played. Duffy also drove in the winning run again with a long two-base hit to left in the sixth that scored Doc Hoblitzel from first base. A feature of this game was the fact that the Phillie shortstop, Dave Bancroft, had not a single fielding chance—the only time in World Series history a shortstop has been out of work in the field.

An effort by the Phillie management to crowd in more paying customers lost the final game for them. They had built temporary bleachers in center field and Harry Hooper, who uppercut a lot of pitches, bounced two "Chinese" home runs into those stands. Duffy Lewis hit an honest home run into the left-field seats. Nowadays Hooper's hits would have been "ground-rule" doubles.

Manager Moran gave the Phillie fans something to groan about immediately in this game when he ordered a squeeze bunt in the first inning with the count three-and-two on Cravath and the bases full. With all the runners moving Gavvy laid down a swinging bunt that George Foster, the Boston pitcher, managed to scoop up in time to nail the lead runner at home. Slow-boat Cravath then was easy pickings at first for a double play.

60

Leading hitters:

BOSTON RED SOX
Lewis: .444

PHILADELPHIA PHILLIES
Luderus: .438

Winning pitchers:

BOSTON RED SOX
Shore: won 1, lost 1
Foster: won 2, lost 0
Leonard: won 1, lost 0

PHILADELPHIA PHILLIES
Alexander: won 1, lost 1

1916

BOSTON A.L. vs. BROOKLYN N.L.

<small>WON BY BOSTON, 4 GAMES TO 1</small>

Game Scores:

Boston 6	Brooklyn 5	October 7 at Boston
Boston 2	Brooklyn 1	October 9 at Boston
(14 innings)		
Brooklyn 4	Boston 3	October 10 at Brooklyn
Boston 6	Brooklyn 2	October 11 at Brooklyn
Boston 4	Brooklyn 1	October 12 at Boston

In 1916, the Boston Red Sox made it four league pennants without losing a World Series. It was the first World Series for Brooklyn. The first in which Babe Ruth appeared as a regular, and the richest series to date, with the attendance record set in the final game at Braves Field: 42,620. It was also the first World Series for a kid outfielder named Casey Stengel, who was Brooklyn's star of the series with a batting average of .364.

The Boston hero at bat was again Duffy Lewis, with Harry Hooper right behind him. Ernie Shore pitched and won two games and Dutch Leonard won one. The most brilliant pitching, however, was done by Babe Ruth, the husky left-hander. In the second game Babe pitched thirteen scoreless innings, after giving up a home run in the first inning. In spite of the fact that

62

it was acknowledged he "hit pretty good for a pitcher," Babe went hitless in five times at bat. He struck out twice.

This was also the first World Series in which the spectator had to pay as much as five dollars for a grandstand seat. Heretofore it had been the practice to double the regular fee. But Charlie Ebbets in Brooklyn felt he had to do something, in his small park, to balance the gate receipts at oversize Braves Field.

The first game in Boston, however, did not fill the park because someone had been ill-advised enough to schedule it for Yom Kippur, when the Jewish fans had to stay home. The Sox scored first in this game and were never headed, although a four-run ninth inning by the Dodgers nearly overtook them. Casey Stengel scored the first Brooklyn run, that tied the score 1 to 1 in the fourth inning. The Sox went ahead in the fifth. In the seventh inning, the Brooklyn infield, on whom the Red Sox were depending for some sloppy play, produced two errors that helped the Red Sox score three runs; they added another run in the eighth, just enough to hold off the final effort by the Brooklyn sluggers.

Game number two brought out a full-sized crowd and gave Babe Ruth the chance he had been begging for—a World Series start. Babe had won twenty-three games that season and led the league with an earned-run average of 1.75. On this bright October day he was at his best. Hi Myers of Brooklyn hit a long drive in the first inning that bounced crazily over Tilly Walker's head in center field and bounded on and on and on across the endless green. Myers legged it into a home run. "It only ought to have been a single," Babe growled. Then Babe buckled down and gave up no more scores, and even drove in a run with an infield out to make up for Myers' run, in the third. The final inning was played in dusk so deep that Bill Klem said, if he had been working, he'd have called the game. Pinch-hitter Del Gainer won the game with a double that drove in pinch-runner Mike McNally. The ball disappeared on its way to the outfield but it was a good clean hit.

When the series moved to Brooklyn, the weather turned bitter cold and fans brought blankets to the park. Old Jack Coombs, who had won a twenty-four-inning game in 1906 for Connie

63

Mack, pitched for Brooklyn and rugged Carl Mays, the underhand pitcher, worked for the Red Sox. At the end of five innings, the Dodgers were ahead 4 to 0 and Mays was given the rest of the day off. George Foster came in then and allowed no more runs. But the Red Sox could not gather enough to catch up, despite a triple by Hooper and a home run by Larry Gardner.

The fourth game, played at Ebbets Field, was a chilly one too. The Dodgers this time kicked the ball around as they had been expected to, making four errors. Dutch Leonard toyed with the Brooklyn batters. They made two runs off him in the first inning but after that he forced them to pop up one after another, until he counted fifteen pop flies. Duffy Lewis, in left field, made six putouts. With Rube Marquard, the Brooklyn pitcher, matters worked out in just the opposite way. He fielded Hooper's weak grounder for the first out and struck out the next two batters. But in the second inning Larry Gardner got his second home run of the series, scoring Hoblitzel and Duffy Lewis ahead of him. Altogether the Red Sox made ten hits which, carefully blended with the Brooklyn errors, added up to six runs. The final Red Sox run came on a three-base error—an overthrow of first base by pitcher Larry Cheney that let Boston second baseman Hal Janvrin run all the rest of the way home.

The fifth game, played on Columbus Day in Boston, set an attendance record that stood until the Yankee Stadium was opened: 42,620. Thousands who traveled to the park were turned away and the gate receipts were the largest ever. Brooklyn never had a look-in at this game. Ernie Shore, returning to look for his third World Series victory and his second in this series, pitched the best World Series game he ever worked—a three-hitter in which the only Brooklyn run came as the result of a walk, a sacrifice, an infield out, and a passed ball. Brooklyn errors, misjudgments, and awkwardness in the field turned a single into a triple and allowed a runner to score on a short outfield fly. The Red Sox gathered only seven hits off Brooklyn's top pitcher Jeff Pfeffer, who had appeared twice in relief and once as a pinch-hitter (he struck out in the fourth game). But

Jeff made two wild pitches to add to the three Brooklyn errors so the Red Sox ran off with the championship.

Leading hitters:

BOSTON RED SOX
Lewis: .353

BROOKLYN DODGERS
Stengel: .364

Winning pitchers:

BOSTON RED SOX
Shore: won 2, lost 0
Ruth: won 1, lost 0
Leonard: won 1, lost 0

BROOKLYN DODGERS
Coombs: won 1, lost 0

1917

CHICAGO A.L. vs. NEW YORK N.L.

WON BY CHICAGO, 4 GAMES TO 2

Game Scores:

Chicago 2	New York 1	October 6 at Chicago
Chicago 7	New York 2	October 7 at Chicago
New York 2	Chicago 0	October 10 at New York
New York 5	Chicago 0	October 11 at New York
Chicago 8	New York 5	October 13 at Chicago
Chicago 4	New York 2	October 15 at New York

The feature of the 1917 World Series, the first wartime World Series in the nation's history, was "Zimmerman's chase" in which the Giant third baseman, holding the baseball, chased Eddie Collins across home plate with a run in the sixth game. This was long recalled as Zimmerman's Boner, and classified with Merkle's forgetting to touch second in 1908. But Manager Mc-Graw of the Giants never blamed Zimmerman. The New York pitcher, Rube Benton, and the first baseman, Walter Holke, apparently could not decide which one was to cover home, so the mighty Zim had no one to throw to except the umpire.

Eddie Collins, Connie Mack's former star, was the star of this series for Chicago. He hit .409 and stole three bases, and he set a new record by playing in his 26th World Series game.

War or no, Comiskey Park was jammed for the opening game

66

in Chicago. The White Sox, hungry, underpaid, hard-hitting, and tough, were the best team in baseball, and they promptly showed it by beating left-handed Slim Sallee, with the help of a home run by Hap Felsch. Sallee pitched a strong game but Eddie Cicotte pitched just as strongly. Both pitchers allowed seven hits. Both struck out two. The home run made the difference.

Game number two was also played before a full house and once more McGraw started a left-hander, as he did in every game in the series. But this left-hander, Ferdie Schupp, gave up four hits while getting four men out, and was lifted in the second inning. The White Sox kept right on hitting and scored five runs in the fourth to put the game on ice. There was not a single extra-base blow in this game but Eddie Collins stole two bases.

Back at the Polo Grounds three days later, with his left-handers rested and his players rejoicing in their home heath, McGraw found a way to beat the White Sox: He started another left-hander, Rube Benton, and Rube gave Chicago only five hits and no runs. The Giants meanwhile combed Ed Cicotte for eight hits, three of them by Davy Robertson, New York's right fielder. The crowd at this game was the biggest yet for the series, a full house, with standees on the ramps, but still not so large as the mob that filled Braves Field the year before.

The next day, before a somewhat smaller crowd, Ferdie Schupp, the happy-go-lucky lefty, came back and found his control. He shut the White Sox out this time, with seven hits, and fanned seven. McGraw's pet, Bennie Kauff, the reformed Federal Leaguer, who had gone hitless in the first two games, came to life too and swatted two home runs, driving in three runs and briefly suggesting that maybe he *was* going to be the world's greatest hitter, just as he always said.

When they went back to Chicago for the fifth game, McGraw's men acted as if they were about to keep the White Sox on the run. Reb Russell could not get a single Giant out in the first inning and Ed Cicotte rescued him after the Giants had scored two runs. In the seventh inning the Giants were leading 5 to 2 and Slim Sallee looked invincible. But he was suddenly set upon in the home half of the inning and gave up three runs. Next inning, before he could get more than one man out, he gave up three runs more and the Giant lead had faded for good. Pol Perritt yielded only a single hit thereafter. The White Sox needed no more. Bennie Kauff had got two hits again but this time there had been no home runs. These were his last hits of the series, which he finished with a batting average of .160.

The sixth game was an all-around disaster for McGraw, and the race between Zimmerman and Eddie Collins was the least of it. In the fourth inning, with both sides scoreless, Heinie Zimmerman threw the ball into the outfield in trying to put out Eddie Collins. Then Dave Robertson, who was the Giants' hitting leader in the series, dropped an easy fly by Joe Jackson. With Collins on third and Jackson on first, Hap Felsch hit a high bounding ball to the pitcher, Rube Benton. Rube threw quickly to Zimmerman, and Collins was caught yards off the base. The catcher, Bill Rariden, closed in quickly to catch Collins in a rundown. But neither Benton nor first baseman Walter Holke made a move to cover the plate. Collins then quickly brushed by Rariden and beat Zimmerman home, with no one at the plate but umpire Bill Klem. The White Sox got two more runs then on only two hits and the Giants never caught up. The biggest crowd of the season in the Polo Grounds watched this travesty and added their own groans to McGraw's anguished cries.

This was the end of the line for a number of ball players, who went into service before the next season began. Bennie Kauff came back for three more seasons with McGraw but he never played in another World Series.

Leading hitters:

CHICAGO WHITE SOX
Eddie Collins: .409

NEW YORK GIANTS
Robertson: .500

Winning pitchers:

CHICAGO WHITE SOX
Cicotte: won 1, lost 1
Faber: won 3, lost 1

NEW YORK GIANTS
Schupp: won 1, lost 0
Benton: won 1, lost 1

1918

BOSTON A.L. vs. CHICAGO N.L.

WON BY BOSTON, 4 GAMES TO 2

Game Scores:

Boston 1	Chicago 0	September 5 at Chicago
Chicago 3	Boston 1	September 6 at Chicago
Boston 2	Chicago 1	September 7 at Chicago
Boston 3	Chicago 2	September 9 at Boston
Chicago 3	Boston 0	September 10 at Boston
Boston 2	Chicago 1	September 11 at Boston

The 1918 season was cut off abruptly by the "work-or-fight" order of Major General Enoch Crowder, the Provost Marshal General of the United States Army. The country by the summer of 1918 was deep in the war, many baseball stars were in uniform, and many fans as well, while there was a general conviction that the war had years to go. Food rationing, Blue Mondays, and long casualty lists had diminished the interest in baseball anyway and the shortened season had provided no buildup of excitement. As a result the series was poorly attended, with empty seats at every game. Yet it was tightly played, as the scores indicate. Every Red Sox victory was by a one-run margin and no club scored more than three times in any game.

The country's greatest pitcher, Grover Cleveland Alexander, recently purchased by the Cubs, should have starred in the

70

series. But he was in military uniform, as were most of the men who had starred in the 1916 series for the Red Sox. Of the famous outfield trio of Lewis-Speaker-Hooper, only Harry Hooper remained. Babe Ruth was playing for the Red Sox and, as a part-time outfielder, he had hit eleven home runs in the short season, tying for the league lead. But he had still not started to pull crowds into the park and he was still, for the series at least, the leading Red Sox left-handed pitcher. The gate receipts were the smallest since 1910.

Boston's hero of the series was a thirty-five-year-old outfielder who had played four games for the Red Sox in 1907, had played eleven games for the Yankees in 1913, and was destined never to play another major league game after the series was over. He was George Whiteman from Peoria. He hit .267 in the season and made five hits and several spectacular catches in the series.

The first three games were played in Chicago, to keep traveling at a minimum. They were played at Comiskey Park, the home of the White Sox, because there were more seats there. But the extra seats stood empty.

In the first game Babe Ruth continued his string of scoreless innings, begun when he pitched thirteen of them in the 1916 series. He gave up six hits, all singles, and no runs. The Chicago manager, Fred Mitchell, whose real name was Fred Yapp, used left-handers in hopes of keeping Ruth out of the lineup; in the fourth game Babe pitched just to two batters in the ninth and then went to left field to allow Joe Bush to clean up.

Lefty George Tyler, hero of the 1914 series when he was with the Braves, won the second game for the Cubs, giving up but six hits (one to George Whiteman) and allowing no run until the ninth inning. Joe Bush gave only seven hits to the Cubs, but the tail end of the Chicago order got to him in the second inning for three runs, all they needed to win.

Carl Mays won game number three for Boston. This season he had excellent control of his underhand pitch, although not always of his temper. He struck out four in this game and gave up only a single base on balls. Boston hitting was light too, for

Hippo Vaughn scattered seven hits among them, with only Wally Schang, the Boston catcher, one of several players bought from Philadelphia, getting more than one.

The fourth game, the first one played at Boston, was another victory for Ruth, who received credit even though Joe Bush had to bail him out in the ninth. In this game, Babe got his only hit of the series, a long triple. He also added $7\frac{1}{3}$ more scoreless innings to his string, to set up a World Series record that stood until Whitey Ford broke it in 1961. Ruth hit seventh in the lineup in this game and his hit played an important part in the scoring. With two strikes on him, in the fourth inning, and Whiteman and McInnis on base, Ruth drove the next pitch out over the head of the Cub right fielder, sending two runs home. This was one time when it would have been excellent strategy to walk the pitcher, for the next batter was shortstop Everett Scott, who had made one hit in the previous twelve times at bat.

Before the fifth game was played, the players of both clubs held an indignation meeting and elected representatives to protest the new divvy that would cut the second- and third-place clubs into the receipts of the first four games. With prices kept low to invite attendance and with attendance low anyway, the cuts were going to be small enough without this extra slice. The clubs were already griped at having to leave Comiskey Park, where attendance was picking up, to play in Fenway Park, with its smaller capacity. The National Commission, however, would not give in and the unhappy players took the field an hour late, with a few hundred extra police on hand to prevent the predicted "riot." Hippo Vaughn won this one over Sad Sam Jones, who had been tossed in as a make-weight when the Red Sox had traded Tris Speaker to Cleveland. Jones nearly matched big Hippo until the eighth inning, when two Chicago runs put the game out of reach. Shortstop Charley Hollocher won this game for Vaughn, with his hitting and base-running. The light-footed infielder, who was always "not feeling too well," ran away from a pickoff at first to steal second base, made three of the Cubs' seven hits, and scored two of their three runs.

The final game was played before the smallest crowd yet, the local fans having turned against the ball players for their "greed" and "commercialism" in wanting to take home almost as much from the series as the club officials did. Carl Mays let the Cubs have only three hits in this game. George Tyler gave the Red Sox only five hits but he provided five walks too and beat himself with his wildness. In the third inning he walked the opposing pitcher, who was promptly pushed to second with a bunt, then walked the Red Sox second baseman, Dave Shean, putting on two runs for George Whiteman to drive home with a fierce blow to right that the Cub fielder could not hold on to.

The winning players in this series took home only $1100 each this season, with the pot sliced up among the first-division clubs and war charities.

Leading hitters:

BOSTON RED SOX
Schang: .444

CHICAGO CUBS
Pick: .389

Winning pitchers:

BOSTON RED SOX
Ruth: won 2, lost 0
Mays: won 2, lost 0

CHICAGO CUBS
Vaughn: won 1, lost 2
Tyler: won 1, lost 1

1919

CINCINNATI N.L. vs. CHICAGO A.L.

WON BY CINCINNATI, 5 GAMES TO 3

Game Scores:

Cincinnati 9	Chicago 1	October 1 at Cincinnati
Cincinnati 4	Chicago 2	October 2 at Cincinnati
Chicago 3	Cincinnati 0	October 3 at Chicago
Cincinnati 2	Chicago 0	October 4 at Chicago
Cincinnati 5	Chicago 0	October 6 at Chicago
Chicago 5	Cincinnati 4	October 7 at Cincinnati
Chicago 4	Cincinnati 1	October 8 at Cincinnati
Cincinnati 10	Chicago 5	October 9 at Chicago

Nineteen-nineteen was the first year of peace. It was the year the Boston police went on strike and the year Babe Ruth set a new home run record (29) with the Red Sox. It was the first year Cincinnati had won a pennant. It was the first year, since 1903, that a club had to win five games to take the championship. And it was the year the Black Sox sold out to the gamblers.

With the tremendous resurgence of interest in baseball, now that the boys were home from the wars, and especially now that Cincinnati, professional baseball's birthplace, had a chance to win first prize, the club owners decided to cash in while the cashing was good. They scheduled the 1919 World Series as a five-out-of-nine contest. The players, bound by the reserve rule and paid far less than men earned in the wartime shipyards (where

74

the work was sometimes playing baseball!), wanted to cash in too. So some of them listened to the gamblers who promised them sudden wealth if they agreed to give less than their best efforts on the diamond.

As it turned out, one or two of the players made $10,000 on the deal while some of the "conspirators" got nothing at all. And many people thought that the players had not thrown more than one game—that they had decided to cross up the gamblers who had double-crossed them. But this was not really the first instance of games being thrown at the behest of gamblers. In Cincinnati the previous season, as later investigation proved without a doubt, two ballplayers had made at least one and probably many more efforts to "do business" on ball games. The gamblers had really begun to make inroads among the players, who had become very conscious of the profits that baseball produced and the unhappy contrast between profits and ballplayers' salaries. (A star in that day might earn $7500 a season.) The Black Sox scandal brought the whole business into the open and prompted immediate corrective action.

There had been only 140 games in the 1919 regular season. (The club owners were not sure if General Enoch Crowder was still looking over their shoulders.) So the series got off to an early start. But there was an air of suspicion around the game already, for the gamblers had made the Reds the favorites over the best team in baseball, the slugging White Sox. The park, however, was jammed with the first really big baseball crowd since before the war. When the Reds knocked out Eddie Cicotte, Chicago's 29-game winner, in the fourth inning, several observers thought they smelled something bad. The mighty White Sox had collected only six hits, while the Reds had made fourteen—half of them off Cicotte. And the White Sox manager, Kid Gleason, thought his men were "acting strangely." Cicotte's testimony before the grand jury admitted he had lobbed the ball to the batters.

After the second game went to the Reds, the whispers and suspicions increased. But Pat Moran (called Old Whiskey Face by his friends) always insisted that his club won on its merits. They were not a pushover club by any means. Dutch Ruether, who won the first game, and Slim Sallee, who won the second (although he allowed ten hits), had won forty games between them during the season.

In the second game, Lefty Williams of the White Sox (who was supposed to have received $10,000) gave up only four hits, but he walked six. One of the men later suspended for being involved in the fix, Chick Gandil, actually stole a base in this game and there was no apparent lack of effort to win.

Dickie Kerr, who was never suspected of either guilty knowledge or participation in the fraud, shut out Cincinnati in game number three. The White Sox played errorless ball. Joe Jackson, one of the Black Sox, got two hits, while Swede Risberg, who was also to become an outcast, hit a triple. There was dissension on the club at this time with some of the players not talking to the rest; but all agreed that little Dickie Kerr pitched his heart out for this game and all admired him for it.

Game number four went to Cincinnati, but it was difficult to think of it as a put-up job. Eddie Cicotte, suspect-in-chief, pitched this game and allowed the Reds only five hits, while the White Sox gathered only three off Cincinnati's Jimmy Ring. All the Chicago hits were made by three other supposed plotters: Jackson, Gandil, and Hap Felsch. Cicotte did not yield a single base on balls.

Cincinnati shut out the White Sox in game number five, with Hod Eller, who had won nineteen games for the Reds in the season, holding the White Sox to only three hits again. This time, Buck Weaver, another black sheep, got two of the hits and one was a triple. Claude Williams, accused of engineering the fix, pitched for Chicago and gave the Reds only four hits and walked two men. What suspicion attached to this game centered on costly errors by third baseman Buck Weaver and center fielder Felsch. It was hard to imagine, however, that Lefty Williams could have worked any harder to win.

Dickie Kerr won the sixth game despite more errors by Felsch and Swede Risberg, but he did allow eleven hits. According to some grand jury testimony that was later disowned, however, the ballplayers did make an effort to kick this one away by holding the ball a little bit longer than need be when fielding a ground ball and by other tactics not so crude as deliberately booting the ball. But whatever they did, it was not enough to beat Dickie Kerr. In this game, the hard-core Black Sox—Weaver, Jackson, and Felsch—did particularly well at the plate, with Weaver getting two doubles and a single.

In game number seven, it was the innocents from Cincinnati who kicked the ball around. They committed four errors against only one for the White Sox, and they were never close to winning the game after Chicago had collected four runs in the first five innings. The final game, however, saw the complete collapse of the White Sox, whether from design or from simple demoralization, who can say? It surely helped confirm the suspicions of many baseball men—including Chicago owner Charles Comiskey, who spent several thousand dollars in an investigation that turned up a good deal of unpleasant evidence. What looked most suspicious perhaps was the failure of Chick Gandil even to come back to the club in the spring. The other seven who were eventually suspended did show up, however, and put in a good season before they were adjudged guilty and suspended for life by baseball's new High Commissioner, Kenesaw Mountain Landis.

Leading hitters:

CINCINNATI REDS
Neale: .357

CHICAGO WHITE SOX
Jackson: .375

Winning pitchers:

CINCINNATI REDS
Ruether: won 1, lost 0
Sallee: won 1, lost 1
Ring: won 1, lost 1
Eller: won 2, lost 0

CHICAGO WHITE SOX
Cicotte: won 1, lost 2
Kerr: won 2, lost 0

1920

CLEVELAND A.L. vs. BROOKLYN N.L.

WON BY CLEVELAND, 5 GAMES TO 2

Game Scores:

Cleveland 3	Brooklyn 1	October 5 at Brooklyn
Brooklyn 3	Cleveland 0	October 6 at Brooklyn
Brooklyn 2	Cleveland 1	October 7 at Brooklyn
Cleveland 5	Brooklyn 1	October 9 at Cleveland
Cleveland 8	Brooklyn 1	October 10 at Cleveland
Cleveland 1	Brooklyn 0	October 11 at Cleveland
Cleveland 3	Brooklyn 0	October 12 at Cleveland

The 1920 series became celebrated as the one in which Bill Wambsganss, the Cleveland shortstop, performed an unassisted triple play, the only man ever to pull such a stunt in a World Series, and Elmer Smith, Cleveland right fielder, hit the first grand slam home run in series history. But 1920 lives in baseball fame for other reasons. It was the year that Brooklyn and Boston played the longest game in history—twenty-six innings to a tie. It was the year Cleveland shortstop Ray Chapman was killed at the plate by a pitch from Carl Mays. It was the last time that the National Commission ran the World Series (the Commissioner took over after that). And it was the year (about two weeks before the series) that the Black Sox scandal broke.

Fans were not notably affected by the scandal, for they

crowded the small ball parks in both cities. Brooklyn had the strongest pitching staff in baseball, it was said, and Cleveland was led by one of baseball's deities—Tris Speaker, still active and still fearsome at the plate. As it turned out, Cleveland supplied the real pitching thrills and Brooklyn turned up a man, pitcher Clarence Mitchell, who hit into five putouts in two trips to the plate. He was the one who hit into the triple play and he hit into a double play next time up.

Cleveland's hero was their mighty pitcher, Stan Coveleski, whose older brother, Harry, had starred for Detroit a few years earlier. Stan, a big strong Polish boy from Pennsylvania, where he was known as Stanislaus Kowalewski, outpitched all of the Dodger stars—outpitched everyone, in fact, who had ever worked in a World Series except the matchless Christy Mathewson. Stan won three games from Brooklyn. In the three games he gave up a total of fifteen hits, two runs, and two bases on balls. He struck out eight.

Coveleski won the first game from Brooklyn Manager Wilbert Robinson's ace, Rube Marquard, with each club making five hits. But Steve O'Neill, Cleveland's veteran catcher who still had many baseball years ahead of him, did the most damage, with two doubles.

Spitballer Burleigh Grimes, one of Brooklyn's immortals, stood the Indians on their ears in the second game, in which Jim Bagby, the thirty-one-game winner, pitched for Cleveland. Burleigh, as always, made believe every pitch was a spitter, yet he actually was sparing of it. A lot of Clevelanders got on base, but none of them got home. The spitball had been outlawed this year, although all the pitchers who depended on it were permitted to use it as long as they stayed in organized ball. Burleigh became the last of the spitballers. He threw his final juicy pitch when he was working for the Yankees in 1934.

When Sherry Smith, Uncle Robby's other veteran left-hander, took the third game for Brooklyn, the local fans saw total victory around the corner. Smith, who had won only eleven games in the season, gave the Indians only three hits and a single run. But in the next game Stan Coveleski came back and doled out his ration of five small hits, while the Indians battered iron man Leon Cadore, who had pitched the entire twenty-six-inning game in May, for four hits and two runs in one inning.

Jim Bagby, Cleveland's top pitcher, was hit hard in the fifth game, but so many miracles were wrought around him that he was never in danger of losing the game. He gave up thirteen hits, including a three-bagger by Brooklyn first baseman Ed Konetchy. But Elmer Smith hit his bases-full home run in the first inning and gave Bagby a nice cushion to ride on. Then, when too many Brooklyns got on base, Bill Wambsganss wiped them all off in one agile move.

In the fifth inning, with no one out, Brooklyn had put second baseman Kilduff and catcher Otto Miller on base. Clarence Mitchell, the pitcher, was the batter, and the hit-and-run was on. Both runners started on the dead run down the baselines as Bagby unleashed his pitch. Mitchell drove it on a line to Wambsganss, who had broken toward second base and was almost there when the ball reached him. He grabbed the ball for one out, stepped on the base to double Kilduff, and then spun around to put the tag on Miller. It took everyone several seconds to realize he had put the whole side out, and then the Cleveland stands exploded even more wildly than they had for Elmer Smith's blow. Jim Bagby put frosting on his own cake by hitting a home run, the first ever hit by a pitcher in a World Series game.

Elmer Smith, besides his home run, hit a triple and a single.

Game number six was a typical World Series surprise, with a castoff pitcher throwing a nearly hitless shutout against his former teammates. Duster Mails had been with Brooklyn in 1915 and 1916 without ever winning them a game. Now, four years later, he had helped win the pennant for Cleveland—seven wins and no losses in nine starts. Matched with Sherry Smith, left-handed Duster dusted the Dodgers off properly, allowing them two singles and a double, well-separated, and no runs at all. Smith pitched one of the best games of the series for Brooklyn, allowing seven singles, giving up one walk, and granting just the lone run that was needed to beat him. This was Brooklyn's last chance.

Bearded Burleigh Grimes made a valiant effort to climb back uphill in the final game, but his mates could not get past first base on Stan Coveleski. Shortstop Ivey Olson, notorious for his spells of erratic fielding, forecast the Dodger defeat early in the afternoon when he got in the way of a batted ball in the third inning and was called out.

Joe Wood, former star pitcher with the Red Sox when Speaker was there, played right field against the Dodgers but batted only .200. (Next season he gave up pitching altogether and batted .366.)

Leading hitters:

CLEVELAND INDIANS
Jamieson and O'Neill: .333

BROOKLYN DODGERS
Wheat: .333

Winning pitchers:

CLEVELAND INDIANS
Coveleski: won 3, lost 0
Bagby: won 1, lost 1
Mails: won 1, lost 0

BROOKLYN DODGERS
Grimes: won 1, lost 2
Smith: won 1, lost 1

1921

NEW YORK N.L. vs. NEW YORK A.L.

WON BY GIANTS, 5 GAMES TO 3

Game Scores:

		All games at Polo Grounds, New York
Yankees 3	Giants 0	October 5
Yankees 3	Giants 0	October 6
Giants 13	Yankees 5	October 7
Giants 4	Yankees 2	October 9
Yankees 3	Giants 1	October 10
Giants 8	Yankees 5	October 11
Giants 2	Yankees 1	October 12
Giants 1	Yankees 0	October 13

This was a series for firsts. It was the first time in history that all the World Series games were played in the same park. It was the first series that included the Yankees. It was the first time that New York fans were able to attend a World Series game on Sunday. It was the first World Series held under the auspices of the new Commissioner. It was the first time the series was won by the club that dropped the first two games. It was the first World Series in which two runners stole home (McNally of the Yankees in the first game and Meusel of the Yankees in the second). It was the first time the winner's share had exceeded $5000 per man. But it was the *last* five-out-of-nine series ever played.

The hero of this series should have been Waite Hoyt, strong Yankee right-hander who had been John McGraw's "schoolboy pitcher" three years earlier, when he made his debut at the Polo Grounds by striking out the final batter in the only game he worked. Hoyt, traded to the Yankees by the Red Sox, won nineteen games for the Yankees in 1921, won two games in the World Series, and came within a deep breath of winning a third game.

There was a crucial character to this series that had nothing to do with the players engaged in it. The Yankees, for the first time in history, had actually been outdrawing the Giants (using the same park), and McGraw was grimly determined to show the city that his Giants were still number one—despite Babe Ruth and his fifty-nine home runs. George Kelly of the Giants had led the older league with twenty-three home runs, and the contrast was accepted by many fans as an indication of how the leagues compared.

Actually the clubs were remarkably well matched. The Giants had the edge in fielding, but the Yankees—with hitters like Ruth, Bob Meusel, Wally Pipp (he led the league in homers in 1916 and 1917), and Home Run Baker—were stronger at the plate. Each club had a fine pitching staff: Carl Mays, the league leader; Waite Hoyt; and Bob Shawkey for the Yankees; Art Nehf; Shuffling Phil Douglas; and Fred Toney for the Giants.

In the first game, Carl Mays showed all the form that had won him twenty-seven games that season. He gave the Giants five hits and did not walk a man. He hit one batsman. The Yankees made only seven hits off Phil Douglas and Jess Barnes, but they put them close enough together to turn them into three runs.

Game number two was a duplicate of the first in score but even more sensational in pitching. Waite Hoyt was at his very best, and he needed to be, because Art Nehf was just about as good. The difference lay in the fielding, where the Giants were supposed to excel. There were three errors by the Giants, one by the catcher, Earl Smith, one by Nehf, and one by Frankie Frisch, the second baseman. That was all the Yankees needed. Nehf gave them only three hits to work on. But he walked seven. Waite Hoyt, who walked five men himself, allowed only two hits and struck out five.

According to tradition, the Giants, having lost the first two games, were the same as done for. And the third game started as if this fact were well-established. Fred Toney looked like just the pitcher the Yanks had been waiting for. They clubbed his delivery here and there, making four runs in the third inning and hustling Fred to the showers. With a four-run lead Bob Shawkey seemed ready to plop the third game into the bag. And then the Giant tornado struck him. Coming to bat last in the third inning (they were the home club today) the Giants did just what the Yankees had done—belted in four runs and sent the enemy pitcher back to the center-field clubhouse. But the Giants never let up until they had collected twenty hits, including triples by Ross Youngs and George Burns and doubles by Youngs, Burns, and Irish Meusel. Babe Ruth so far had hardly been in it when it came to hitting.

In game number four, Carl Mays tried to trim Phil Douglas again, and this time Ruth came through with his only home run of the series. But it was not enough. The Giants reached Mays for nine hits, including doubles by Burns and Kelly, while Shuffling Phil Douglas struck out eight Yankees.

The fifth game brought together the two aces—Nehf and Hoyt —and once more rugged Waite, the hero of Brooklyn's Erasmus High, outpitched the veteran Nehf—even though Nehf allowed only six hits to the Giants' ten off Hoyt. Hoyt was just invincible with Giants on base, and the one run he did permit was not earned. This game was especially costly to the Yankees, for in it they lost Babe Ruth. Babe wrenched his knee badly and had to sit out the game. He had started out with an infected arm but he did not let this slow him. In game number one he had hurled himself recklessly into slides to steal second and third bases in succession. But the knee finished him and he appeared again only as a pinch-hitter in the final game, when he grounded out feebly to the shortstop.

84

The Yankees tried a wild man named Harry Harper in the sixth game and they greeted the Giants' Fred Toney just as they had in the third game, with hits enough, including a home run by Fewster, to send the Giants' pitcher back to the clubhouse before the inning was over. The Giants repeated too, tying the score promptly, in their next at-bats, and sending Harper to join Toney in the showers. Harry, who got only four men out, allowed three hits, walked two, and gave up three runs. Then Shawkey came on and looked as if he might last, especially when the Yankees provided two more runs in their half of the second (they were the home club this time). But the Giants came on strong again in the fourth and added four more runs, then another in the sixth to put the game on ice. Jess Barnes, who took over for the Giants in the first inning, gave up only four hits and struck out ten.

Game number seven brought Douglas and Mays together again and one was as good as the other. The Giants got only six hits off Mays, while Douglas gave up eight. But the Giants this time got theirs when it counted, while the Yanks left seven men on base. Early in the game, the Yankees' leaping third baseman, Mike McNally, injured his throwing arm and had to let Baker take over. Baker hit as well as Mike but he slowed the team down on the baselines.

The final game was one of Waite Hoyt's finest pitching efforts, and when he lost it his stout heart nearly cracked. He again allowed not a single earned run. The Giants scored in the very first inning on an error by Roger Peckinpaugh. The rest of the way, Hoyt kept them far from the scoring column, while he struck out seven. Art Nehf, however, was just as strong as Hoyt and he did not let the Yankee base runners get near home plate. The game was saved for the Giants in the final inning by a truly sensational stop by second baseman Johnny Rawlings of a blow by Frank Baker that looked like a certain hit. Johnny nailed the ball on the edge of the right-field grass, far to his left, sprawled on the ground, got up, and threw out slow-footed Frank at first. Aaron Ward, who had been on first, counted the ball a hit and lit out for third base. But long George Kelly, with a rifle throw, cut him down there and won the series.

Leading hitters:

NEW YORK GIANTS
Snyder: .364

NEW YORK YANKEES
Ruth: .313

Winning pitchers:

NEW YORK GIANTS
Barnes: won 2, lost 0
Douglas: won 2, lost 1
Nehf: won 1, lost 2

NEW YORK YANKEES
Hoyt: won 2, lost 1
Mays: won 1, lost 2

1922

NEW YORK N.L. vs. NEW YORK A.L.

WON BY GIANTS, 4 GAMES TO 0 (ONE TIE GAME)

Game Scores:

		All games at Polo Grounds, New York
Giants 3	Yankees 2	October 4
Giants 3	Yankees 3	October 5
Giants 3	Yankees 0	October 6
Giants 4	Yankees 3	October 7
Giants 5	Yankees 3	October 8

John McGraw settled the question of superiority in 1922 with firmness and dispatch. The best the Yanks could do this time was hang on in the second game for a ten-inning tie. They never were able to score more than three runs against Giant pitching in any game. Babe Ruth was especially feeble at the plate, with just a double and single in seventeen times at bat. Babe had missed the first two months of the season, as punishment for going on a barnstorming tour after the 1921 World Series, in open defiance of an edict by Commissioner Landis. He lost his home run leadership to Ken Williams of St. Louis, who hit 39 homers to Babe's 35. And Babe's season average had dropped from a .378 in 1921 to .315 in 1922.

The Giants' hitters, led by second baseman Frankie Frisch and third baseman Heinie Groh, grew fat on Yankee pitching in the four games. They had a club average of .309; Groh hit .474 for the series while Frisch hit .471.

The tie game was a wholly mysterious business, for the sun was still at least a half-hour above the horizon when umpire George Hildebrand called the game "on account of darkness." Some said that he did so at the urging of veteran umpire Bill Klem, who still remembered the fourteen-inning Red Sox-Brooklyn game in 1916 that was finished in the dusk. But dusk was far away when they halted this game and the patrons suspected that someone had called it off just to earn another fat gate (there were thirty-seven thousand in the stands). Commissioner Landis, who was present and who received most of the customers' boos, ordered the clubs to donate the entire receipts to charity.

The Giants came close to losing the first game, for they were behind 2 to 0 when they came to bat in the last of the eighth. In that inning, Bancroft, Groh, Frisch, and Irish Meusel all laid into Joe Bush and scored three runs. Waite Hoyt relieved and silenced the Giant bats. But the Yanks could do nothing with relief pitcher Rosy Ryan.

The second game was the tie game. Bob Shawkey really did some of his finest work in this game. After a rough first inning, in which Irish Meusel teed off for a home run with Groh and Frisch on base, Shawkey shut the Giants out for nine innings in a row. Jess Barnes pitched the whole game for the Giants and struck out six. Aaron Ward got a home run in this game, the only one the famous Murderers' Row could produce in the series.

Game number three was a triumph for Jack Scott, the tobacco farmer who came back to baseball in a desperate effort to recoup the money he lost when his barns burned down. Scott faced the best the Yanks could offer, Waite Hoyt, nineteen-game winner, who had yet to allow an earned run in World Series competition. But today the Giants figured out Hoyt while Scott was a mystery to the Yankees. He gave them just four hits while the Giants pried eleven away from Hoyt in seven innings. Still, of the three runs the Giants scored, only one was earned.

For the fourth game, the Giants had pitcher Hughie McQuillan, a cheerful, light-hearted young Irishman from Queens, New York, who had been a flop with the last-place Braves and had come to the Giants in midseason. Handsome Hugh gave up two runs to start with and seemed on the verge of giving up a lot more. But a hair-raising catch in deepest center field made by substitute outfielder Bill Cunningham of a howling blow by Babe Ruth put a sudden end to the Yankee rally. Later on Aaron Ward made his second hit of the series, another home run. But the Giants, led by Beauty Bancroft, Irish Meusel, and Ross Youngs, really assaulted Carl Mays in the fifth inning and put four runs together—enough to win the game.

The final game was an overdue victory for Art Nehf, who had had to let Rosy Ryan win the first game for him. Nehf this time held the Yanks to five hits, all singles, and for the third time in World Series history the American League entry had failed to win a single game. Joe Bush pitched for the Yankees and lost his second game.

The humiliation of the Yankees caused an uproar in the front office, where one of the "colonels" who owned the club, Tillinghast Huston, insisted that little Miller Huggins, the manager, be fired because of the Yanks' poor showing. What really came about, however, was that Huston himself had to sell out to his partner Colonel Ruppert, who immediately gave Huggins the authority he needed to discipline the Yankee playboys. Huston, himself a man who liked to look upon illicit wine when it was red, had been inclined to forgive the boys all their derelictions. But Huggins, once the boss told him he had the power, set out to whip his lads into line.

This World Series victory was the last one for John McGraw, whose hatred for the Yankees grew deeper and more bitter, despite the fact that he had trimmed them twice head-to-head. The Yankees continued to outpull the Giants and the fans clearly did not agree with McGraw's assessment of Ruth—that he was not one-third the hitter Rogers Hornsby was. Exasperated by the continued success of the Yanks, McGraw and the Giant management told them to go find a park of their own to play in—and thus they instigated the creation of the Yankee Stadium, the first really modern baseball plant, that eventually grew big enough to hold almost twice as many as the Polo Grounds.

Leading hitters:

NEW YORK GIANTS
Groh: .474

NEW YORK YANKEES
R. Meusel: .300

Winning pitchers:

NEW YORK GIANTS
Ryan:	won 1, lost 0
Nehf:	won 1, lost 0
McQuillan:	won 1, lost 0
Scott:	won 1, lost 0

1923

NEW YORK A.L. vs. NEW YORK N.L.

WON BY YANKEES, 4 GAMES TO 2

Game Scores:

Giants 5	Yankees 4	October 10 at Yankee Stadium
Yankees 4	Giants 2	October 11 at Polo Grounds
Giants 1	Yankees 0	October 12 at Yankee Stadium
Yankees 8	Giants 4	October 13 at Polo Grounds
Yankees 8	Giants 1	October 14 at Yankee Stadium
Yankees 6	Giants 4	October 15 at Polo Grounds

In 1923, when the Yankees moved into their new park, and promptly set out to spread-eagle the rest of their league in the race for the pennant, the Giants were determined to put their rivals down for the third and, they hoped, the final time. So scornful was McGraw of all things connected with the Yankees that he had his club dress in their own locker room at the Polo Grounds for all games, then cross the bridge to the Stadium for the Yanks' home games. He allowed his players to shift sweat shirts in the Stadium clubhouse, and nothing more.

The Yankees, however, really made hay in the Polo Grounds. They lost two of the three games played at Yankee Stadium, but they won all three of the games played at McGraw's home park.

The only authentic hero the Giants produced in this series was an aging outfielder they had rescued from the Phillies two seasons before. He was Charles Dillon (Casey) Stengel, and he helped convince the fans of both clubs that they were getting their money's worth. Known as a wit and a man who could rasp an opponent's hide with a wisecrack, Stengel belted a long long drive in the first game at Yankee Stadium. It did not go out of the park (no fair ball ever has, except one that trickled out through an unfinished fence), but Stengel made a home run out of it and the Yankees all screamed their hatred of him. It was the one run the Giants needed to win that first game. They had finished off Waite Hoyt in the third inning, when they scored four runs, thanks largely to a triple by Heinie Groh. The Yanks tied it in the seventh and Stengel won it for the Giants.

In the third game, when Art Nehf and Sad Sam Jones were locked in a scoreless duel, Casey Stengel, with the yelps of the bench jockeys ringing in his ears, poked one of Jones' pitches into the right-field stands at Yankee Stadium. He thumbed his nose at his tormentors as he touched all the bases. Colonel Ruppert was all for having Casey stripped of his uniform and flayed in public for his insulting conduct, but someone persuaded him that there was no statutory basis for such punishment. It was the only run of the game, so Casey actually won all the games the Giants made off with.

In previous World Series, when an accident had taken a key player off the roster, as when Ray Chapman of Cleveland was killed in 1920 and when Jimmy Johnston of the Dodgers was injured prior to the same series, opposing managers had always agreed to the eligibility of substitutes. This season, Wally Pipp, the Yankee first baseman, sprained his ankle just before the series and Miller Huggins wanted to use a kid named Lou Gehrig, just up from Hartford. But tough John McGraw would not agree. He was giving nothing away to the dirty Yankees. So Pipp played, and got five hits, batting in two runs.

This was the first series in which Babe Ruth starred as a hitter. He made three home runs, a triple, a double, and three singles, for a series average of .368 (he had hit .393 for the season). Two of his home runs came one after the other in the second game. He also received eight free trips to first base.

92

The pitching star for the Yankees was the Squire of Kennett Square, Herb Pennock, a Red Sox graduate and one of the game's great left-handers. This was his eleventh season in the majors and his best yet. He had won nineteen games for the Yanks in the regular campaign. Herb won the second and sixth games. Although he gave up nine hits in the sixth game, he struck out six and managed to stay ahead of the struggling Giants through seven innings. After that Sad Sam Jones came in and held McGraw's snarling minions at bay. Pennock had saved the fourth game for Bob Shawkey by holding the Giants to one hit for the final four outs.

In this series the Yankees introduced one of their specialties —the big inning. Their runs usually came in sudden bunches and their pitchers were then charged with the job of hanging on to a fat lead.

The first three games were exceptions, particularly the third game, won by the Giants, in which the Yanks got only six hits and the Giants only four. But in game number four the Yanks provided six runs in the second inning, added one more in the third, and another in the fourth. They hung tight then until the eighth and ninth when, with the score 8 to 0 against them, Youngs, Stengel, and George Kelly pushed four runs across for McGraw.

In the fifth game, the only one at Yankee Stadium that the Giants lost, the Yankees put together seven runs in the first two innings. Then Joe Bush, after giving up a triple to Irish Meusel, on which Irish scored as Stengel grounded out, allowed only two more hits to the Giants all the rest of the way.

The big inning in the final game was the eighth. The Yanks were down 4 to 1 in this one (Ruth having made the only Yank run with a homer) when Art Nehf suddenly lost his stuff, after Wally Schang, the Yankee catcher, and Everett Scott, the iron man shortstop, had hit successive singles. On eight straight pitches, allowing no time for McGraw to warm up a relief pitcher, Nehf walked two pinch-hitters, catcher Fred Hofmann and pitcher Joe Bush, thus forcing in a run. By this time McGraw felt he had Rosy Ryan ready to fling into the breach. But Rosy was not quite ready, for he promptly walked Joe Dugan, forcing in one more run and leaving the bases full. Then Rosy pulled himself together and struck out Babe Ruth. Perhaps then he might have thought that the worst was over. If he did think that, he thought wrong, for the next member of Murderers' Row to step to the plate was Bob Meusel. Bob slapped a ball right at Ryan. It took a wild bounce over the pitcher's head and scooted to center field, where Bill Cunningham managed to kick it around long enough to let all three runners in. That made eight runs batted in for Bob Meusel, a series record. In their half of the eighth and in the ninth the Giants could do nothing against Sam Jones and the Yanks took home their first World Championship.

Leading hitters:

NEW YORK YANKEES
Ward: .417

NEW YORK GIANTS
Frisch: .400

Winning pitchers:

NEW YORK YANKEES
Pennock: won 2, lost 0
Shawkey: won 1, lost 0
Bush: won 1, lost 1

NEW YORK GIANTS
Ryan: won 1, lost 0
Nehf: won 1, lost 1

1924

WASHINGTON A.L. vs. NEW YORK N.L.

WON BY WASHINGTON, 4 GAMES TO 3

Game Scores:

New York 4 (12 innings)	Washington 3	October 4 at Washington
Washington 4	New York 3	October 5 at Washington
New York 6	Washington 4	October 6 at New York
Washington 7	New York 4	October 7 at New York
New York 6	Washington 2	October 8 at New York
Washington 2	New York 1	October 9 at Washington
Washington 4 (12 innings)	New York 3	October 10 at Washington

In 1924, John McGraw won his tenth and last National League pennant. Washington, in the American League, under her boy manager, twenty-seven-year-old Stanley (Bucky) Harris, won her first. Harris, who still played second base full time for the Senators, was one of the best-liked men in baseball and he outshone President Coolidge in Washington. But the sentimental favorite, and the most nervous man on the field, was thirty-six-year-old Walter Johnson, baseball's fastest pitcher, who was entering his first World Series after a spectacular big-league career that had begun with Washington in 1907. The whole town, indeed fans everywhere, rejoiced that this "old man," so long without honors that he had so long deserved, was going to have his chance to earn world fame and a cut in the series money. Walter had won twenty or more games for Washington ten years in a row (1910–19), had won thirty-six games one year, and this season had won twenty-three. He still had the speed of an express train and the nature of a gentle big brother. He was actually trembling when he walked out on the field to pitch the first game, and he was never at his best in the series. He held the Giants even for eleven innings in the first game and struck out twelve, only to lose the game to Art Nehf when the Senators could not come up with the tying run in the last of the twelfth. The Giants got fourteen hits off Walter's fast ball.

The second game almost went the way of the first when the Giants tied the game with two runs in the ninth inning. But the Senators, last at bat, came through with the needed run and went to New York all even.

The clubs then took turns winning. Firpo Marberry, a mediocre performer during the season, was wild as a mountain goat when he took the mound for Washington. In three innings, he allowed five hits, walked two men, hit Frankie Frisch with a pitch, and gave up three runs. The Senators never caught up, although they made two runs in the fourth and added one in the eighth, on a pinch single by an obscure first baseman named Mule Shirley, and then another in the ninth. To choke off the final threat, the Giants used two pitchers, Claude Jonnard, who never won more than six big league games in any season, and their own Mule, Mule Watson, who never pitched another big league game.

Next it was the Senators' turn. This time they started George Mogridge, a sixteen-game winner, and after the Giants got the first run, the Senators gave George three runs to work with. The Senators added two runs in the fifth, to give George a four-run lead; after the Giants had scored a run in the bottom of the sixth, the Senators added two runs in the eighth. In the Giants' half, however, George could only get one man out, the Giants scored a run, and Harris lifted him quickly to bring in Firpo Marberry, all warmed up from his work the day before. Firpo gave up a run in the ninth but came out ahead all the same.

9. This young man, called Jidge by his teammates, and Babe by everyone else, was one of the best left-handed pitchers alive in 1915, but Manager Carrigan would not use him in the World Series except as a pinch-hitter (Ruth grounded out). He did pitch in the series of 1916, when he held the Dodgers scoreless for thirteen innings, and in the series of 1918 when he ran his scoreless innings to twenty-nine. After that Babe Ruth became a home-run hitter. *Culver Pictures, Inc.*

10. John McGraw, in 1911, was still warming up before World Series games. Mathewson at his side. *Brown Brothers.*

11. The man who won the series: Frank "Home-Run" Baker, who hit three home runs for Philadelphia in the 1911 World Series. *Brown Brothers.*

12. Brooklyn battery in the 1916 World Series: Rube Marquard and Chief Meyers. *Brown Brothers.*

13. Jake Daubert scores a run for the Dodgers. Third World Series game against Boston Red Sox, 1916. *Brown Brothers.*

14. Baseball brass in 1910: Byron Bancroft Johnson, President of the American League; Thomas J. Lynch, President of the National League; August Hermann, Chairman of the National Commission, which supervised the World Series. *Brown Brothers.*

The Twenties

15. Muddy Ruel scores the winning run in the 1924 World Series, as home fans, yelling their delight, begin to jump over the barriers to the field to celebrate Washington's first World Championship. A wild bounce on a ground ball by McNeely sent this run across in the twelfth inning. *Brown Brothers.*

16. During the 1925 World Series, Christy Mathewson, greatest Giant pitcher, died in a sanitarium. This group of present and former heroes stood silently before the third game in the Washington ball park to honor Matty. In street clothes are Honus Wagner, on extreme left, then John McGraw, Babe Ruth (in his standard camel's-hair cap), and Christy Walsh, the sportswriter. Bill McKechnie, Pittsburgh manager, stands between Wagner and McGraw. Between McGraw and Ruth is Walter Johnson, hero of the previous World Series. The other uniformed figure is Nick Altrock, pitching hero for the White Sox in the 1906 World Series and now a semi-professional clown with Washington. *Brown Brothers.*

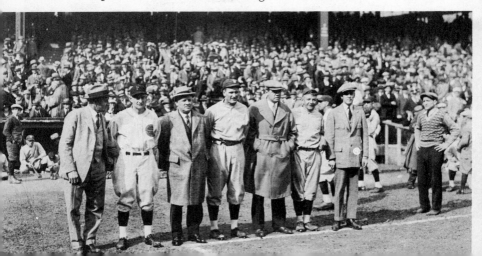

Goose Goslin was the big gun in this game, with four hits in four at-bats. The Giants got six hits altogether against thirteen for the Senators.

The Giants next day started their big handsome hard-hitting pitching find, Jack Bentley, who had come up to them the year before as the most versatile and most popular player in the International League—a pitcher who was in the lineup almost every day, mostly as a first baseman, and a slugger who hit twenty-two home runs while averaging .350 at bat. His earned-run average as a pitcher had been 1.75. Jack had spent four unhappy years with the Senators, with never a winning season, before becoming a first baseman with Baltimore in the International League. With the Giants, however, Jack had so far stuck to pitching and in 1924 he had won sixteen games. Today he squared off against Walter Johnson and he came out ahead, thanks largely to his own home run. Walter struck out only three this time and actually hit Ross Youngs with a pitch, a rare mistake for Johnson to make. Freddy Lindstrom, an eighteen-year-old third baseman whom McGraw had hustled in to take the place of the injured Heinie Groh, made four hits off Johnson, and a new fellow named Bill Terry reached Johnson for a triple. He had got a home run off Johnson in the first game.

The Senators' turn came the next day with a courageous pitching job by Tom Zachary, who gave the Giants one run in the first inning and nothing more. His mates made only four hits off Art Nehf and none at all off Rosy Ryan, but they put them near enough together with a walk to provide two runs in the fifth. Zachary did not walk anyone.

When the Giants' turn came they stumbled into some sort of jinx that took the game away from them when they had it in their grasp. In the eighth inning the Giants were ahead 3 to 1 and needed just to get the Senators out twice more to take home the championship. Jess Barnes had given them only six hits and one run up to that point and he looked strong enough to finish. But, with two men on base, Bucky Harris hit a hard ground ball down the third-base line toward Freddy Lindstrom, who had been playing like a genius. The ball (a lot livelier than it had been five years before) bounced crazily over Freddy's head and two runs came in, tying the ball game. For the second time, the clubs went into twelve innings and for the third time Walter Johnson came in to pitch for the Senators. This time big Walter was invincible. He allowed three hits over the four innings he pitched but he struck out five and permitted no runs. In the twelfth inning, the Giant jinx reappeared. Muddy Ruel, the Washington catcher, who had made only one hit so far in the series, popped a routine foul high over the head of Hank Gowdy. Hank, prompted by Lord knows what, dropped his mask as no veteran catcher ever would—right near his feet. Then, as he was about to glove the ball, he caught his foot in the mask, stumbled badly, and lost the ball. Whereupon Ruel banged a two-base hit and put the winning run out where a single would bring it in. Earl McNeely, the Washington center fielder, then poked what looked like a routine ground ball to Freddy Lindstrom. And again the ball hit a hard spot on the diamond or the foot of an invisible leprechaun and bounced over Lindstrom's head, to drive in the run, and to win the game for Johnson and the World Championship for Washington.

Leading hitters:

WASHINGTON SENATORS
Peckinpaugh: .417

NEW YORK GIANTS
Terry: .429

Winning pitchers:

WASHINGTON SENATORS
Zachary: won 2, lost 0
Mogridge: won 1, lost 0
Johnson: won 1, lost 2

NEW YORK GIANTS
Nehf: won 1, lost 1
McQuillan: won 1, lost 0
Bentley: won 1, lost 2

1925

PITTSBURGH N.L. vs. WASHINGTON A.L.

WON BY PITTSBURGH, 4 GAMES TO 3

Game Scores:

Washington 4	Pittsburgh 1	October 7 at Pittsburgh
Pittsburgh 3	Washington 2	October 8 at Pittsburgh
Washington 4	Pittsburgh 3	October 10 at Washington
Washington 4	Pittsburgh 0	October 11 at Washington
Pittsburgh 6	Washington 3	October 12 at Washington
Pittsburgh 3	Washington 2	October 13 at Pittsburgh
Pittsburgh 9	Washington 7	October 15 at Pittsburgh

The World Series of 1925 seemed to be the 1924 series turned upside down. This time, Walter Johnson, who had just completed his twelfth (and last) twenty-or-better season, came on strong at the start, then hung on too long and lost the series. And the gremlins this time fastened their hold on the Senators, causing veteran shortstop Roger Peckinpaugh, who had been a minor goat in the 1921 series with the Yankees, to set a new World Series record of eight errors in forty chances.

The hitting was hard in this series. Max Carey, field captain of the Pirates, led both clubs with a batting average of .458. Moon Harris, the Senators' thirty-three-year-old right fielder, who had played with the Yankees, Cleveland, and the Red Sox, posted the highest Washington average: .440. Both he and Goose Goslin hit three home runs each, while Edgar Charles (Sam) Rice of Washington made the most hits of anyone—twelve. Sam also made the most spectacular fielding play of the series, a headlong dive into the bleachers to hang on to Earl Smith's drive that would have been a home run.

This was an uphill struggle for the Pittsburgh club, who were behind three games to one at one point. But they perhaps recalled when they had held a similar edge on the Boston club in the first World Series ever played, and that the Boston club still managed to win it. So they played catch-up baseball day after day and finally went ahead in the rain and mud of a dreary October afternoon in Pittsburgh, after being so far behind in *that* game that many of their own fans gave up. After the fourth game, of course, every game was sudden-death so the tension both on the field and in the stands was strung to the splitting point.

Pittsburgh's hero for this series was her sturdy right fielder, Hazen (Kiki) Cuyler, who had completed his finest season with the bat. Cuyler's long and timely blows brought screams of excitement and delight in several games, and his mighty two-base blow off Walter Johnson in the final game drove in three runs to win the championship.

Johnson's pitching looked from the start as if it would be good enough to win the whole series. In the first game he allowed the Pirate sluggers but five hits and struck out ten of them. In the fourth game, played four days later, he shut the Pirates out with six hits, although he struck out only two. Several other old-timers, besides Johnson and Peckinpaugh, put in an appearance in this series and some of them showed a return to their youthful form. The outstanding veteran for Pittsburgh was probably Stuffy McInnis, graduate of the Athletics and the Red Sox in the other league. While George Grantham, age twenty-five, played first base for the Pirates through the first four games and got a total of two hits in fourteen at-bats, Stuffy McInnis, age thirty-five, moved in for the final three games and the Pirates won them all. Stuffy had only two incomplete seasons ahead of him in the big leagues. But he managed to collect four hits in thirteen times at bat and to perform in his usual slick and errorless manner around first base. But Stanley Coveleski, hero of the Cleveland club in the 1920 World Series, and now thirty-five years old, lost both of his starts in the series, even though he had just completed a twenty-victory season for Washington. Big Stanislaus gave only seven hits to Pittsburgh in the second game and still lost. In the fifth game he gave up nine hits in one out more than six innings, walked four men, and was again charged with the loss.

Nemo Leibold of Washington, playing his final games after thirteen seasons in the majors, appeared three times as a pinch-hitter, walked once, doubled once, and popped out. Nemo had trod the outfield for Cleveland, the Chicago White Sox, and the Boston Red Sox before joining the Senators in 1923. Still another ancient (age thirty-seven) who appeared for Washington in what turned out to be his last major league effort was Bob Veach, former star outfielder with the Tigers and long-time teammate of Ty Cobb's. Veach bunted as a pinch-hitter in the second game.

The feature of the series was unquestionably the final game, played before 43,000 fans on a muddy field, with the drizzling dampness taking a good part of the gimp out of Walter Johnson's arm. But the Senators started out as if they meant to pound the Pirates into the mud and walk over them. In the first inning, it looked as if Pirate pitcher Vic Aldridge, who had won the fifth game handily, was not going to get the Senators out at all, with nearly everybody hitting, except Peckinpaugh, who didn't have to because catcher Earl Smith got in his way and the umpire let Peckinpaugh have first base because of interference. Before the inning was over Aldridge was warming himself in the clubhouse and the Senators had four runs. Aldridge had walked three men, given up two hits, and let go with a wild pitch, while getting one man out.

The game seemed to last forever. The drizzle came down steadily. The mud grew deep and Walter Johnson could get no proper purchase in the mud for his cannon-fire sidearm. The Pirates kept chopping at his lead, which was all that kept him in there. In the third inning the Pirates came up with three runs but then the Senators drove out pitcher John Morrison with two runs in the fourth and clung to a lead, despite steady pounding by the

Pirates, until the seventh inning, when two scores brought the Pirates even. Roger Peckinpaugh hit a home run in the eighth to put the Senators in the lead once more. But when the Pirates next came to bat, Johnson could not deal with them. Working with such aching deliberation that the customers moaned, Johnson finally filled the bases. Then Kiki Cuyler stepped up and delivered a smashing two-bagger that emptied the bases and put the Pirates into the lead to stay. Smart-alecs all over the land were soon insisting that Bucky Harris had kept Johnson in there just out of sentiment—which, according to them, "had no place in baseball." But few fans agreed, even though most people were saddened to see the great Walter robbed of his triumph.

Leading hitters:

PITTSBURGH PIRATES
Carey: .458

WASHINGTON SENATORS
J. Harris: .440

Winning pitchers:

PITTSBURGH PIRATES
Aldridge: won 2, lost 0
Kremer: won 2, lost 1

WASHINGTON SENATORS
Johnson: won 2, lost 1
Ferguson: won 1, lost 1

1926

ST. LOUIS N.L. vs. NEW YORK A.L.

WON BY ST. LOUIS, 4 GAMES TO 3

Game Scores:

New York 2	St. Louis 1	October 2 at New York
St. Louis 6	New York 2	October 3 at New York
St. Louis 4	New York 0	October 5 at St. Louis
New York 10	St. Louis 5	October 6 at St. Louis
New York 3	St. Louis 2	October 7 at St. Louis
(10 innings)		
St. Louis 10	New York 2	October 9 at New York
St. Louis 3	New York 2	October 10 at New York

Mention of the 1926 World Series always brings talk of Grover Cleveland Alexander, the veteran drinking pitcher who had been the greatest in the game for a while. And nearly everyone remembers that his exploit had something to do with Tony Lazzeri, the muscular little epileptic who played second base for the best Yankee teams ever fielded. What happened was that Alexander, coming in when disaster loomed to relieve a sore-fingered pitcher for St. Louis, struck out Lazzeri, after Tony had come within inches of driving out a home run that would have broken up the ball game.

Legend sometimes has it that Old Pete Alexander was somewhat the worse for having celebrated the night before and that he had never expected to be called upon to pitch again in the series. But those who played in the game found Old Pete clear-eyed and steady, and his throwing arm alive and strong. He not only struck out Lazzeri in the final game but he pitched almost perfect baseball to the next six batters and won the game going away.

The manager of the St. Louis Cardinals in 1926 was Rogers Hornsby, a cold-eyed and outspoken man who had difficulty getting along with his employer, Branch Rickey. It was he who summoned Old Pete from the bullpen in the seventh inning of the seventh and he made a personal appraisal of his pitcher right on the baselines. (Rogers was playing second base.) He found Alexander in perfect control of his faculties and full of confidence, or he would not have let him take the mound.

When the Cardinals won the pennant in 1926, they brought St. Louis the first National League championship it had ever earned. It was hardly to be expected that the Cards could also knock off the invincible Yankees. But the Cardinals themselves had nothing but confidence and their fans gathered outside the Yankee quarters in St. Louis to tell the visitors they were going to get licked.

It took a long time for the Yankees to believe it. With left-handed Herb Pennock (twenty-three wins that season) pitching for them, they beat the Cards in the first game 2 to 1. The Cardinals collected only three hits and three walks. Wee Willie Sherdel, the St. Louis pitcher, pitched well, allowing only six hits in seven innings and his relief man, Jess Haines, allowed none. But they could not completely stifle the new first baseman the Yankees were showing—a big Bronx kid named Lou Gehrig, who drove in both Yankee runs.

The man called upon to pitch the second game was Alexander, thirty-nine years old and no monument to Spartan training. Alex had come over from the Cubs that year and had won only nine games for the Cardinals. But in the series, which was his second (he had won one and lost one in the 1915 series), he looked like the thirty-game winner of old. He spread four singles among the Yankee Murderers' Row and struck out ten.

The clubs went to St. Louis then, where the Yankees were kept awake most of the night by serenading St. Louis fans. The next day, they were tranquilized by Jess Haines, a man old enough to be called Pop by his teammates. Pop gave the Yankees only five hits, two by Gehrig, and all singles. He hit a home run himself to provide all the edge he really needed.

In the fourth game, with Waite Hoyt none too steady on the mound, the Yankees broke loose and let Hoyt coast to victory. In three official trips to the plate, Babe Ruth hit three home runs, one of them the longest blow ever seen in the park. Everybody in the lineup except Hoyt got a base hit. Ruth and second-string catcher Hank Severeid got three each. The Cards hit the ball as often as the Yankees did, getting fourteen hits among them, but they just did not hit as far or as close together.

Next day, with the local fans thirsting for revenge, Herb Pennock came back and held the Cards at arm's length while his mates picked off one run at a time, until they had enough to win. Ruth went hitless in this game but he continued to pick up bases on balls. He had eleven walks for the series.

Game number six marked the turning point of the series. This time it was the Cardinal bats that exploded and the Cardinals that provided the Big Inning. They got three runs in the first inning and five in the seventh. Bob Shawkey and Urban Shocker, New York's veteran pitchers, were both bombed out by the eighth. Alexander just toyed with the Yankees in this game, holding Ruth hitless again and never feeling any pressure. He struck out six.

The final game was played on a rather hazy day that, one observer said, made Old Pete Alexander, when he did walk in to relieve, look almost half again as big as he really was. And he was bigger than a normal man to start with.

The Yankees got the first run in this game on a third-inning homer by Babe Ruth that streaked into the right-field seats. Waite Hoyt was working well, the Yanks were playing at home, and even the law of averages stood in their favor. But in the fourth inning, the Yanks began to come apart. Shortstop Mark Koenig foozled an easy double play and misjudged a short pop fly. Then Bob Meusel dropped a routine fly in the outfield and the Cards had runs enough on base to go ahead. Shortstop Tommy Thevenow delivered them with a sharp single, making it 3 to 1 in favor of the Cards. This should have been margin enough but Pop Haines broke a blister on his finger and it began to bleed. He struggled with it through an inning or two. Then in the sixth inning, Joe Dugan, Yankee third baseman, doubled and Hank Severeid drove him home with a single, to bring the Yanks uncomfortably close.

But Pop Haines would not quit. Facing the fat part of the Yankee batting order, he worked with excess care, and walked Earle Combs. Mark Koenig laid down a neat sacrifice that put Combs on second with the tying run. Babe Ruth was next at the plate. The fans naturally wanted the big man to hit, but no one in his right mind was going to pitch to the Babe in these circumstances, with first base open, so Babe got his tenth walk. The strategy of setting up a force play paid off in a small degree, for Meusel then hit an easy ground ball to third that forced Babe at second. Now Lou Gehrig approached and he could break a game as wide open as anyone. Haines, bleeding finger and all, quickly got Gehrig down two strikes and then tried to feed him a low pitch out of the strike zone. He tried three times and Gehrig scorned them all. With a full count on and the tying run only ninety feet away, Hornsby ordered Gehrig put on first. This brought up young Tony Lazzeri, in his first year with the Yankees and already a home run hitter and a particularly strong man in the clutch. Hornsby took a look at Haines' finger and decided Pop had had torture enough. Then he called in Old Pete. Alexander had set Lazzeri down four times in a row just the day before, and he had no qualms about trying him again. Tony swung and missed at one pitch then laid into the next one with all the good wood in the bat. The ball rocketed off into left field, obviously headed for the stands, and the New York fans screamed. But, as such blows often do, this blow hooked gracefully to the left and landed about two feet outside the foul line, in the seats. It was strike two. Old Pete put the next pitch on the outside and Tony this time missed it by inches. That ended the threat and

106

Old Pete from then on did such an artistic job of moving his pitches around and flirting with the edges of the strike zone that starting Yankee pitcher Waite Hoyt, out of the game, showered, and seated in the stands now, could only shake his head in admiration.

Leading hitters:

ST. LOUIS CARDINALS
Thevenow: .417

NEW YORK YANKEES
Combs: .357

Winning pitchers:

ST. LOUIS CARDINALS
Alexander: won 2, lost 0
Haines: won 2, lost 0

NEW YORK YANKEES
Pennock: won 2, lost 0
Hoyt: won 1, lost 1

1927

NEW YORK A.L. vs. PITTSBURGH N.L.

WON BY NEW YORK, 4 GAMES TO 0

Game Scores:

New York 5	Pittsburgh 4	October 5 at Pittsburgh
New York 6	Pittsburgh 2	October 6 at Pittsburgh
New York 8	Pittsburgh 1	October 7 at New York
New York 4	Pittsburgh 3	October 8 at New York

The 1927 Yankees were supposed to be the greatest slugging aggregation in baseball history, for they owned nearly all the batting titles that year. Ruth had hit sixty homers and batted .356. Gehrig had hit .373 and led the league in doubles and in runs batted in. Earle Combs, the center fielder, batted .356 and led the league in triples and in total hits. Ruth was also leader in total runs scored. Bob Meusel hit .337 for the season. Tony Lazzeri hit .309. Shortstop Mark Koenig hit .285, third baseman Dugan .269, and catcher Pat Collins .275. This gang set a new record for victories in the American League, winning 110 and taking the pennant with a percentage of .714. And yet when it came to the World Series, it was the pitchers rather than the sluggers who brought home the triumph. Waite Hoyt, top pitcher in the league that year, George Pipgras, Herb Pennock, and Wilcy Moore each won a game and the most hits the Pirates made off any of them was ten.

The Pirates of course had some fierce batsmen of their own, including the Waner brothers, who took home most of the batting honors in the National League: Paul won the batting title with an average of .380, made the most hits and the most triples, and had the most runs batted in. Brother Lloyd tied with Rogers Hornsby for the most runs scored.

But there was one Pirate slugger who had to sit on the bench for this series, to his own dismay, to the bewilderment of his fans, and to the distress of his teammates. That was Kiki Cuyler, the man who broke up the crucial game in the 1925 World Series by batting in three runs in the eighth inning. Cuyler's batting average had suffered from being moved from third to second place in the batting order. He had quarreled with his new manager (Donie Bush) about this but Bush had been determined to show his authority, so Kiki continued to hit in second place and to play left field (his choice was center). Kiki was injured early in the season and his replacement, Clyde Barnhart, a veteran outfielder, hit so well that Cuyler could not get his job back, until another injury left an opening. Then Kiki was fined once for not sliding into base. The fans and other players began to take his side publicly, and Bush apparently decided he did not even want Kiki on the club.

During all the series games played in Pittsburgh, the cries of "We want Cuyler! We want Cuyler!" provided a background in every inning. But it is doubtful if even the doughty Kiki could have staved off the Yankee might. The Waners did the best batting for the Pirates, but did not come close to the Yankee leaders, Koenig and Ruth, who hit .500 and .400 respectively. Many ball players felt that the Pirates had been scared out of winning by the frightening barrage of long hits the Yankee Murderers laid down in batting practice before the first game. Certainly the Pirates looked nervous and inept in the field that day. The Pirates made nine hits off Hoyt and scored four runs but Paul Waner in the first inning missed a shoestring catch that cost a run, then errors by second baseman Grantham and catcher Earl Smith helped provide the Yankees with three more runs in the third inning. Only two of the New York runs were earned.

109

There were some who thought Miller Huggins was crazy to start a rookie like George Pipgras in the second game. George was 27 years old but he had just come back up to the Yankees from St. Paul after having made a few appearances in 1923 and 1924. He had won ten games this season. But today he pitched like a veteran, allowing just seven hits, giving the Waners one apiece. The Yankees built two three-run innings to provide all their runs, and nobody hit any homers.

When the Yankees got back to the Stadium, the pitching choice was Pennock and he pitched the game of his life. The first twenty-two Pirates to face him went down without getting on base. Finally in the eighth inning, after Pennock had to sit long on the bench to watch his mates pile up six runs in the seventh, Pie Traynor, Pittsburgh's rugged third baseman, hit a single and George Grantham followed it with a double that gave the Pirates a run. In the ninth inning Lloyd Waner hit a single, and that was all for Pittsburgh. The big Yankee bats were not really needed this day, but they broke out all the same. Ruth got a home run while Gehrig had a double and a triple.

Miller Huggins, the Yankee manager, pulled a surprise when he started relief pitcher Wilcy Moore in the fourth game. Hardly anyone could recall when Wilcy had ever pitched nine full innings before. But this was to be sort of a reward for Wilcy for saving so many games on the way to the pennant. Wilcy, although he allowed only one earned run, almost did not make it. He needed two runs provided by a Ruth homer to hold him even and then he needed a couple of wild pitches by the enemy to save the day. It was another instance of Yankee reputation winning when Yankee bats failed. The Pirate relief pitcher, John Miljus, who had broken in with the Federal League, had got himself into a minor jam in the last of the ninth by walking Earle Combs and letting Mark Koenig beat out a sacrifice bunt. Then a wild pitch put runners on second and third and Ruth was at bat. With first base open, Babe was purposely passed. Then Miljus worked his heart out on Gehrig and Meusel and fanned them both. He had only Lazzeri to get rid of and he still had plenty of strength left. But he put every ounce of it into his next pitch and the ball sailed over his catcher's head. Gooch, the catcher, leaped to knock it down but could only deflect it and Combs came roaring in with the run that meant the championship.

Leading hitters:

NEW YORK YANKEES
    Koenig: .500
PITTSBURGH PIRATES
    L. Waner: .400

Winning pitchers:

NEW YORK YANKEES
    Hoyt: won 1, lost 0
    Pipgras: won 1, lost 0
    Pennock: won 1, lost 0
    Moore: won 1, lost 0

1928

NEW YORK A.L. vs. ST. LOUIS N.L.

WON BY NEW YORK, 4 GAMES TO 0

Game Scores:

New York 4	St. Louis 1	October 4 at New York
New York 9	St. Louis 3	October 5 at New York
New York 7	St. Louis 3	October 7 at St. Louis
New York 7	St. Louis 3	October 8 at St. Louis

In 1928, the Yankee sluggers finally managed to dominate a World Series. They were badly needed, too, for the Yankee pitching had suffered with the laming of Herb Pennock's arm, and the defense was wobbling because of Earle Combs' broken finger and Tony Lazzeri's bad arm, not to mention Babe Ruth's gimpy ankle. But at the bat Babe was supreme and Lou Gehrig was right close to him. The Babe's batting average of .625 was the highest ever posted for a complete World Series. He hit three home runs in one game while Gehrig got four in three games.

The previous time the Cardinals and the Yanks had met, the Cards had given Babe 11 bases on balls, and beat the Yankees. This time they pitched to him, allowing him just one free trip to first. And they probably wished they had gone back to the original system.

Another forgotten feature of this game was the appearance of a very fresh youngster named Leo Durocher at second base, part-time, for the Yankees. The Cardinals did not realize it then, but this young roughneck was destined to become their own Peerless Leader after he had grown up a little. In this series they were about ready to throttle him for his fresh talk.

The first game was a breeze for Waite Hoyt, who allowed only three hits and struck out six. Two doubles by Ruth, one by Gehrig, and a home run by Bob Meusel gave Hoyt more than he needed to win. The very first run of the series came on successive doubles by Ruth and Gehrig, and if the Cardinals did not realize then that they were cooked, they should have.

In the second game the Yankees quickly gave George Pipgras three runs to lean on. With substitute center fielder Cedric Durst on base and Ruth right there too, Gehrig poled a pitch into the bleachers. Pipgras needed this edge too, for the Cardinals came back with three in the second. This just seemed to irritate the Yankees, who went ahead with one run in their half of the inning and then made three more in the third. After that, Pipgras had no trouble. He allowed only four hits all the way. In St. Louis, with old Tom Zachary, at the end of his eleventh season in the majors, starting for New York, the Cardinals got a head start, scoring two runs in the first inning. In the top of the second, Gehrig reminded them of what was coming by driving a ball into the right-field pavilion for his second homer of the series. In the fourth inning, Ruth hit a single and Gehrig drove a ball far out over center fielder Douthit's head for another home run, this one inside the park, and for two more runs. The Cardinals tied the score in the next inning, so the Yankees got serious and piled three runs across the plate in the inning after that. Ruth scored one of the runs when he knocked the catcher loose from the ball, after the tag had been put on him. It was Ruth's habit, injury or no, to run bases like a demon and to play always to win.

The fourth game, pitched by Hoyt, was the most exciting, the loudest, and the angriest of the series. The Cardinals again started the scoring and again a home run evened things up. This time it was a home run by Ruth, his first of three. In the Yankee half of the seventh, the Cards were leading 2 to 1. With one out, Ruth came to bat and Wee Willie Sherdel immediately put him down two strikes. Then he tried a quick pitch on him, snapping

113

the ball back over the plate the instant he received it from the catcher. It was a strike, but Ruth was not out, because the Commissioner's rules had already declared the quick pitch illegal in the series, although it was legal in the National League. There was an unholy row at the plate, with much pushing and yelling and shaking of angry fingers in angry faces. But there was no changing the rules, as all the umpires agreed. So Babe had one more cut at the ball. And of course he stepped up and drove the next pitch into the stands, to make it 2-all. Then Gehrig came to the plate and drove a pitch even deeper into the seats and the Yankees did not stop until they had made four runs in the inning.

Old Pete Alexander, now forty-one years old, was called in to try to put the pieces back together but Pete could do little better than Sherdel. Cedric Durst started off the eighth inning by hitting a home run and Babe, after Mark Koenig made out, came up and hit another homer. This was too much for the St. Louis fans, who just had to provide Babe the biggest ovation of the series. With the cheers of the enemy sweetening the air around him, Babe, a bursting grin on his face, trotted in his quick little steps around the bases and took his hat off to the crowd. Then, in the final inning, to illustrate that he was the complete baseball player, Babe, lame foot and all, streaked after a foul fly at the very edge of the left-field stand, nailed it one-handed for the final out, and kept right on going into the clubhouse to help celebrate the second four-in-a-row triumph.

Leading hitters:

NEW YORK YANKEES
Ruth: .625

ST. LOUIS CARDINALS
Maranville: .308

Winning pitchers:

NEW YORK YANKEES
Hoyt: won 2, lost 0
Pipgras: won 1, lost 0
Zachary: won 1, lost 0

1929

PHILADELPHIA A.L. vs. CHICAGO N.L.

WON BY PHILADELPHIA, 4 GAMES TO 1

Game Scores:

Philadelphia 3	Chicago 1	October 8 at Chicago
Philadelphia 9	Chicago 3	October 9 at Chicago
Chicago 3	Philadelphia 1	October 11 at Philadelphia
Philadelphia 10	Chicago 8	October 12 at Philadelphia
Philadelphia 3	Chicago 2	October 14 at Philadelphia

There are people who recall October 1929 only as the month of the great stock market collapse. But to a few baseball fans it will always be the month that old Connie Mack took old Howard Ehmke out of mothballs and made a world-beating pitcher out of him for one afternoon. The marvels that Ehmke worked as he posted zero after zero against the enemy's name kept people all over the country open-mouthed.

It had taken Connie a long time to build his club back up to a pennant, after the shame of 1914 when his favored A's lost four in a row to the nobodies from Boston. Howard Ehmke had also been trying since 1914 to land with a major league pennant winner. He started with the Buffalo Federal League club in 1915 and pitched for Detroit and the Red Sox before joining the A's in 1926. He had left his very best days behind him in Boston, where he pitched in 1923 a no-hit game and a one-hit game in succes-

115

sion and won twenty games with a club that was going nowhere. The most he had ever won for the A's was twelve games, and in 1929 he won only seven. He was far back on the roster behind Lefty Grove, George Earnshaw, Rube Walberg, and Ed Rommel. Earnshaw had won twenty-four games; Grove, twenty; Walberg, eighteen; and Rommel, twelve.

When the A's clinched the pennant, a week or so before the season ended, Connie Mack decided to turn Ehmke loose. But the old pitcher (thirty-five) talked his boss into letting him pitch in the series, the first in his career. Connie therefore set Howard the job of staying home to study the Cubs, the National League champions, as they played the Phillies in a final series. Ehmke kept a chart of every pitch and every batting move until he could have recited each Chicago man's weakness by heart.

The series started in Chicago, and everyone at Wrigley Field (except the A's) took for granted that Lefty Grove would start. When Ehmke began to warm up there were many who thought this was another of old Connie's tricks, and that the *real* pitcher had got ready somewhere else. Ehmke had not pitched nine full innings since Lord knows when. But the fact was that Grove had a sore hand and his fast ball would have been just batting practice for sluggers like Kiki Cuyler, Hack Wilson, and Rogers Hornsby, who had blasted the Cubs to the pennant. Howard Ehmke's "nothing-ball," however, had the big hitters all off balance, as he kept throwing to the spots he knew they liked the least.

Charlie Root was pitching well for the Cubs too and for six innings nobody scored. The A's made a run in the seventh and two in the ninth. Ehmke struck out pinch-hitter Gabby Hartnett to turn back a Chicago threat in the seventh and then in the ninth, after the Cubs had scored a run, Ehmke struck out Chick Tolson, another pinch-hitter, to set a World Series strikeout record of thirteen. It stood until 1953.

In game number two Lefty Grove appeared as a relief pitcher, for his injured fingers would last only three or four innings. But for four and a third innings in this game, they lasted very well. After George Earnshaw had begun to wobble badly in the fifth inning, when the Cubs scored three runs to cut the Philadelphia lead in half, Grove took over and added six strikeouts to Earnshaw's seven to give the Cubs another total of thirteen complete misses for the game. The brutes of the Philadelphia batting order meanwhile clubbed four Chicago pitchers for twelve hits, including home runs by Al Simmons and Jimmy Foxx.

George Earnshaw had one day's rest while the teams returned to Philadelphia, then he tried again. This time he struck out ten all by himself and still could not win the ball game. Timely blows by Hornsby and Cuyler in the sixth inning gave the Cubs three runs and the A's could make only one, on a single by Miller that scored Mickey Cochrane in the fifth.

Game number four was the most horrible that Chicago Manager Joe McCarthy ever had to live through. How could a club with an eight-run lead in the seventh inning still lose the ball game? The Cubs made it easy. They blasted ageless Jack Quinn, Rube Walberg, and Ed Rommel for ten hits in seven innings. Cuyler got three hits and Hornsby, Wilson, and Charlie Grimm had two each, including a home run for Grimm. They were ready to coast home for the victory that would tie the series when all the A's hit them at once. Al Simmons opened the home half of the seventh with a home run and it looked then as if the Cubs would never get the side out. When a man failed to hit cleanly, there was always someone to turn the wallop into a score. Hack Wilson, floundering in the bright sun of center field, lost two easy fly balls in the sun and one of them went for a home run that scored three runs. Fifteen A's went to bat in this inning. Fortunately for the Cubs one of them was a pinch-hitter who made out twice or they might be counting runs still. When the A's had all the runs they needed, Lefty Grove came in and threw his lightning ball for two innings, in which he struck out four and gave no hits.

The final game may have hit Manager McCarthy just as hard, for once more the Cubs had the game won when the A's took it away from them. With one out in the last of the ninth, the score was 2 to 0 in favor of Chicago. Pat Malone, the Cubs' twenty-two-game winner, had allowed only two hits so far and he opened

117

the ninth by striking out Walter French, who was pinch-hitting for Rube Walberg. God was in His Heaven, President Hoover was in the grandstand, and even the stock market had shown no signs, yet, of collapsing. But then, of a sudden, Max Bishop singled. Mule Haas, the A's center fielder, was next up and he drove a ball right out of the park, to tie the score. Malone got Mickey Cochrane out but Al Simmons then hit a double. Malone filled the open base by walking Jimmy Foxx, whereupon right fielder Bing Miller hit another double to bring in the winning run and douse the Cub hopes for keeps.

Leading hitters:

PHILADELPHIA ATHLETICS
Dykes: .421

CHICAGO CUBS
Wilson: .471

Winning pitchers:

PHILADELPHIA ATHLETICS
Ehmke:	won 1,	lost 0
Earnshaw:	won 1,	lost 1
Rommel:	won 1,	lost 0
Walberg:	won 1,	lost 0

CHICAGO CUBS
Bush:	won 1,	lost 0

1930

PHILADELPHIA A.L. vs. ST. LOUIS N.L.

WON BY PHILADELPHIA, 4 GAMES TO 2

Game Scores:

Philadelphia 5	St. Louis 2	October 1 at Philadelphia
Philadelphia 6	St. Louis 1	October 2 at Philadelphia
St. Louis 5	Philadelphia 0	October 4 at St. Louis
St. Louis 3	Philadelphia 1	October 5 at St. Louis
Philadelphia 2	St. Louis 0	October 6 at St. Louis
Philadelphia 7	St. Louis 1	October 8 at Philadelphia

In 1930, Connie Mack's great pitchers were all well and they illustrated that first by running away with the American League pennant by a margin of eight games, with Lefty Grove winning twenty-eight games and George Earnshaw winning twenty-two. The A's had expected to meet the Cubs again, or possibly the Giants or Dodgers. But instead they came up against a St. Louis club that roared out of nowhere to win twenty-one games in September and grab the National League flag from all the favorites.

The A's, however, soon cooled down the Cards. Their mighty batsmen kept hitting for extra bases, making a few wallops go a long way. And their pitchers were even better than the year before. In the first game, Burleigh Grimes of St. Louis, the swarthy spitballer, really pitched well enough to win—if only the ball had

119

not gone so far the few times it was hit. The A's got only five hits, as against the nine that St. Louis made off Grove, but all the A's' hits were for extra bases and each one meant a score. Cochrane and Simmons hit home runs. Foxx and Haas each hit a triple and Dykes hit a two-bagger. The Cards scored twice in the third inning when they put together three singles and a sacrifice. Grove had no trouble with them thereafter.

The pitching was tighter in the second game than the score indicated. The A's made only seven hits to build their six runs, getting them two at a time. The Cards made only six hits. But all the Philadelphia hits were made off Flint Rhem in ten at-bats in the first four innings, while Earnshaw scattered the Card hits through the game. The only Card run came on a homer by rookie right fielder George Watkins, who was never again to have as good a season as the one he just put in. (He hit .373 in 119 games.)

In the third game the Cards turned Wild Bill Hallahan loose and he put an immediate stop to this extra-base nonsense. Only Simmons, with his two-bagger, tagged him for more than a single as he limited the A's to seven hits and struck out six. Walberg, who started strongly, began to wobble in the fourth and fifth, when the Cards scored a run each inning. Bill Shores and Jack Quinn did no better, but it hardly mattered because Hallahan only needed one run to win.

Pop Haines, going on thirty-eight, pitched for St. Louis in the fourth game and did better than Bob Grove, who had turned thirty. Grove allowed the Cardinals only five hits but Haines let go of only four, and the only extra-base hits in the game were made by the Cardinals. Each right fielder in this game made seven putouts.

Burleigh Grimes came back tougher than ever in game number five and by all rights he should have won it. He should have, that is, just to uphold the tradition of victories by veterans in the series. Burleigh had started in the National League in 1916. The big man pitched a fine game too, holding the A's to only four hits through eight innings. In the ninth inning, however, he put Mickey Cochrane on base with a walk. He did away with Simmons without trouble, but Jimmy Foxx, up next, sent a real screamer into the left-field seats that broke the hearts of nearly everyone in St. Louis, particularly that of Burleigh Grimes, who had now lost his last four World Series starts. He had won the second game in the 1920 series. George Earnshaw, pitching his second game of the series, was at his best. He pitched seven innings before giving way to a pinch-hitter (who walked), and he allowed only two hits. Grove pitched the last two innings and allowed only one hit. Grove got the victory.

The crucial game then had to be played back in Philadelphia and Earnshaw had time enough to rest and try for his second win.

This time the A's gave big George a cushion to ride on by hitting nothing but extra-base hits once more. And again every hit meant a run. By the sixth inning the A's were leading 7 to 0. By the ninth, Earnshaw had allowed only three hits. Then Andy High singled and Chick Hafey drove him home with his second double of the day. But it was far too late to save the series and Connie had won his fifth World Championship—a record at that time.

Leading hitters:

PHILADELPHIA ATHLETICS
Simmons: .364

ST. LOUIS CARDINALS
Gelbert: .353

Winning pitchers:

PHILADELPHIA ATHLETICS
Grove: won 2, lost 1
Earnshaw: won 2, lost 0

ST. LOUIS CARDINALS
Hallahan: won 1, lost 1
Haines: won 1, lost 0

1931

ST. LOUIS N.L. vs. PHILADELPHIA A.L.

WON BY ST. LOUIS, 4 GAMES TO 3

Game Scores:

Philadelphia 6	St. Louis 2	October 1 at St. Louis
St. Louis 2	Philadelphia 0	October 2 at St. Louis
St. Louis 5	Philadelphia 2	October 5 at Philadelphia
Philadelphia 3	St. Louis 0	October 6 at Philadelphia
St. Louis 5	Philadelphia 1	October 7 at Philadelphia
Philadelphia 8	St. Louis 1	October 9 at St. Louis
St. Louis 4	Philadelphia 2	October 10 at St. Louis

There was something poetically gratifying about the 1931 World Series. Baseball's forgotten men, the underpaid, the superannuated, and the out-of-luck all had their day together, it seemed, and their triumph was shared by hundreds of thousands, made jobless by the depression, who could not even pay their way into the park.

The man who dominated the series, and whose name will be connected with it as long as men talk about baseball, was twenty-seven-year-old John "Pepper" Martin, outfielder-third baseman and sometime pitcher for the St. Louis Cardinals. Martin ran wild on the bases and exploded at the plate. Then, to top it all off, he ended the series with a spectacular catch in the outfield for the final Philadelphia out.

The Cardinals had dominated their league, but few people really believed they had a chance against the gold-plated Athletics, who had just won their eighth league championship. The A's' top pitcher, Lefty Grove, had completed the greatest season of his career, with thirty-one wins and only four losses, and he had led the league in strikeouts, with 175. The A's' Al Simmons had led the league with a batting average of .390. (Chick Hafey of the Cards had led his league with .349.) Mickey Cochrane of Philadelphia had had one of his best years with a .349 batting average. And Mule Haas, the A's center fielder, had posted the best batting average of his career: .323. George Earnshaw had won twenty-one games for Connie Mack and Rube Walberg, attaining the top mark of his career, had won twenty. Connie had even got ten victories from a rejuvenated Waite Hoyt, who had come from the Yankees via Detroit.

The series started as if the favorites would run off with it again. Lefty Grove spotted the Cards two runs in the first inning and then choked them off completely the rest of the way. His mates delivered four in the third inning, with the help of a home run by Al Simmons. They added two in the seventh. But there was one omen, in this game, of things to come. Pepper Martin, batting sixth in the Cardinal order, reached Lefty Grove for three hits and stole a base.

In game number two, Martin cut loose. He made a single and a double in three trips to the plate and stole two bases. He scored both runs that St. Louis made. Meanwhile Wild Bill Hallahan held the mighty A's to three hits, all singles, and struck out eight.

Martin was still batting sixth in the third game, when 38-year-old Burleigh Grimes got another chance to win a World Series game, after years of frustration. Burleigh today really spun a masterpiece, allowing the A's only two hits among them, thoroughly outpitching Lefty Grove, and not giving up a run until Al Simmons poled a homer in the last of the ninth. Martin today kicked in with a single and a double.

Game number four was George Earnshaw's turn to build a masterpiece. He held all the Cards hitless, except for one guy who got two hits. That of course was Pepper Martin, who also

123

stole a base. But none of the Cards came close to scoring. By this time, however, Manager Gabby Street of the Cardinals was convinced, and he moved Martin up to fourth spot in the batting order. The effect on Pepper was like lighting a fuse. In the fifth game, with Wild Bill Hallahan holding the A's in check, Pepper went to bat four times, made three hits, including a home run, and drove in four of the Cards' five runs.

When the clubs returned to St. Louis, Pepper seemed to have cooled down. Against Lefty Grove, he could not scratch up a hit. The rest of the Cards made only five and Grove struck out seven. The next day, against George Earnshaw, Pepper still could get no traction. He walked once and stole a base. But he could not hit the ball safely. He didn't need to, however, for old Burleigh, looking for his second win of the series, threw eight scoreless innings at the A's. In the ninth inning, they began to get to the old man. With his lead cut in two, and the tying runs on base, Gabby Street replaced Burleigh with Bill Hallahan, who got the last man out, with the help of Pepper Martin. Pepper, who had struck out his last time at bat, came streaking in from deepest center after Max Bishop's sinking drive, nailed it with one hand, and tucked away the championship.

After the series, Pepper was inundated with gifts and offers. Baseball Commissioner Kenesaw Mountain Landis wrung his hand and told him earnestly: "I wish I could change places with you, young man." Unabashed, Martin agreed: "Okay, if you'll swap your fifty grand a year for my forty-five hundred." And many a jobless fan, reading of Pepper's exploits and seeing his picture, an obviously impecunious ball player with dirty uniform and dirty face, or hearing of the wonders old cast-off Burleigh Grimes performed, felt his own heart lift up for the first time in months.

Leading hitters:

ST. LOUIS CARDINALS
Martin: .500

PHILADELPHIA ATHLETICS
Foxx: .348

Winning pitchers:

ST. LOUIS CARDINALS
Hallahan: won 2, lost 0
Grimes: won 2, lost 0

PHILADELPHIA ATHLETICS
Grove: won 2, lost 1
Earnshaw: won 1, lost 2

1932

NEW YORK A.L. vs. CHICAGO N.L.

WON BY NEW YORK, 4 GAMES TO 0

Game Scores:

New York 12	Chicago 6	September 28 at New York
New York 5	Chicago 2	September 29 at New York
New York 7	Chicago 5	October 1 at Chicago
New York 13	Chicago 6	October 2 at Chicago

The World Series of 1932 was a hitters' series, with even the losers thrilling their fans by belting the baseball out of the lot, or all around it. The Cubs, however, were really never in the fight. Gehrig was a monster at the plate, this time outstripping teammate Babe Ruth by many percentage points at bat. He hit for .529, made nine hits in seventeen at-bats, hit three homers, drove in eight runs, and scored nine times. Ruth, playing in his last World Series, performed one of the most memorable feats of his life by pointing to a spot where he meant to hit a home run, and then hitting it there. Some said he was not really pointing, but those who knew Babe best insisted that he was, for he had done the same thing once before, against the Red Sox. It was the perfect response to the bitter heckling the Chicago bench was giving him and it won Babe the cheers of all the enemy fans.

It was a bitter and vengeful series in many ways. The manager of the Yankees was Joe McCarthy, who had been fired by the Cubs for failure to win a World Series, and he openly relished the way in which the Cubs were humiliated. The Yankees as a club were angry at the Cubs because of the shabby treatment of Mark Koenig, former Yank shortstop who had gone to the Cubs via the Detroit Tigers and the Pacific Coast League. Mark had played in only 33 games for the Cubs but he had hit .353 and had been a big factor in the Cubs' narrow win of the pennant. The Cubs, however, had voted Mark only a half-share of the World Series pot, and Mark's old friends named them cheapskates, for thus violating Yankee tradition.

For a moment in the first game, the Cubs thought they had a chance, and again in the fourth game their fans hoped they might at least extend the series. But each time the fates, in the persons of the Yankees' new Murderers' Row, caught up with them. In game number one, the Cubs reached Red Ruffing for two runs in the first inning, thanks to a timely blow by Riggs Stephenson, the only Cub hitter who really got fat on Yankee pitching. And veteran Cub pitcher Guy Bush held the Yankees in check for the first three innings. But in the fourth the Yankees ganged up on him for three runs and did not stop until they had piled up nine runs more in the next four innings. Yankee pitching meanwhile did not have to be particularly good but it was good enough. Ruffing handed ten hits out among the Cubs, including a triple by Koenig, who was playing as well as he ever had, or a little better. But the Yankees altogether needed only eight hits to make twelve runs, because their hits kept coming with men on base. Burleigh Grimes, now thirty-nine years old but still a couple of years away from retirement, made a brief appearance in this game and appeared at his worst. He hit Bill Dickey with a pitch and let go a wild pitch, walked a man, and gave up three hits while making only five outs.

Game number two saw the World Series debut of Vernon (Lefty) Gomez, the antic Californian who was nearly as good a story-teller as he was a pitcher. Gomez, who had won twenty-four games that season, faced Lon Warneke, twenty-two-game winner for the Cubs. Although the Cubs jumped on Lefty for a run in the first inning, thanks again to that pesky Stephenson, who hit .444 in the series, the Yanks got the run back double in their half of the first and from that time forth they were never headed.

The third game, played in Chicago before a hostile and vocal crowd of nearly 50,000, was the game in which Ruth called his home run. This was actually the closest game of the series, although the Yankees started off with a three-run first inning. The Cubs scored a run in their half of the first inning and Yankee pitcher George Pipgras seemed a shade unsteady, so the crowd had hopes. In the third inning, pitcher Charlie Root fired a fastball strike to Babe Ruth and Babe lifted one finger, grinning at the Chicago bench. Root fired another fast ball right down the middle and Ruth, still unperturbed, lifted two fingers to indicate two strikes. Then, as the catcalls descended on him from every corner of the park, he gestured grandly toward the center-field wall. This called forth a deafening crescendo of howls. Charlie Root unwisely accepted the challenge and uncorked another fast ball. Babe belted it right in the heart with the fat part of his tremendous bat and it streaked like a vanishing star out over the wall in right-center field, exactly where Ruth had pointed. The fans came to their feet in a body and as Babe trotted around, thumbing his nose from time to time at the Chicago bench, the applause drowned every other noise for half a block. The World Series had never seen anything so audacious, nor any promise so perfectly fulfilled. It was the roaring climax to a swashbuckling career. The Cubs did get two runs in their half of the same inning, one in the fourth, and another in the ninth, but when they looked likely to catch up with the Yankees, Pipgras was lifted and veteran Herb Pennock, now thirty-eight, and completing his twentieth big league season, moved in, struck out a pinch-hitter, and got rid of the Cubs without allowing another hit.

Before George Pipgras left the scene, he did set a sort of record of his own. He had gone to bat five times in the game and struck out every time.

Game number four is the one Chicagoans thought they were sure to win. Johnny Allen, a star in his first year in the majors, pitched for New York and the Yanks gave him one run to start with. The Cubs, however, immediately landed on him for five base hits and four runs, completing his World Series chore for him very quickly. His job was taken over by aging Wilcy Moore who, since winning the final game in the 1927 World Series, had been to the Red Sox and back. Wilcy's sinker ball operated effectively for most of six innings, during which he allowed but two hits. By the time the Cubs managed to get a run off him, the score was 5 to 4 in favor of the Yankees. After the Cubs tied it up, Herb Pennock came back once more to finish up. The hitters, however, did the finishing, Lazzeri's two home runs doing most of the damage. The Yanks made four runs in the seventh and four more in the ninth. And that made it twelve World Series victories in a row.

Leading hitters:

NEW YORK YANKEES
 Gehrig: .529

CHICAGO CUBS
 Stephenson: .444

Winning pitchers:

NEW YORK YANKEES
 Ruffing: won 1, lost 0
 Gomez: won 1, lost 0
 Pipgras: won 1, lost 0
 Moore: won 1, lost 0

1933

NEW YORK N.L. vs. WASHINGTON A.L.

WON BY NEW YORK, 4 GAMES TO 1

Game Scores:

New York 4	Washington 2	October 3 at New York
New York 6	Washington 1	October 4 at New York
Washington 4	New York 0	October 5 at Washington
New York 2	Washington 1	October 6 at Washington
(11 innings)		
New York 4	Washington 3	October 7 at Washington
(10 innings)		

Two youthful managers, both of whom were still active on the field and played in every series game, led the opposing clubs in the 1933 World Series. The National League pennant had been won, to nearly everyone's surprise, by John McGraw's hand-picked successor, Bill Terry, age thirty-four, who had hit .322 that season. And another long-odds bet had won in the American League: twenty-seven-year-old Joe Cronin, Clark Griffith's son-in-law and successor as manager. Joe played the full season at shortstop and batted .309. It was Bill's second season as manager and Joe's first.

The Giants had some hard hitters but they won the pennant on their pitching. They won the series that way too. The Senators won mainly on their hitting, by Heinie Manush (.336), Goose

130

Goslin (.297), and Cronin himself. But they had added two great pitchers to their staff too: Alvin Crowder, who won twenty-four games, and Earl Whitehill, who won twenty-two games and filled in in the outfield. There was nothing in the American League that year, however, to match Carl Hubbell, king of the screwball, a pitch that resembled Mathewson's famous fadeaway and one that Hubbell could throw at three different speeds.

The batting hero of the series was Mel Ott of the Giants, with two home runs and a batting average of .389. And the chief disappointment was Washington's Alvin Crowder, who failed in both his starts and never lasted through the sixth inning. Earl Whitehill, however, did turn in the best pitching job of the series, with a five-hit shutout for the Senators' only victory.

Hubbell gave only five hits in the first game, but the losing Senators made two runs, although nobody hit more than a single off him. Ott put this game on ice with a home run, his first time up. With four hits in four at-bats he drove in three of the Giants' four runs. The man who had been the inspiration of the Giants' pennant drive, Blondy Ryan, the shortstop, took no part in the scoring and committed an error. But fans and players still talked about his famous telegram, sent when he was rejoining the team on its final western trip, after Blondy had been laid up with a spike wound: "They cannot beat us. En route. J. C. Ryan." So it was "They can't beat us" all through the final days of the season and right on through the series.

Hal Schumacher allowed just five hits in game number two, but again the Senators at least managed a score when Goose Goslin teed off for a home run in the third inning, to put his club temporarily ahead. In the sixth inning, however, the Giants got all their runs, all six of them, blasting poor Alvin Crowder out of the box with a sudden burst of power, including a pinch-hit single by Lefty O'Doul with the bases full. That was the blow that sent Crowder to the showers.

The hero of the third game, in the eyes of the ball players and most of the fans, was President Franklin D. Roosevelt, who brought down the house when he was rolled into the park in his wheel chair to throw out the first ball. The ball was tossed and

131

every player on both squads scrambled wildly for it, like kids after a quarter. The fans howled with excitement as the ball players shoved, scrambled, butted, and fought one another for the prize. It was finally retrieved by Washington outfielder Heinie Manush. After the game, which was one of the best Earl Whitehill ever pitched, Heinie presented the ball to Whitehill. But that was the only chance the Senators had to rejoice, for the Giant pitchers then closed the door tight, opening it only a small crack now and then to let a lone run trickle through.

It was Hubbell again in the fourth game, and he allowed no Senator runs until the seventh inning. The Giants had already posted one run on Bill Terry's homer. The tying run was largely Hubbell's fault, for his fumble of a simple bunt by Joe Kuhel put the tying run into scoring position. Now it was Blondy Ryan's turn to be a hero at last. In the eleventh inning, he came through with a sharp single to center field that sent Travis Jackson home with the tying run. The true hero, however, may well have been a utility infielder recently dragged up from the minor leagues, Charlie Dressen, formerly with the Cincinnati Reds. When the Senators, with the bases full in their half of the eleventh, sent up as a pinch-hitter a young catcher recently with Chattanooga in the Southern Association, the Giants had no "book" on him. But Dressen, who had played most of the season in the Southern Association, knew the young catcher, Cliff Bolton, well. What he knew best about him was that he ran like an ice cart. Dressen hastened to Terry with the word: "Make him hit on the ground and you've got a cinch double play." Hubbell spun in a low pitch, Bolton whacked it on the ground to Blondy Ryan at shortstop. Ryan tossed to Critz at second and Critz fired down to Terry for the easiest double play of the day, and the Giants had their third victory.

The final game was a nerve-stretcher too, with tight pitching on both sides and another Frank Merriwell finish. Alvin Crowder started this one for the Senators but stumbled a bit in the second inning when pitcher Hal Schumacher of the Giants drove in two runs with a single. Crowder hung on, however, until the sixth, when Gus Mancuso's double scored a run. Schumacher up to this point had allowed several hits but had not been in danger. In the bottom half of the sixth, however, Fred Schulte, Washington's center fielder and the Senators' batting star in the series, clouted a home run with Manush and Cronin on base to tie the score. Then Bill Terry called in his cool Cuban, Adolfo Luque, to halt the uprising. At the age of forty-three, Luque was not supposed to have a great deal left. His last World Series appearance had been in 1919 when he had pitched five strong innings for the Reds in two different games, allowing only one hit and striking out five. Now, fourteen years later, he called up all his old cunning. He held off the Senators until the tenth, when Mel Ott put the Giants ahead with a home run. By the time the Senators had two out in the bottom of the tenth, they had made only one hit off Luque and he had struck out four of them. Now he began to show his age. Joe Cronin tapped him for a clean single. He walked Fred Schulte. Next at bat was Joe Kuhel, who had hit .322 that season. A solid hit by Kuhel and the series would go back to New York. But Adolfo wanted to go home. So he hitched up his belt and struck out Kuhel on three pitches.

Leading hitters:

NEW YORK GIANTS
Ott: .389

WASHINGTON SENATORS
Schulte: .333

Winning pitchers:

NEW YORK GIANTS
Hubbell: won 2, lost 0
Schumacher: won 1, lost 0
Luque: won 1, lost 0

WASHINGTON SENATORS
Whitehill: won 1, lost 0

1934

ST. LOUIS N.L. vs. DETROIT A.L.

WON BY ST. LOUIS, 4 GAMES TO 3

Game Scores:

St. Louis 8	Detroit 3	October 3 at Detroit
Detroit 3	St. Louis 2	October 4 at Detroit
(12 innings)		
St. Louis 4	Detroit 1	October 5 at St. Louis
Detroit 10	St. Louis 4	October 6 at St. Louis
Detroit 3	St. Louis 1	October 7 at St. Louis
St. Louis 4	Detroit 3	October 8 at Detroit
St. Louis 11	Detroit 0	October 9 at Detroit

Besides being one of the most closely fought, one of the most violent, and one of the most thrilling of all World Series, the 1934 World Series was perhaps the most artistic, in that it ended with an eruption that left no doubt of the superiority of the winner over the loser. The 1932 series between New York and Chicago had been full of hard feelings and personal invective. But that was a Boy Scout outing compared to this one. So loud were the catcalls, and so prominently displayed were the boasts of Dizzy Dean, the Cards' thirty-game winner, that hardly anyone had time to notice that this series was also a rematch of Pepper Martin and catcher Mickey Cochrane. Pepper, who had stolen five bases off Mickey in the 1931 series when Cochrane was catching for Philadelphia, stole two more in this set. He also hit for .355.

But there were plenty of sluggers in this series. Ducky Medwick, the rugged left fielder for the Cards, made eleven hits for an average of .379. Charlie Gehringer, Detroit's Mechanical Man, also hit .379. Hank Greenberg, the big Detroit first baseman who had led the league in two-baggers that year, hit .321. But he struck out nine times, to the open and raucous delight of Dizzy Dean. Dizzy, besides starring in the series on the pitching mound, where he won two games, also managed to hold the spotlight most of the rest of the time. In the first game, he helped make the nervous Tigers more miserable by belting a fat two-bagger off relief pitcher Firpo Marberry. Laughing merrily as he perched on second base, Dizzy called to Marberry: "What was that you throwed me?"

In the fourth game, he got into the fray as a pinch-runner, was forced at second, and managed to get his head in the way of Billy Rogell's throw. He was knocked completely cold and did not recover until he had lain for several minutes on the baseline and had been carried, limp as a potato sack, into the clubhouse. While everyone had been staring aghast at his prostrate body, Durocher had sneaked over the plate with the run that tied the game for St. Louis. And when Dizzy came to, he promptly asked: "Did I break up that double play?"

This was the spirit that had won the pennant for the St. Louis Gashouse Gang, who had been counted out of the pennant race two weeks before the season was over. And it was the spirit that eventually overcame the sparkling Detroit ball club, which was the "paper" favorite everywhere.

In the first game, Mickey Cochrane pulled a Connie Mack-type surprise by starting, of all people, Alvin Crowder, late of the Senators, who had failed to finish his two games in the last World Series. Alvin really should have won this one but the Detroit club, still a-flutter at having won their first American League Championship in twenty-five years, kicked the ball game away. There were five infield errors by Detroit, with two of them by Marvin Owen, the third baseman. Even Charlie Gehringer, the greatest second baseman alive, foozled an easy toss for a force-out that should have ended the inning. Then Owen followed with a wide throw to first on the next play, and the gates were open for the Cards to score two unearned runs. Of the eight runs the Cards made, against Crowder, Marberry, and Hogsett, five were earned. The Tigers earned three, and that was not enough. Dizzy Dean gave up eight hits while he and his mates got thirteen. Dizzy also struck out six, one of his victims being Hank Greenberg, who fanned with runners on second and third.

The second game was one of the finest ever pitched by Detroit's number one pitcher, Schoolboy Rowe, who had the misfortune to ask of his wife, during a pregame radio broadcast, "How'm I doing, Edna?" If Rowe had been given a dollar for every time he heard that phrase screamed, bellowed, and whined into his ear by the St. Louis bench jockeys, he'd have had more than his cut of the series pot. Nevertheless, after momentary unsteadiness, Rowe settled down to knock off twenty-two St. Louis batters in a row, while his teammates picked away at Wild Bill Hallahan and Lefty Bill Walker for one run at a time, until in the last of the twelfth, they got the extra one they needed, thanks to a run-scoring single by left fielder Goose Goslin.

The third game, the first in St. Louis, was wild and wooly. Paul Dean pitched it and seemed always just about to let the game get away from him. The Detroit club left thirteen men on base, enough to have won the game twice over. But they could not get anyone across the plate until the top of the ninth, when it was far too late. The St. Louis fans, and the Gashouse Gang, whooped and howled as the futile Tigers tried to turn their eight hits and five walks into runs. And the place exploded when, in the fifth inning, Pepper Martin opened with a double, to be followed by a triple from Rothrock, and a single by Frisch. Tommy Bridges, the starting Detroit pitcher, gave way to Hogsett then, and the Indian gave up only one hit for the rest of the game. But the Cards needed no more.

In the fourth game, the angry Tigers broke loose with all the might in their bats and not even Dizzy Dean's sacrificial breaking-up of a double play could get the Cards into the ball game.

Hank Greenberg hit two doubles, and two singles to drive in three runs. Elden Auker, the underhand pitcher, gave the Cards ten hits, and he was all even as late as the seventh inning. But then poor Pepper Martin made his third error of the day and the Tigers went ahead to stay. In the eighth inning they scored five times.

Game number five looked like the turning point for Detroit. Winning this one on the enemy's field, to go ahead, three games to two, seemed to have given them the edge. And in this they beat the Cards' best, Dizzy Dean, who gave way to Tex Carleton in the final inning. The Cards came close and catcher Bill Delancey hit a home run. But then he struck out three times, and called the umpire a lot of bad names that later cost him $50.

The sixth game was supposed to be Schoolboy Rowe's triumph. He had never looked stronger than he had in the second game. But in this one he started unsteadily. He held his own for a while, after allowing a run in the first. But in the fifth inning the improbable happened: Leo Durocher got a single. After that, Paul Dean bunted Leo on to second and Pepper Martin drove him home with a long single to left. When the return throw was wild, Pepper kept on going to third and scored soon on an infield out. Then in the seventh Durocher performed the impossible: he got a *two*-base hit. Paul Dean scored him with a single and won the game.

The final game was a victory parade for the Cards, who made seventeen hits while Dizzy Dean was toying with the Tigers. The feature of the game was the wild explosion after Ducky Medwick and Marv Owen collided at third base, following a Medwick triple. No serious blows were struck then but when Medwick took his position in left field, the Detroit bleacher bugs doused him with garbage, paper, odd pieces of trash, and dirty language. The game could not progress while the junk showered on the field and finally Judge Landis, after a conference with all the umpires, ordered Medwick removed from the park. This was hardly justice, but it got the game over and St. Louis won anyway.

After the series it turned out that Judge Landis had also fined umpire Bill Klem for using bad language—not on the ball field but in a hotel elevator.

Leading hitters:

ST. LOUIS CARDINALS
Medwick: .379

DETROIT TIGERS
Gehringer: .379

Winning pitchers:

ST. LOUIS CARDINALS
J. Dean: won 2, lost 1
P. Dean: won 2, lost 0

DETROIT TIGERS
Rowe: won 1, lost 1
Auker: won 1, lost 1
Bridges: won 1, lost 1

1935

DETROIT A.L. vs. CHICAGO N.L.

WON BY DETROIT, 4 GAMES TO 2

Game Scores:

Chicago 3	Detroit 0	October 2 at Detroit
Detroit 8	Chicago 3	October 3 at Detroit
Detroit 6	Chicago 5	October 4 at Chicago
(11 innings)		
Detroit 2	Chicago 1	October 5 at Chicago
Chicago 3	Detroit 1	October 6 at Chicago
Detroit 4	Chicago 3	October 7 at Detroit

It was a good thing for Mickey Cochrane's peace of mind that Detroit got another chance, in 1935, to win the Championship of the World. This time, the Tigers were underdogs and the club was somewhat less keyed up. But there were plenty of hard feelings and lots of hard words in the series, with the Cubs almost constantly at war against the umpire. Judge Landis had overheard or been told about plenty of vulgar language in the 1934 series. This time his ears were really singed and when the affair was over he imposed fines on four Chicago ballplayers and on umpire George Moriarty, all of whom were eligible to have their mouths washed out with soap.

The games were nearly all tight ones, and Chicago lost all the one-run games, which may have accounted for the fiery tongues. But the Detroit fans relished every moment and when the series was over they kept the city awake all night while they celebrated.

A feature of the series, to Alvin Crowder at least, was that after so many attempts he finally won a World Series game. And Lon Warneke, who had lost his only previous World Series start, against the Yankees in 1932, this time got credit for two wins, although he did not finish his second start. Slugging Hank Greenberg, who had led the league in runs batted in (170), had to sit most of this series out, for he broke his wrist in a collision with Chicago catcher Gabby Hartnett at the plate in the second game. But Ervin (Pete) Fox, Detroit right fielder, made 10 hits in 22 at-bats, and Gehringer, in his perfectionist manner, posted almost the same series batting average as he had the year before: .375 (against .379 in 1934).

The Cubs were heavy favorites to start with, largely because of the momentum of the long winning streak that had carried them to the pennant. In the first game, the Cubs seemed bent on rolling right along. With their lean Arkansas ace, twenty-game-winner Lon Warneke on the mound, they outclassed the Tigers completely. Schoolboy Rowe pitched a fine game, giving seven hits and striking out eight. But he took the first step toward disaster himself when, with one out in the first inning, and Augie Galan, Chicago left fielder, on base after a leadoff double, Rowe hurried his throw on a bunt by Billy Herman and threw the ball into right field. The Cubs scored twice soon after that and they needed only one run to win. Warneke allowed only four hits and Pete Fox got two of those.

In the second game the angry Tigers did not waste a moment. Jo-Jo White, the leadoff man, who had opened with a strikeout in the first game, started this one with a single. Then Mickey Cochrane drove a two-bagger to the fence that brought Jo-Jo across the plate. Gehringer scored Cochrane with a clean single to center. Then cleanup man Hank Greenberg cleaned off the bases with a home run into Greenberg Gardens—the left-field stands. At this point Manager Charlie Grimm of the Cubs removed Charlie Root and put in a tiny left-hander, Roy Hen-

140

shaw. The Tigers let this tidbit live until the fourth inning, then they ate him alive.

Henshaw started the trouble himself, with two out, when he hit Marvin Owen with a pitch. The pitcher then bounced one past the mound that Henshaw just missed. Roy gave Jo-Jo White a walk and that filled the bases, all the pitcher's own doing. Henshaw next came up with a wild pitch, letting Owen score, then he walked Cochrane to fill the bases again. This time Gehringer really hit the ball for a single that brought in two more runs. With the score 7 to 0, Detroit's Tommy Bridges eased up enough to let the Cubs get a few runs of their own. But he never let them get close.

The loss of Greenberg gave the Tigers problems. They had to move Owen from third to first and put Herman (the Flea) Clifton at third base. Both these fellows hit about the size of their neckbands. But the Tigers were determined. In the third game the heavy hitters all contributed solid blows, while three different pitchers struggled to keep the Cubs from overrunning the defense perimeter. In this game the rough heckling the Cubs had been handing the Tigers grew rough beyond belief. When Phil Cavaretta was called out on a close play, the whole Chicago crew bore down on the umpire and managed among them to fish up every obscene word in the well. It cost them all $200 and it did not win them the game. The Tigers pulled that out in the eleventh inning on a single by Jo-Jo White.

The fourth game was another tight one, won almost unaided by Alvin Crowder, who gave the Cubs only five hits. The winning run in this game scored on a succession of errors, with Crowder himself poking the crucial ball at the shortstop and the shortstop letting it elude him, while a run scored.

Schoolboy Rowe, who had helped win the eleven-inning game, just did not seem cut out for World Series work. He tried again in the fifth game, pitched well, but still not well enough. Lon Warneke, who had to quit with a wrenched muscle after the sixth inning, gave the Tigers only three hits and his successor Bill Lee, while yielding four hits, let no Tiger get near the plate.

The series then had to be won at home, which suited the Detroit fans completely. The best crowd of the series packed the stands to watch the Tigers pull victory out of the jaws of defeat in the last few minutes. The two clubs were tied at 3-all when the ninth inning came. And every Detroit heart hit bottom when Stan Hack, Chicago third baseman, opened the inning with a screaming three-bagger into deepest center field. When Hack pulled up at third, the stands were so silent that a man could hear the crunch of peanut shells ten rows away. Tommy Bridges, Detroit's great curve-ball pitcher, who had won the second game, dug up the final ounce of his strength to keep Hack from crossing the plate. First he struck out Bill Jurges. Then he teased the pitcher, Larry French, into sending a roller back to the mound, which Bridges fielded easily and tossed to first for out number two. There must have been several hundred fans who gave thanks at that point that Grimm had not used a pinch-hitter. The next man was a real threat—Augie Galan, who had opened up the series with a two-bagger. But the best Augie could do was lift a long fly to Goose Goslin, good for a score if there had not been two out already. Now the silence was broken with a roar and Tommy Bridges, dripping sweat, stalked happily into the dugout.

The Tigers, impatient to end it, nearly fell on their faces in their inning. Clifton, who was reputedly unable to hit a bull in the rear end with a shovel, struck out for the second time. But then the mighty Mickey Cochrane managed to bounce a ball which the second baseman just could not field cleanly. With Cochrane on first, Gehringer bounced to the shortstop. Mickey dashed wildly down to second, making a double play impossible, and Gehringer was out at first. Goose Goslin, an old hand at such matters, then stepped up and drove out a solid hit that brought the winning run straight home, and with it the Championship.

Leading hitters:

DETROIT TIGERS
Fox: .385

CHICAGO CUBS
Herman and Klein: .333

Winning pitchers:

DETROIT TIGERS
    Bridges: won 2, lost 0
    Rowe: won 1, lost 2
    Crowder: won 1, lost 0

CHICAGO CUBS
    Warneke: won 2, lost 0

1936

NEW YORK A.L. vs. NEW YORK N.L.

WON BY YANKEES, 4 GAMES TO 2

Game Scores:

Giants 6	Yankees 1	September 30 at Polo Grounds
Yankees 18	Giants 4	October 2 at Polo Grounds
Yankees 2	Giants 1	October 3 at Yankee Stadium
Yankees 5	Giants 2	October 4 at Yankee Stadium
Giants 5	Yankees 4	October 5 at Yankee Stadium
Yankees 13	Giants 5	October 6 at Polo Grounds

Thirteen years elapsed between the last subway series and the series of 1936. Now there was no more Babe Ruth or Bob Meusel or Whitey Witt. Instead of Joe Dugan there was a college boy called Red Rolfe at third base. Instead of Wally Pipp at first there was Lou Gehrig, already a veteran. Instead of old Everett Scott, the Yankees played a California kid named Frank Crosetti at short. Joe DiMaggio trod the grass where Whitey Witt had galloped in other years. And out in Ruth's pasture there was a speedboy named George Selkirk. Ross Youngs of the Giants had been replaced by the Shetland Pony, Mel Ott. Bill Terry held Long George Kelly's job at first base for the Giants, while John McGraw and Miller Huggins were both long dead.

In this series, as in previous years, the Yankees had the sluggers and the Giants had the pitchers. But the pitchers pitched in hard luck and the sluggers grew fat. As always before it was

144

The Thirties

17. Ernie Lombardi, bowled over by Charlie Keller of the Yankees in the final game of the 1939 World Series between New York and Cincinnati, sits dazed by the plate while Joe DiMaggio also scores. Billy Werber of the Reds tries to dig the ball out from under Lombardi. Frank Crosetti, who scored ahead of Keller, stands between Lombardi and the camera, with Bill Dickey, still giving the "stand-up" signal, in front of him, and Joe DiMaggio in the background. Umpire Babe Pinelli remains squatting to view a close play that never developed. *Wide World Photos.*

18. The play that started a riot. In the seventh game of the 1934 World Series, Ducky Medwick of St. Louis slides into third. Detroit third baseman Marv Owen lifts right leg high while awaiting throw, to avoid Medwick's spikes. He set his foot down on Medwick and the fight began. When Medwick took his position in the outfield fans threw hot dog buns, cushions, bottles, and assorted impedimenta until Commissioner Landis ordered Ducky from the field. *Wide World Photos.*

19. Connie Mack's last great team, the American League Champions of 1931, who lost the series to Pepper Martin's gang from St. Louis. This club included Waite Hoyt (fourth from the left in back row), former Yankee star who made a strong comeback after two dismal seasons with Detroit; and Mickey Cochrane, third from left in center row, who would go on to become Detroit's Great Leader. Lefty Grove is at the extreme left of the center row, Eddie Collins is sitting at Connie's right elbow. Rube Walberg is sitting at Connie's right ankle. *Brown Brothers.*

20. Mickey Cochrane, fighting manager of the Detroit Tigers, yells a few comments at his charges during the 1934 World Series, while Pepper Martin of St. Louis slides safely home behind him. *Brown Brothers.*

21. Dizzy Dean, after shutting out the Tigers in the final game of the 1934 World Series, shows Will Rogers how he twists a tiger's tail. *Brown Brothers.*

22. Joe DiMaggio, in 1937 World Series against the Giants, hits a single for the Yankees his first time up. *Brown Brothers.*

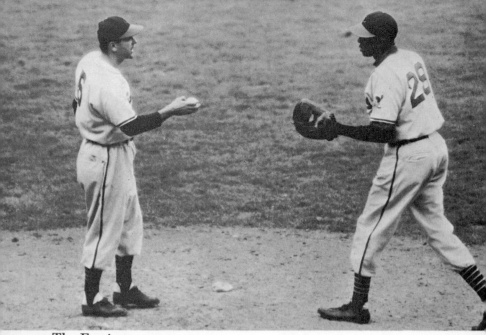

The Forties

23. The end of a long long trail. Satchel Paige, one of the greatest pitchers the country ever produced, finally gets into a major League World Series game, at the age of forty-two. In the fifth game of the 1948 World Series, Paige came in to pitch for Cleveland in the seventh inning and put two Boston batters out without allowing a hit. Lou Boudreau hands him the ball. *Brown Brothers.*

24. The run that sank the Red Sox. Enos Slaughter of St. Louis scored all the way from first to bring in the winning run in the final game of the 1946 World Series. Culberson, the Red Sox outfielder, never dreamed Slaughter would try to go all the way and he just lobbed the ball in to cut-off man Johnny Pesky after Walker singled. *Wide World Photos.*

a close series and a hard-fought one, despite some lopsided scores in games two and six. The Giants just would not give up until they had been pounded right into the sod by the Yankee bats.

The Giants, having won the pennant in a rush, were supposed to have the momentum in this series. The Yankees had opened up a wide lead over their rivals and won the pennant so easily they just coasted home. The substitute for Babe Ruth in this series, as far as color and excitement went, was to be young Joe DiMaggio, George Weiss's prize catch, who had hit .323 in this, his freshman season. And next best seemed certain to be Lou Gehrig. But the slugging star turned out to be Yankee left fielder Jake Powell, who had been brought in from Washington in midseason (and who was destined to go back there several seasons later). Jake hit for an average of .455. DiMaggio got nine hits and Gehrig made two home runs. The Giants' top slugger was shortstop Dick Bartell, with an average of .381. Bill Terry, who failed to break any fences, played his last game of professional ball in this series. It also marked the final major league appearance of Mark Koenig, who this time played second base and pinch-hit for the Giants.

The first game of the series was played according to the script. The invincible Carl Hubbell, who had won twenty-six games that season, won easily over Red Ruffing. Red was just not at his best and the Yankee hitters could not unwind Hubbell's screwball. Jake Powell, however, was able to reach Hubbell for three hits, but he was batting sixth in the order and did the Giants no damage. The rest of the Yankees together got four hits and Hubbell struck out eight. It was a rainy, miserable day and the base paths were dark with mud. But Hubbell never faltered. The Yankees started off with a run in the third when George Selkirk put a ball in the stands. But that completed the Yankee scoring. The Giants tied the game in the fifth, went ahead in the sixth, and broke loose in the eighth for four runs, with Frank Crosetti and Bill Dickey helping the enemy by committing an error apiece.

In the second game, the Yankees saw fast-ball pitching and that is what they doted on. They landed on Hal Schumacher for three hits in the first two innings, and Hal added a wild pitch and four walks. Then the Yanks destroyed pitchers Al Smith and Dick Coffman in the third inning, during which they scored seven runs. Bill Dickey contributed a home run and pitcher Lefty Gomez startled everyone, including himself, by actually driving in two runs with a base hit. In the ninth inning Lazzeri hit a home run with the bases full to put the game so far out of reach that it was no longer laughable. It was the easiest victory Gomez ever earned, and President Roosevelt was there to witness it.

Game number three was a heartbreaker in a different way, for in this poor Freddy Fitzsimmons outpitched two Yankee hurlers—Bump Hadley and Pat Malone—yet could not come in first. Altogether, the Yanks made only four hits off Freddy, while the Giants took Hadley for ten hits and Malone for one. Yet the only run the Giants could push across was a home run by rookie outfielder Jimmy Ripple. That just matched a home run by Gehrig and the game was won by the Yankees when Crosetti's scratch single, with two men already out in the eighth, bounced off Fitzsimmons' glove and pushed Jake Powell across the plate.

The fourth game matched Carl Hubbell with Monte Pearson, the Yanks' nineteen-game winner. This time Carl's screwball failed him at a crucial point, in the third inning, when the Yanks made three runs, one on a home run by Lou Gehrig. That made it 4 to 1 in favor of the Yankees. The Giants, largely through Jimmy Ripple's efforts, could scratch up only two runs before the game was over.

The Giants fought back, however, and won game number five for Hal Schumacher, beating off a Yankee effort to snatch the game away. Schumacher was hit hard in this game, particularly by George Selkirk, who hit a home run and a single, but Hal managed to strand nine Yanks on base. The Giants gave Hal a three-run lead to start with and added one in the sixth but the Yankees tied the score and sent the game into overtime. In the top of the tenth, Jo-Jo Moore opened with a double, Dick Bartell put him on third base with a sacrifice, then Bill Terry drove a long fly to Joe DiMaggio and Moore scored the winning run after the catch.

The Giants started off strong in the final game too, with two runs in the first inning. But the Yankees quickly caught up, with a murderous attack on Freddy Fitzsimmons that gave them five runs in three innings. Clydell Castleman, who had worked hard in relief that season but had won only four games for the Giants, relieved Freddy and held the Yanks at bay while the Giants tried to even matters up. The Giants were only one run behind when they went into the ninth. They lifted Castleman at the start of the eighth to pinch-hit for him but his pinch-hitter had flied out. In the ninth they wished they had kept Clydell on the job. His substitute, Dick Coffman, never got anybody out. The Yanks posted seven runs in the ninth and Johnny Murphy shut the door on the Giants.

Leading hitters:

NEW YORK YANKEES
Powell: .455

NEW YORK GIANTS
Bartell: .381

Winning pitchers:

NEW YORK YANKEES
Gomez: won 2, lost 0
Hadley: won 1, lost 0
Pearson: won 1, lost 0

NEW YORK GIANTS
Hubbell: won 1, lost 1
Schumacher: won 1, lost 1

1937

NEW YORK A.L. vs. NEW YORK N.L.

WON BY YANKEES, 4 GAMES TO 1

Game Scores:

Yankees 8	Giants 1	October 6 at Yankee Stadium
Yankees 8	Giants 1	October 7 at Yankee Stadium
Yankees 5	Giants 1	October 8 at Polo Grounds
Giants 7	Yankees 3	October 9 at Polo Grounds
Yankees 4	Giants 2	October 10 at Polo Grounds

In the 1937 series, the Giants, who had kept the contest exciting in previous years by their persistence in coming from behind, were subdued almost without a struggle. Carl Hubbell won a game, with the help of a six-run inning, but in all the other contests Yankee superiority, at the plate and on the mound, was painfully clear. Hubbell looked good for a time in the opening game but no better than Lefty Gomez, who had led his league in strikeouts and in earned-run average that year. When the Yankees ganged up for their habitual big inning, it was too much for Hubbell, and for his relievers as well.

The 1937 club was deemed by some the best Yankee team of all. In winning 102 games, for a thirteen-game edge over second-place Detroit, the Yankees hung up high marks in almost every department. DiMaggio led the league in homers and in runs scored, while Gomez was the most effective pitcher. But Red Ruffing had his best year to date, with twenty wins against only

148

seven losses, while relief pitcher Johnny Murphy won thirteen games and saved countless others. Rookie Tommy Henrich hit .320 and Myril Hoag hit .301. Gehrig hit .351, Dickey .332, and George Selkirk, with a month out for injuries, hit .328.

Yankee hitting and Yankee pitching and Yankee managing dominated the All-Star game that year, and there was already talk of the need to break up the Yankee organization, which now seemed to win its pennants in the spring, and then coast home. But actually shrewd trading and careful grooming of rookies had much to do with the Yank success. DiMaggio could have been bought by many other clubs, but no one other than George Weiss wanted to take a chance on his supposedly weak knee. Tommy Henrich was "rescued" from the Cleveland organization, when they failed to move him out of the minors in time and he was made a free agent. Ivy Paul Andrews, who won some key games for the Yankees, could not make a job for himself in Cleveland. Red Rolfe had been picked off a college campus, where other clubs hardly bothered looking for talent.

The Giants had had to struggle for the pennant this season but they came up to the series full of fight. The big inning in the first game, however, sending Hubbell to the showers, gave the Yankees a psychological edge. The second game nearly duplicated the first, except that the lone Giant run came in the first inning on a double by Bartell and a single by Mel Ott, the National League's most valuable player. The Yankees put all their runs in three innings this time, with Red Ruffing, who hit a single and a double, batting in three.

In the third game the Yankee bats were relatively quiet. But the Giants could not muster hits enough to score off Monte Pearson until the seventh inning when Jimmy Ripple and first baseman Johnny McCarthy combined to shove a run across. The Yanks had already made five, and when the Giants mounted a mild threat in the ninth Johnny Murphy came in and put the last man out.

Game number four belonged to Carl Hubbell, who gave the Yankees one run at a time while his teammates got six in a bunch. A little-noticed feature of this game was a home run by

Lou Gehrig, the last one he would ever hit in a World Series game. The big guns for the Giants were Hank Leiber, center fielder, and Harry Danning, the big catcher whose mates called him "Horse."

Lefty Gomez came back to win the fifth game and clinch the championship, the sixth for the Yankees. This was a game of home runs, but Gehrig did not contribute any. Myril Hoag hit a homer in the second inning and Joe DiMaggio hit one in the third. But the Giants immediately tied the score in their half of the third when Ott's home run scored Dick Bartell. In the fifth inning the matter was settled in the most unlikely fashion imaginable. Gomez, who usually accepted congratulations if he hit a long foul, followed up Tony Lazzeri's triple with a single of his own. Then Gehrig brought Lefty home with a two-bagger. That was all the scoring. Lazzeri's triple was his sixth hit of the series. He hit safely in every game and ended his Yankee career as a star. No one at that time could have foretold that two seasons later he would be filling in at third base for the enemy—the New York Giants. But no one knew then either that Lou Gehrig's lumbago, which seemed to have hampered him only a little, was the forerunner of an ailment that would bring his career to a sudden end after one more World Series.

Leading hitters:

NEW YORK YANKEES
Lazzeri: .400

NEW YORK GIANTS
Moore: .391

Winning pitchers:

NEW YORK YANKEES
Gomez: won 2, lost 0
Ruffing: won 1, lost 0
Pearson: won 1, lost 0

NEW YORK GIANTS
Hubbell: won 1, lost 1

1938

NEW YORK A.L. vs. CHICAGO N.L.

WON BY NEW YORK, 4 GAMES TO 0

Game Scores:

New York 3	Chicago 1	October 5 at Chicago
New York 6	Chicago 3	October 6 at Chicago
New York 5	Chicago 2	October 8 at New York
New York 8	Chicago 3	October 9 at New York

The 1938 Yankees did not breeze home to the pennant with quite the ease of the year before. Joe DiMaggio held out (in vain) for a raise in salary in the spring and did not begin to perform at the top of his skills until June. So instead of grabbing first place in May and hanging tight, the Yanks did not make it to the top until the middle of July. After that there was no catching them, and they spent the last weeks marking time. Meanwhile, back in the older league, the Cubs staged a breakneck come-from-behind battle to overtake the Pirates. They had the momentum when they entered the series. But that's all they had, and the Yankees soon took that away.

This pennant enabled McCarthy to become the first major league manager to win three World Championships in a row and it gave him another chance to remind the Chicago owners of how shortsighted they had been to fire him for not winning a World Series.

This was the last World Series for Lou Gehrig, who had posted his lowest season batting average since 1925 (.295). He made only four singles in the four games and was noticeably slower in the field. Lazzeri made two appearances in the series in a Chicago uniform, grounded out once and struck out once. The Yankees used only one relief pitcher in the series. The Cubs used nine. Still the Yankee bats did not explode as everyone expected. Bill Dickey and Joe Gordon both hit .400 and there were five home runs. But DiMaggio got only four hits in the series, and Red Rolfe got only three.

The Yankees got an immediate jump on the Cubs with two runs in the second inning of the first game, against Bill Lee, the Chicago ace, who had won twenty-two games in the season. That was really all they needed, for the Cubs made only one run off Red Ruffing on hits by Rip Collins and Stan Hack.

The Cub pitcher for the second game looked to be a soft touch for the Yankees. He was Dizzy Dean, whose whirring fast ball and sizzling curve were mere memories now. The Yankee sluggers licked their lips in anticipation as they stepped up to face him. But Old Diz managed to keep them all off stride with his next-to-nothing ball and his ten-cent curve. The Yankees did score twice in the second inning but that could be laid to the slow thinking of his infielders more than to Dean. When the eighth inning opened, the Cubs had got the runs back and were leading the Yankees 3 to 2, having tagged Gomez for nine hits. Center fielder Joe Marty got three of those, a double and two singles, and drove in all the Chicago runs.

In the eighth inning, the old arm began to give out. George Selkirk opened up with a single, his first hit of the game. But Dizzy Dean teased Joe Gordon and pinch-hitter Myril Hoag into hitting ground balls for forceouts. With two out and Hoag on first base, Frank Crosetti drove a pitch over the left-field fence to put the Yanks ahead to stay. Old Diz made the third out by fanning Red Rolfe, however, and the Cubs were at least within reach of victory. But in the ninth, the pattern was repeated. Henrich opened with a single and then, with no outs in between, Joe DiMaggio drove a ball right where Crosetti had hit his and the score became Yankees 6, Cubs 3. Old Diz was taken out then and except for a brief appearance in the fourth game, he never appeared in a World Series again.

The third game was the finest pitching job in the series, and it was performed by Monte Pearson, who had adorned his record that season with a no-hit game against his former teammates, the Cleveland Indians. Monte, whose square name was Marcellus Montgomery Pearson, and who would hardly ever admit to feeling anything but a bit off his feed, nearly threw a perfect game that day, for he walked only two men and faced only twenty-seven. He should have been in bed, too, he allowed. He gave the Cubs only five hits and struck out nine. Meanwhile Bill Dickey and Joe Gordon, who had replaced Lazzeri at second base, each hit a home run, Gordon's coming with a man on base. Joe Marty hit a home run for Chicago. He collected three of the five Chicago hits.

The final game was more the Yankee style than any of the others. It clinched the championship with a bang and a roar, as every single Yankee made at least one hit, while Crosetti and Myril Hoag drove in five runs between them, with two hits apiece. Tommy Henrich contributed his first World Series home run, Crosetti hit a double and a triple. The official victim again was General Bill Lee, but Tex Carleton was the pitcher the Yanks seemed to dote on most. Tex was unable to get a man out in the eighth inning and he let two wild pitches fly while he was trying.

Gomez' victory in this series tied him with Waite Hoyt and Chief Albert Bender at six wins. He never completed another World Series game. And he always gave full credit to Fireman Johnny Murphy for the victory in the second game, when he gave up nine hits in seven innings in his duel with Dean. Murphy pitched the last two innings and managed to keep the Bears from the door, even though pinch-hitter Phil Cavaretta reached him for a single in the ninth.

This was also the sixth straight World Series loss for the Cubs.

153

Leading hitters:

NEW YORK YANKEES
Dickey and Gordon: .400

CHICAGO CUBS
Marty: .500

Winning pitchers:

Ruffing: won 2, lost 0
Gomez: won 1, lost 0
Pearson: won 1, lost 0

1939

NEW YORK A.L. vs. CINCINNATI N.L.

WON BY NEW YORK, 4 GAMES TO 0

Game Scores:

New York 2	Cincinnati 1	October 4 at New York
New York 4	Cincinnati 0	October 5 at New York
New York 7	Cincinnati 3	October 7 at Cincinnati
New York 7	Cincinnati 4	October 8 at Cincinnati
(10 innings)		

The 1939 Yankees continued to set World Series records—the first club to win four World Championships in a row; the fifth four-in-a-row victory in eleven meetings; the eighth World Championship in their history. The hitting in this series was comparatively sparse and the clubs proved far more closely matched than the result would indicate. But the hardest and longest hitting was done by the Yankees, and particularly by a beetle-browed and powerful young man from the University of Maryland, via the Newark Bears. He was rookie right fielder Charlie Keller, George Weiss's prize discovery, who looked like the new Babe Ruth (and might have become one but for a back injury that shortened his career). Keller hit .334 for the season and in the series he hit .438, with three home runs, a triple, and a double.

The prize exhibit from the National League was a converted

third baseman (and one of the tallest men ever to play that position), pitcher Bucky Walters, who had won twenty-seven games in the season, striking out 137. His teammate Paul Derringer had an even better won-lost percentage, to lead the league with twenty-five wins and seven defeats. These two men could not check the Yankees but they came close enough to thrill their fans and earn the respect of the New Yorkers. The most famous Cincinnati player of them all did not even appear in the series. He was Johnny Vander Meer, the miracle pitcher who had won two no-hit games in a row the year before. This year Johnny was nowhere. He had won only five games for the Reds and was not counted on to throw a pitch.

Perhaps if Johnny had been ready the Reds could have made off with a game or two. But nothing the Reds had working for them could stop the Yankees. Paul Derringer did start off as if he might, for he set down eight men in a row to begin the first game. But big Red Ruffing was doing almost the same for the Yankees, until the fourth inning when a walk, a stolen base, and a single gave the Reds one run. The Yanks took that right back in the next inning when Joe Gordon's single was followed by a Babe Dahlgren double—Dahlgren being the fill-in for ailing Lou Gehrig, now a non-playing captain on the club. The game was won in Yankee fashion—power hitting plus lucky breaks. In the last of the ninth a long long blow by Charlie Keller was misjudged by center fielder Ival Goodman and dropped for a triple. DiMaggio was purposely passed then, but Dickey, who was supposed to hit into a double play, hit a single instead and won the ball game.

In game number two, Monte Pearson, again full of aches and pains, was matched against the Reds' Bucky Walters. Monte must have been feeling exceptionally poorly this day for he gave up not a single hit until the eighth inning. Ernie Lombardi got a single in the eighth and Billy Werber got one in the ninth. One Cincinnati man got on base with a walk. Dahlgren, who wasn't supposed to hit home runs, hit one in this game, as well as a double. The homer would have been enough.

The third game gave Lefty Gomez his last World Series

156

chance. He had never lost to a National League club, but this day he had not much more than a batting practice pitch to offer. He did not advertise the fact, but he was pitching with a girdle on—an elastic strap to hold in place a torn tendon that gave him constant pain. The Yankees gave him two runs to begin with but the Reds took one right back with three singles. The Reds added two more in the next inning off Bump Hadley but from that time forth, they could not do business with Bump. The Yankees did not hit often either. In fact, they made only five hits off Gene Thompson and none at all off Leo Grissom and Whitey Moore. But oh, those five hits! Two of them were home runs by Charlie Keller. One was a home run by Joe DiMaggio and one a home run by Bill Dickey. The other one was a single by Red Rolfe who rode in on one of Keller's home runs. The sum total of bases on those hits was seventeen.

In the final game, the Reds received very good pitching too, from their topliners, Derringer and Walters. Derringer gave up only three hits in seven innings. Walters gave up four. The Reds meanwhile piled up eleven hits off Oral Hildebrand, Steve Sundra, and Johnny Murphy. But when they came to count up the runs, guess who was far ahead? The Yankees, naturally. The Reds were leading in the eighth inning, despite home runs by Keller and Dickey. But in the top of the ninth, the Yanks again took advantage of the breaks. Keller singled through the pitcher's box for his second hit of the game. DiMaggio singled to left and Keller moved to third. Again it was Dickey at the plate, the man who hit into double plays because he was so slow getting down to first. And this time Dickey did as he was supposed to—trundled a nice ground ball to Lonnie Frey at second base. Lonnie snapped it to second, but Billy Myers was off the base. Some said the high throw pulled him off. The official scorer said it was Billy's error that allowed Keller to score. But the fans said, "Here we go again." And the fans guessed right. With this opening provided, the next Yank, Joe Gordon, beat a merciless ground ball at Billy Werber, the third baseman, and by the time Billy had knocked it down and tamed it, DiMaggio had brought home the tying run.

In the tenth inning, the game turned into a nightmare, or into a vaudeville sketch with tragic overtones. It began with a base on balls to Frank Crosetti, a man who was schooled to grab the extra base whenever it was offered. Red Rolfe's sacrifice moved Cro to second. Then followed an error by Billy Myers, a man noted for his fits of unsteadiness in the field. This allowed Crosetti to get to third and it put on base big Charlie Keller, known as King Kong, and noted as a man who hit hard, ran hard, and played hard. DiMaggio then provided an honest single to center field, more than enough to score Crosetti. In center field, Ival Goodman allowed the ball to bounce by him, and Keller, never slowing down, roared on for home, where Ernie Lombardi awaited the throw. He received the ball in his glove but almost instantly he received Charlie Keller in his midsection. The final blow separated big Ernie from the ball and from his senses. To the horror of his teammates and all the fans, big Ernie crumpled to the ground, unconscious, with the ball an arm's length away, while DiMaggio loped in with an extra run. It made no real difference, for the Reds did not score again.

Leading hitters:

NEW YORK YANKEES
Keller: .438

CINCINNATI REDS
McCormick: .400

Winning pitchers:

Ruffing:	won 1, lost 0
Pearson:	won 1, lost 0
Hadley:	won 1, lost 0
Murphy:	won 1, lost 0

1940

CINCINNATI N.L. vs. DETROIT A.L.

WON BY CINCINNATI, 4 GAMES TO 3

Game Scores:

Detroit 7	Cincinnati 2	October 2 at Cincinnati
Cincinnati 5	Detroit 3	October 3 at Cincinnati
Detroit 7	Cincinnati 4	October 4 at Detroit
Cincinnati 5	Detroit 2	October 5 at Detroit
Detroit 8	Cincinnati 0	October 6 at Detroit
Cincinnati 4	Detroit 0	October 7 at Cincinnati
Cincinnati 2	Detroit 1	October 8 at Cincinnati

In 1940, the scramble was in the American League, while the breeze was in the National. The Tigers had to claw and snarl their way to the flag right up to two days before the end. The Reds clinched the pennant on September 18 and had the rest of the month to play catch. So the Tigers this time had the momentum. The result was the best series since Bobo Newsom was a kid. And Bobo Newsom himself was very nearly the hero of this one. Perhaps if the fates who have the outcome of ball games in their keeping had had any sense of what was fair and right, they'd have let Newsom (called Bobo because he used that name for everybody, including himself) win that final game. Newsom's father died during the series and if anyone deserved help from the fates it was Bobo.

This time both teams looked good, both pitching staffs looked strong, and each team had its batting heroes. The Reds had an extra hero in the person of forty-year-old Jimmy Wilson, who deserted the coaching lines to replace injured Ernie Lombardi in the second game, then went on to hit .353 and take the only stolen base in the series.

The Tigers were managed this season by Del Baker, who had spent his entire active major league career (three years) catching for Detroit a quarter century before. He moved Hank Greenberg to the outfield and put on first base a big tough Indian named Rudy York. Between the two of them they made almost all the home runs in the league. (Actually they drove out seventy-four.)

Paul Derringer pitched the first game for the Reds, trying for his first World Series victory after three defeats. Paul had pitched strongly in his previous defeats. This time he pitched badly. Using the old-fashioned method of throwing his second-best pitch first, Paul was like barbecued meat to the Tigers, who all began to land on that first pitch and drive it for distance. In the second inning, Greenberg, leading off, drove a clean single to left. Rudy York hit the very next pitch for another single to center. Bruce Campbell, the Tigers' right fielder, bunted the third pitch of the inning for a sacrifice, and was safe at first when Werber threw wide. Pinky Higgins hit the fourth pitch of the inning cleanly into center field and two runs scored. Then Derringer walked a man, got one out on a force play at the plate, and faced Rowdy Dick Bartell, the shortstop. Dick hit a single on pitch number one, scoring two more, and Barney McCosky, the center fielder, singled on the next pitch, bringing in run number five. This also brought in Manager McKechnie from the Red bench and he brought Derringer out of the game.

Old Bobo Newsom had it soft from then on and the Tigers made it softer with two more runs on Campbell's homer in the fifth. But Bobo's father, who had watched the game, died that night from the excitement.

The next day, the Tigers were ready to give Bucky Walters some more of what they had fed Paul Derringer. But Bucky was not of a mind to have any. He started off a little wild, walking two men in the first inning and giving up a single to Gehringer that brought both men across the plate. But after that he could spare the Tigers only two more hits, a double by Greenberg and a single by Pinky Higgins. Greenberg's double drove in a run for the Tigers but by that time the Reds had scored five times and had sent Schoolboy Rowe back to the clubhouse. A home run by Jimmy Ripple scored two of the runs, while Billy Werber's double and singles by Eddie Joost and Billy Myers sent in the rest.

Game number three, the first in Detroit, started off as a pitchers' duel between Jim Turner and Tommy Bridges. At the end of six innings, each club had scored only once. Then the Detroit seventh inning opened in the good old-fashioned way, with every Tiger landing on the first pitch and some of them driving it out of sight. Greenberg started the inning with a stinging blow to center field for a single. Then Rudy York sent a line drive into the lower left-field stands for a home run. The Detroit fans had hardly recovered from their delirium when the next two batters repeated the performance. Bruce Campbell, the right fielder, singled to left, then Pinky Higgins, the third baseman, drove a ball higher and farther than York had, to add two more runs. The Reds scored an extra run in the eighth, but the Campbell-Higgins crew collected two more runs in their share of that inning, after a triple by Greenberg, and that put the game beyond the reach of the Reds.

Game number four was Paul Derringer's fifth try for a World Series victory. Before dropping game number one in this series he had lost two games in the 1931 World Series, when he pitched for the Cards against the Athletics, and he had lost the first game in the 1939 series. This time he finally got the American Leaguers down. He gave the Tigers just five hits, only two of them for extra bases, and never let them have the lead. The Reds took a head start off Dizzy Trout, who probably would not have pitched if the Tigers had not been so sure they could beat Derringer. Mike McCormick, Jimmy Ripple, and Ival Goodman did the heavy hitting for the Reds, while only Higgins and Greenberg seemed able to zero in on Paul Derringer.

The next game was to be Bobo Newsom's tribute to his father. Working harder than he ever had in his life, and demonstrating how completely invincible he might have been if he had always been willing to make this degree of effort, Newsom combed everything out of the Cincinnati batting order except three puny singles. His mates meanwhile belabored pitcher Gene Thompson for eight hits and seven runs in the first four innings. Most of the Reds got on the base for free as Thompson and Whitey Moore gave out free tickets to the baselines almost any time there was room. But a home run by Greenberg and a double by Dick Bartell kept the traffic moving.

Bucky Walters brought the Reds up even in the next game, by pitching almost as well as Newsom had. The Tigers tried Schoolboy Rowe again but he could not make an out except on a sacrifice bunt. The Reds, as if at batting practice, leaned into his medium pitches with appetite. Werber opened the game by bouncing a two-bagger off the fence. Mike McCormick sacrificed him to third and Goodman got a safe hit on a bouncer to the first baseman when Rowe forgot to cover first. Frank McCormick and Ripple hit safely then and Rowe hastened to the comfort of the showers. It made little difference then because the Tigers never scored at all. Walters, who hit a home run in his last time at bat, gave the Tigers only five hits.

The final game of the series was the one that Bobo should have won. Working after a single day off, Newsom was as grim and as skilled as ever. Although he would have ten more seasons in baseball, moving from one league to the other and back again, and pitching for all three clubs in New York, 1940 was his finest year and winning the World's Championship for the Tigers would have properly climaxed it. But Derringer had already tasted blood and he was a pushover no longer. He gave up only seven hits, the same number as Newsom, and he struck out only one, while Newsom fanned six. But what luck there was in the game landed in the lap of Derringer. The Tigers scored their only run on a scratch single in the infield, a sacrifice, and an error, in the third inning. In the seventh, Frank McCormick drove a ball to the left-field wall for a double. Jimmy

Ripple then lofted a ball that looked for a time as if it might be caught. McCormick waited on the baseline until the ball hit the top of the screen in right field. Then Frank took off for home. Dick Bartell hustled out on to the grass to make the relay from the outfield, but when the ball came to him he did not know what to do with it. While the screams of the wild Cincinnati crowd drowned out the frantic cries of his teammates, Dick, who had his back to the plate when he took the throw, just hung on to the ball while McCormick scored. And that run made the Reds the champions.

Leading hitters:

CINCINNATI REDS
Werber: .370

DETROIT TIGERS
Campbell: .360

Winning pitchers:

CINCINNATI REDS
Walters: won 2, lost 0
Derringer: won 2, lost 1

DETROIT TIGERS
Newsom: won 2, lost 1
Bridges: won 1, lost 0

1941

NEW YORK A.L. vs. BROOKLYN N.L.

WON BY NEW YORK, 4 GAMES TO 1

Game Scores:

New York 3	Brooklyn 2	October 1 at New York
New York 3	Brooklyn 2	October 1 at New York
Brooklyn 3	New York 2	October 2 at New York
New York 2	Brooklyn 1	October 4 at Brooklyn
New York 7	Brooklyn 4	October 5 at Brooklyn
New York 3	Brooklyn 1	October 6 at Brooklyn

The 1941 series was the last series that many young men would ever see and it was the final series for some ballplayers too. Yet there was no knell of doom nor voices prophesying war echoing over Yankee Stadium and Ebbets Field those days. The first peacetime draft had been in effect for over a year but already it was slacking off, and many of the recruits were about ready to come home. So all hearts in Brooklyn, or almost all, were centered on the doings of the Dodgers, who had got into the World Series for the first time in the lifetime of many fans. Yet about all the Dodgers could accomplish was to interrupt the Yankee series of World Series victories, which had reached ten before the Dodgers took game number two.

The Yankees had an upsetting habit of winning ball games in the other fellow's ball park, even getting the breaks there which should have gone to the home team. They won every game at Ebbets Field this year. Many Dodger fans like to recall this series as one the Dodgers almost won. But they really did not come close. They were soundly outhit and roundly outpitched, and they were badly outlucked in the fourth game, played at Ebbets Field. They had all but won this game, with a score of 4 to 3, and were ready to pack it in and go celebrate, when a wild bit of misfortune opened the gates to the Yankees, who poured through with more than enough runs to win. Had the Dodgers won that game, they would have held an edge, it is true. But what they would have used to hold off the Yankees for the rest of the series, who knows?

Leading the Dodgers this year was the ex-Yankee, ex-Gashouse Gangster, Leo Durocher, who wanted nothing more in the world right now than to beat the club that had scorned him and flung him out of the American League. Leo had two 22-game winners, Kirby Higbe and Whitlow Wyatt, to match a whole gallery of Yankee pitchers, only one of whom had won more than fourteen games. And they had a few sluggers of their own, or thought they had, in Pistol Pete Reiser (.343), Dolf Camilli (.285), Ducky Medwick (.318), and Dixie Walker (.311). But they had no one of even half the stature of Joe DiMaggio, who had hit safely in fifty-six consecutive games that year, with a season average of .357. Still, the Dodgers did seem to have the edge in pitching, and they had the scrappiest manager in the leagues.

In the first game, Brooklyn's third-best pitcher, Curt Davis, faced the Yankees' best, Red Ruffing. Brooklyn needed two other pitchers to get through the game, not because the Yanks hit Davis so hard, but because the Brooklyns could not get far enough ahead to be safe. The Yankees made only six hits off Davis and Hugh Casey, and none off Johnny Allen. The Dodgers made the same number off Ruffing. But the Yankees started things off with a home run in the second inning by Joe Gordon and the next time they had a man in scoring position (first base) they scored him on a two-bagger by Dickey. The Dodgers did not even get a hit until the fifth inning, when Pee Wee Reese made a single. Mickey Owen scored him from first base on a triple. The Yankees came back promptly with a run made out of a walk and two singles, to put them two runs ahead. An error, followed by two singles, gave the Dodgers one more run in the seventh but they made no more. Hugh Casey meanwhile was holding off the Yankees, but they still came in ahead.

In the second game, the Yankees used Spud Chandler, who had won ten whole games that year, while the Dodgers sent in Whitlow Wyatt, who had won more than twice as many. Chandler held the Dodgers to six hits while the Yankees made nine. But after Wyatt let the Yankees get two runs—one in the second and one in the third—he turned off the faucet completely. In the fifth, on a walk, a double, a walk, a forceout, and a single, the Dodgers tied the score. In the sixth, they got rid of Chandler when an error and a single put runners on first and third. Johnny Murphy hastened to the rescue. He struck out the mighty Pistol Pete Reiser, despite the throaty exhortations and constant bell-ringing of the Dodgers' famous fan, Hilda Chester. But then Dolf Camilli (who had been nominated for the Presidency on many welcoming placards when the Dodgers brought home the pennant) drove a safe hit to right field and scored the run that soon won the game.

So the clubs were tied when the Dodgers returned to Ebbets Field, away from the strange shadows and the unwelcome distances of the Stadium. And the Dodger players had a feeling that they now held the upper hand. They did indeed hold the upper hand too, until the fates moved in and nearly broke Fat Freddy Fitzsimmons' knee. Freddy had not contributed much to the Brooklyn pennant drive, but he had won six of the thirteen games he worked in and had lost only one. This day he was full of fight, guile, and determination. The crowd had expected to see Kirby Higbe do the pitching but they welcomed Freddy all the same. Freddy had worked in the World Series before. Pitching for the Giants against the Yankees in 1936, he had held the Yanks to four hits and still lost the game. Perhaps Durocher felt he just could not be that unlucky again. But he could be and he was. In the seventh inning, with Fitzsimmons having held the Yanks to four hits, and no runs, a line drive by the enemy pitcher, Marius Russo, struck Freddy on the knee. The ball popped high in the air and was caught by Reese for the third out. But it put Freddy out of action for the duration. Hugh Casey (14 and 11 for the season) warmed up during the Dodger seventh, then came in to hold the line. He did not have quite time enough, apparently, for the Yankee artillery nearly blew him from the mound. He got one man out. Then Rolfe, Henrich, DiMaggio, and Keller all hit singles and nothing could keep two of them from crossing the plate. Larry French came in then and finished up the inning with a double play. The Dodgers fought back but fought in vain. Dixie Walker, hitless up to this point, walloped a double. Reese singled, bringing Dixie home. But then Russo got everybody else out and the Dodger fans had one more near-miss to mourn about.

Their disappointment at this game, however, was as nothing compared to their dismay at game number four, which was already in the bag when they lost it. Hugh Casey was properly warmed up for this one but he did not get into it until the Yanks had disposed of Higbe and French. The Yanks had three runs, to none for the Dodgers, when the home half of the fourth began. Mickey Owen started the inning with a walk. Then Pete Coscarart, the substitute second baseman, who went hitless in the series, got a free ride too. With runners on first and second, Leo Durocher sent in a twenty-six-year-old ex-Washington Senator named Wasdell. Wasdell hit the right-field wall with a safe drive and brought two runs in for Brooklyn. In the next inning the Dodgers did away with Yankee starter Atley Donald altogether when Dixie Walker doubled and Pete Reiser hit a home run. This was the sort of stuff the Dodgers had won the pennant with and the fans just knew the tide had turned. Hugh Casey could surely hold things even for three innings. Hugh did too. He even struck out the third batter in the ninth inning, with the Dodgers still ahead, 4 to 3. But the third strike, breaking down and away in the best curve Casey had thrown all day, got away from catcher Mickey Owen and when Mickey turned to retrieve the ball he found himself hampered by the cops who had hustled up to guard the ballplayers now that the game was

167

"over." So Tommy Henrich, who had swung and missed, sprinted for first and made it safely. Casey then blew up. Too angry even to count the cost, he banged the ball in straight and hard and the Yankees banged it back straight and harder. DiMaggio singled, Keller doubled, Dickey walked, Gordon doubled, Rizzuto walked, and then Johnny Murphy, the pitcher, ended the inning again with a weak roller to short.

Everyone knew then that the Dodgers were done for, and the next day they were for fair. The Dodgers tried for this one, Wyatt called DiMaggio a dirty name and almost started a riot, Durocher fought with the umpires. But all was in vain. Ernie Bonham, who had hardly won any games at all in the season, gave up only four hits to six off Wyatt, and the Dodgers could score only once.

Leading hitters:

NEW YORK YANKEES
Gordon: .500

BROOKLYN DODGERS
Medwick: .235

Winning pitchers:

NEW YORK YANKEES
Ruffing: won 1, lost 0
Russo: won 1, lost 0
Murphy: won 1, lost 0
Bonham: won 1, lost 0

BROOKLYN DODGERS
Wyatt: won 1, lost 1

25. This call cost Cleveland and Bob Feller a World Series victory in 1948, according to Lou Boudreau, who is shown here looking expectantly at umpire Bill Stewart, after Lou has put the tag on Boston base runner Phil Masi. A carefully practiced pick-off play caught both Masi and the umpire unawares. Umpire Stewart was the only man in the park who thought Masi was safe. *Wide World Photos.*

26. Dam bursts in Brooklyn. The umpire has already signaled the third out in the ninth inning of the fourth World Series game in 1941. But the final strike has eluded Dodger catcher Mickey Owen and the ball lies yards away while Tommy Henrich is sprinting for first base. Henrich was safe. The Yankees tied the score and went on to win. *World Wide Photos.*

The Fifties

27. Oh joy! Oh rapture! The Yankee battery in the final World Series game against Milwaukee in 1958 hug each other after winning 6 to 2. Bob Turley came in to pitch runless relief. Catcher Elston Howard's single broke a 2–2 tie. *Wide World Photos.*

28. Caught fly becomes a home run in the 1957 World Series. A Milwaukee fan just about to make a neat bare-handed catch of a blow by Ed Mathews that won the fourth game for the Braves, 7 to 5. Right fielder Hank Bauer of the Yankees is already on his way to the showers. *Wide World Photos.*

29. Manager Leo Durocher of the New York Giants counts hairs remaining on his head after his club barely escaped from bases-loaded situation in eighth inning of opening game of 1954 World Series against Cleveland. *Wide World Photos.*

30. A sample of the grim effort that went into Carl Erskine's record-breaking fourteen World Series strikeouts. This is the eighth inning of the third game of the 1953 World Series against the Yankees. *Wide World Photos.*

31. Yogi Berra tenderly escorts Don Larsen through the crowd, after Don had completed the only perfect World Series game in history. A fan has already captured Don's cap. Fifth game, 1956 World Series. *Brown Brothers.*

32. Umpire boots one. Art Passarella called Johnny Sain out on this play in tenth inning of the fifth World Series game in 1952. *Wide World Photos.*

1942

ST. LOUIS N.L. vs. NEW YORK A.L.

WON BY ST. LOUIS, 4 GAMES TO 1

Game Scores:

New York 7	St. Louis 4	September 30 at St. Louis
St. Louis 4	New York 3	October 1 at St. Louis
St. Louis 2	New York 0	October 3 at New York
St. Louis 9	New York 6	October 4 at New York
St. Louis 4	New York 2	October 5 at New York

The first wartime World Series still found the major league clubs at nearly full strength. The draft had swept off many a rookie but it had not yet bitten deep into the roster of regulars. So the Yankees had no reason to believe that any National League club, even one that had won 106 games in the season, as the Cardinals had, would stand a chance against Yankee power and Yankee luck. But most of the power in this series was supplied by St. Louis. And Yankee luck was almost consistently bad.

It may very well have been that the Yankees had just found winning too easy and were no longer able to get "up" for the World Series. Certainly they seemed anything but the slick, alert, and opportunistic combine that had slaughtered the Dodgers the year before. Yet the only regular missing was Johnny Sturm, who had completed the only major league season he was destined to play. His replacement, Buddy Hassett, looked much better at the plate in the regular season, and the rest of the infield was, as usual, invincible. It was not until the second game of the series that they began to look vincible. Joe Gordon had an especially woeful series, with a batting average of .095.

The first game could have persuaded the Yankees that it was once more just a matter of showing up at the park, for the Yanks demolished Mort Cooper, the Cards' twenty-two-game winner. In the nearly eight innings that Mort stood up against the Yankees, they assaulted him with ten hits, and took advantage of four St. Louis errors. The Cards could do nothing with Red Ruffing until the last of the ninth, when they were already seven runs behind. Then Red suddenly weakened and the Cards came within three runs of tying it before Spud Chandler came in and got the last man out. That final attack was really a foretaste of things to come. The bases were full and the winning run was at bat when Chandler finally put out the fire. The Yankees had not seen such an uprising for a long time and they began to suspect that the natives had grown restless indeed. It was just as if they had lost the ball game, for they showed up next day nervous, irritable, still shaken by the near disaster.

Ordinarily they should have found the second game a breeze, for the Cards used a pitcher named Johnny Beazley, a twenty-three-year-old who had just completed his first full season in the majors. He had won twenty-one games. But he had never faced anything like the Yankees. The Yankees, however, did not frighten Johnny, who had not had time to study up on their reputations. He just mowed them down as if they were a bunch of National Leaguers and he did not give up a run until the eighth. By that time the Cards were leading 3 to 0. The Yankees, in Yankee fashion, got all their runs at once in the eighth inning, when Charlie Keller hit a home run, after DiMaggio had driven in a run with a single. But the Cards promptly scored another run, thanks to a three-bagger, which the Yanks insisted was foul, by a youngster named Whitey Kurowski, whom the Yanks had never heard of.

The games were even now, but sportswriters sprouted a hunch

that the Yankees had lost their edge. The next game, in New York, convinced them. A left-handed pitcher named Ernie White, who had won seven games for the Cards that season, pitched this one against Spud Chandler, who had won sixteen for the Yankees. White gave the Yanks six hits and no runs at all. It was the first time the Yanks had been shut out in a World Series game since 1926—when old Pop Haines of this same ball club had done it. White struck out six, walked none, and gave not a single extra-base blow to the Yankee strong men. In this contest, the St. Louis outfield, which contained a couple of kids named Musial and Slaughter, as well as a charging center fielder named Terry Moore, skipped, danced, spun, and flew about the Stadium outfield as if they had been brought up there. Among them they pulled in eight long fly balls. The Yanks talked themselves out of this game by protesting a sacrifice by Marty Marion. Marty hit again and beat out his next bunt. Then Chandler, who pitched near-perfect ball otherwise, gave up his only run. The Cards got another in the ninth but did not need it.

In the fourth game, the Cards belted rookie Hank Borowy from here to there. In the fourth inning he just could not get anyone out and Atley Donald had to hasten to his rescue after the first six men had got on base. They all scored, too, and put the Cards five runs ahead. The Yanks tied the score with a big inning of their own, but the Cards never let up. When Atley Donald was unable to get a man out in the seventh, Ernie Bonham came in and the Cards misused him too. The final score was 9 to 6.

Red Ruffing, who had set a new record in the first game by scoring his seventh World Series victory, was sent out after the victory that would keep the Yankees alive. In game number one he had come very close to throwing a no-hitter, giving up his first hit with two out in the eighth. In the final game he faced that annoying youngster Beazley. Having pitched hard in the first game, and having appeared twice as a pinch-hitter, Ruffing, at the age of thirty-eight, was just about tired out. Beazley, however, was straining at the halter. He gave up a home run to Phil Rizzuto, who seemed to be doing most of the Yankee slugging in this series, but this did not rock him. Ruffing, while his strength lasted, throttled the Cardinals as of old. But in the fourth Enos Slaughter evened the score with a home run and Red began to labor. The Yanks moved ahead immediately when Joe DiMaggio's single drove Red Rolfe home in the bottom of the fourth inning. Walker Cooper made it all square again in the sixth inning with a single that chased Terry Moore home. It stayed a tie game then until the top of the ninth with Big Red sweating, puffing, and aching his way through the Cardinal batting order. In the Cardinal ninth, Walker Cooper singled, Johnny Hopp pushed him up with a sacrifice, and then up came Whitey Kurowski, the "unknown" third baseman whose triple (and the Yanks *still* insisted it was foul) had sunk New York in the second game. This was Whitey's first full season in the majors and he had broken very few fences during the pennant race, when he sometimes played short, sometimes outfield, and sometimes third base. It was Red Ruffing's nineteenth season. Red was a strong right-handed pitcher and Whitey a mediocre right-handed batter. It should have been no contest. But Red made a pitch too good and Whitey belted it right in the guts. The ball streaked for the distant seats and into them. This time there was no question about its being fair. Two runs scored and put the Cards ahead to stay. Beazley finished off the Yankees in their final effort by forcing George Selkirk to bounce an easy chance to second baseman Jimmy Brown.

What may have griped the Yankees the most about this series was that they wound up with a statistical victory. On paper, they *were* the best-hitting club, and the best-fielding one too. They had knocked the best Cardinal pitcher out of the box twice. They had two high-average hitters—Phil Rizzuto and Red Rolfe —while the Cards had only Jimmy Brown, who hit a meager .300 against Rizzuto's .381 and Rolfe's .353. All they trailed in was the score and in that they were far behind. It was the greatest crash since the unbeatable Athletics went down without a single win before the Nobodies from Boston in 1914.

Leading hitters:

ST. LOUIS CARDINALS
Brown: .300

NEW YORK YANKEES
Rizzuto: .381

Winning pitchers:

ST. LOUIS CARDINALS
Beazley: won 2, lost 0
White: won 1, lost 0
Lanier: won 1, lost 0

NEW YORK YANKEES
Ruffing: won 1, lost 1

1943

NEW YORK A.L. vs. ST. LOUIS N.L.

WON BY NEW YORK, 4 GAMES TO 1

Game Scores:

New York 4	St. Louis 2	October 5 at New York
St. Louis 4	New York 3	October 6 at New York
New York 6	St. Louis 2	October 7 at New York
New York 2	St. Louis 1	October 10 at St. Louis
New York 2	St. Louis 0	October 11 at St. Louis

Joe McCarthy, Yankee Manager, must have prayed all season that the Cards would win the pennant in the National League. It was not so much that he minded the licking, for he had taken those before. He was irritated at the press reaction that spoke of the end of a dynasty and harped on the supposed errors McCarthy had made. Joe longed for a chance to show that the Yanks were not done for, that he was not outdated, and that the club that could win nine World Championships could win more.

Of course it was not really the same club, any more than it was the same world. Star after star had gone off to war, or into war service of some kind. Even the men safe from the draft felt impelled to get into war jobs where they could make some contribution to the country's struggle to survive. Red Ruffing was taken into the Army, creaking joints and all. George Selkirk and

174

Phil Rizzuto joined the Navy. Frank Crosetti, under suspension for losing his temper at an umpire in the previous World Series, did not report until late. Buddy Hassett held a Navy commission. Red Rolfe, tortured by digestive ailments, had quit baseball. Joe DiMaggio had enlisted in the Army.

The Cardinals were missing Jimmy Brown and Terry Moore and Johnny Beazley, who would come back from the war with most of his effectiveness missing. The Cards did have their other secret weapon, Whitey Kurowski, however. But Whitey got only one extra-base blow in the whole series. Then the Cooper brothers suffered a tragedy like Bobo Newsom's, when their father died on the morning of the second game. They worked that game for their father, with Mort pitching and Walker catching, and they won the game too, the only game the Cards could take.

Joe Gordon, playing his last few games before joining the Army, came back to life in this series. His home run in the opening game helped put that one in the refrigerator for the Yankees. Max Lanier pitched almost well enough to win this one for St. Louis but his own mistakes helped boot it away. He foozled a ball in the fourth inning that gave the Yanks the chance they needed to score a run. In the sixth inning, with Frank Crosetti on third base, Max let go a wild pitch that allowed Cro to scurry home with the run that broke the tie.

The second game was the Coopers' game. Ernie Bonham worked hard for it, giving six hits in eight innings and striking out nine. But the hits he gave to Cardinal shortstop Marty Marion and Ray Sanders, the first baseman, were home runs and they accounted for nearly enough runs to win. Mort Cooper gave only six hits to the Yankees, the big one being a triple by Charlie Keller.

The series seemed to crack in two in game number three, played in New York because wartime restrictions on travel would not permit more than one trip between cities. Hank Borowy pitched for the Yanks against an aging (twenty-nine years old) rookie from Oklahoma named Alpha Brazle. The left-hander had the edge on Borowy right up to the eighth inning, when

Johnny Lindell, the new Yankee center fielder (he had been a pitcher the previous year) opened up with a single which Harry Walker fumbled into a double. George Stirnweiss, the new second baseman, then hit for Borowy and tried to bunt Lindell on to third. Ray Sanders, the Card first baseman, gobbled the ball quickly and rifled it to Kurowski at third, beating Lindell by a boat-length. But John was not a man to surrender easily. He kept going full throttle straight into the waiting Kurowski, and sent third baseman bouncing one way and baseball bouncing the other. Stirnweiss and Lindell were both safe then. Tuck Stainback, another strange name on the Yankee roster, who had spent many years in the opposite league, then flied out, with Stirnweiss taking second after the catch, while the throw-in held Lindell fast. The Cards decided to put Frank Crosetti on the open base because Cro had been a real menace at the plate this series. The man they chose to work on was Bill Johnson, a flashy rookie brought up that year from the Newark farm. Bill, also called Bull, then hit the ball for three bases, bringing in everybody who was out there. After that the Cards seemed to deflate. Brazle was unable to get anyone else out and after right-handed Spud Krist had come in and given up still another hit, and Harry Brecheen had arrived to put the side out, the Yanks had made five runs. It was one more instance of the Yanks finding a chink in the enemy armor and blasting it into a double door.

Game number four was a private triumph for Marius Russo, who had put in a most unsuccessful season, with five wins and ten losses. But for errors by shortstop Crosetti and third baseman Johnson, Russo would not have allowed the Cards any runs at all. But in the seventh inning Ray Sanders got on base for free and then got a free ride home. Russo did not let this annoy him, however. He made two two-base hits on his own and scored one of the Yankee runs.

The final game was a Walter Johnson-style game—lots of hits and no runs for the enemy. Spud Chandler, who had won the opener, made this one seem easy. The Cards got ten hits and both their pinch-hitters came through for them. But they could not get anyone across the plate. Chandler struck out seven Cardinals, gave only two walks, and provided his infield plenty of pop-ups. Eleven St. Louisans died on the baselines, after only a distant view of home. The Yankee runs were accomplished in Yankee style, on a home run by Bill Dickey with Charlie Keller on base.

This series really marked the end of good baseball for the duration. In the coming months most of the major stars would change into uniforms of a different hue. Some would never come back to baseball. Some would return with their skills so diminished as to be unable to last a season. And the great Cardinals and Yankees of the past decade would have to sit back and let a new gang take over.

Leading hitters:

NEW YORK YANKEES
Johnson: .300

ST. LOUIS CARDINALS
Marion: .357

Winning pitchers:

NEW YORK YANKEES
Chandler: won 2, lost 0
Borowy: won 1, lost 0
Russo: won 1, lost 0

ST. LOUIS CARDINALS
M. Cooper: won 1, lost 1

1944

ST. LOUIS N.L. vs. ST. LOUIS A.L.

WON BY CARDINALS, 4 GAMES TO 2

Game Scores:

		All games at Sportsman's Park, St. Louis
Browns 2	Cardinals 1	October 4
Cardinals 3	Browns 2	October 5
(11 innings)		
Browns 6	Cardinals 2	October 6
Cardinals 5	Browns 1	October 7
Cardinals 2	Browns 0	October 8
Cardinals 3	Browns 1	October 9

The 1944 series was the first and only in history played between two St. Louis clubs. It was a hard-fought series too and well-attended, and it was marked by some magnificent pitching. It was also featured by some of the most outrageous fielding ever seen outside a high school ball field.

The caliber of the play all over the league was two notches above dismal, with four thousand major leaguers, active, veteran, and prospective, in the service and more going every month. There were average, and overweight ballplayers trying to act

178

like youngsters again, and there were youngsters trying to act grown-up. Cincinnati brought in pitcher Joe Nuxhall, age fifteen, the youngest man ever to make the majors. The Browns perhaps fared best of all the clubs in holding on to their regulars, possibly because they had gathered in a lot of draft-proof characters over the seasons. Hardly anyone was surprised therefore when they triumphed over the Yankees, who had men like Nick Etten, Art Metheny, and Tuck Stainback holding down the jobs once filled by Gehrig, DiMaggio, Henrich, and Keller.

The Cards too held on to their strength at least through the series. And they were able to exhibit some front-rank pitchers, who eventually proved too much for the Browns. Not that the Browns did not have good pitching themselves. The opening game, in which Mort Cooper faced Denny Galehouse, was a thriller. Cooper allowed the Browns but two hits, and walked three. But the two hits came one on top of the other in the fourth inning, a single by Gene Moore and a home run by First baseman George McQuinn, scoring two runs, all that the Browns needed. Denny Galehouse kept the Cards runless until the ninth, when a sacrifice fly by pinch-hitter Ken O'Dea brought in Marty Marion, who had doubled and moved up on an out. This may possibly have been Denny's finest hour, for his career did not list too many winning seasons and he played with second-division teams for a good part of his lifetime. His next clash with Mort Cooper was not quite so successful.

The second game saw more slick pitching and it also saw some very unslick fielding, as the Browns helped the Cardinals to their victory by committing four errors, all of which contributed in some measure to the scoring. Nelson Potter, the Browns' nineteen-game winner, allowed but four hits in the six innings he worked. But he also committed two errors in that stretch and let in two runs. The Browns tied the score in the seventh inning, when a double by thirty-nine-year-old catcher Ray Hayworth and a single by pinch-hitter Gus Mancuso (age thirty-eight) drove in a pair of runs. Max Lanier, the Cardinal starting pitcher, who allowed just five hits in seven innings, was lifted in the eighth when a two-bagger by Mike Kreevich looked as if it might turn into a run. Then right-handed Bob Muncrief, of the Browns, and rookie Blix Donnelly, also a right-hander, stood each other off for four innings. In the eleventh, Muncrief cracked when pinch-hitter Ken O'Dea showed up again and singled to drive in Ray Sanders with the winning run. Sanders, on base on a safe hit, had been sacrificed to second by Whitey Kurowski.

Game number three saw two more Brownie errors that helped the Cardinals. But the Browns were hitting in this game and had given the pitcher, Jack Kramer, plenty of margin, with a four-run burst in the third, featuring scoring singles by George McQuinn, Al Zarilla, rookie right fielder, and third baseman Mark Christman. McQuinn got three hits this day in three times at bat.

The next day, the Cards got the pitching, in the person of a quick left-hander named Harry Brecheen, who had found himself this season after two false starts. Harry got plenty of solid hitting behind him and by the third inning he had a four-run lead, thanks largely to a home run by Stan Musial. Thereafter he toyed with the Browns, striking out only four but forcing a number of high flies. His outfield made eight putouts. Harry's opponent in this game was Sig Jakucki, a wartime pitcher who dropped out of major league ball the following season.

Mort Cooper, in the fifth game, had a chance to square matters up with Denny Galehouse. Again they both pitched well enough to win, with Denny giving six hits while Cooper gave seven. But two of the hits off Galehouse were screaming home runs by Ray Sanders and Dan Litwhiler, for all the runs that were scored in the ball game. Between them Galehouse and Cooper struck out twenty-two men, ten for Denny and twelve for Mort. Denny walked just one man and Cooper walked two. While it was a heartbreaker for Galehouse, it was a fair and square defeat and it made up to Cooper for his two-hit loss in the opener.

The deciding game matched Potter and Lanier again but this time a hair-raising error by shortstop Vernon Stephens spoiled Potter's day. He held the Cardinals scoreless for the first three innings, but when the Cardinals began to hit him in the fourth Stephens, after fielding an easy ground ball, heaved it far into the outfield. The Cardinals made all their runs right there. Max Lanier let nobody cross the plate, except Chet Laabs, the Browns' left fielder, whom George McQuinn drove in in the second inning. But Max let go a wild pitch and began to look shaky in the sixth. Whereupon Ted Wilks, a sturdy rookie, came in and dazzled everyone in the park by pitching no-hit ball the rest of the way. The Browns sent four pinch-hitters up against him and he struck out all four, to wind up the series with a touch of style, worthy of the great St. Louis teams of other years.

Leading hitters:

ST. LOUIS CARDINALS
Verban: .412

ST. LOUIS BROWNS
McQuinn: .438

Winning pitchers:

ST. LOUIS CARDINALS
Donnelly: won 1, lost 0
Brecheen: won 1, lost 0
Cooper: won 1, lost 1
Lanier: won 1, lost 0

ST. LOUIS BROWNS
Galehouse: won 1, lost 1
Kramer: won 1, lost 0

1945

DETROIT A.L. vs. CHICAGO N.L.

WON BY DETROIT, 4 GAMES TO 3

Game Scores:

Chicago 9	Detroit 0	October 3 at Detroit
Detroit 4	Chicago 1	October 4 at Detroit
Chicago 3	Detroit 0	October 5 at Detroit
Detroit 4	Chicago 1	October 6 at Chicago
Detroit 8	Chicago 4	October 7 at Chicago
Chicago 8 (12 innings)	Detroit 7	October 8 at Chicago
Detroit 9	Chicago 3	October 10 at Chicago

Baseball, in the 1945 season, with the war still on, reached its depths, both as a spectacle and as a business. It offered, besides catchers with chest protectors built-in, spring-halt infielders, a pitcher with one leg, and an outfielder with one arm. But when the war came to a sudden close, many of the ball-playing veterans, through some miracle of military planning, achieved early discharges and managed to finish out the seasons with their clubs. As many of them had played baseball throughout the war, they returned lean, sharp, and ready to play.

Both the pennant winners in 1945 were lucky in the matter of getting their ballplayers back from the service. But perhaps the Detroit Tigers were the luckier, for what they got back was

Hank Greenberg, strong, sharp-eyed, and full of home runs. He promptly won the pennant for them on the final day of the season by hitting a home run with the bases loaded against the St. Louis Browns. Still, the Cubs had a bit of bonanza of their own in Hank Borowy, bought from the Yankees after he had won ten games for New York, waived out of the American League, it seemed, in the dark, and immediately able to win games for Chicago. He accounted for eleven altogether and without him there would have been no pennant for the Cubs.

Both these gentlemen starred in the series, which was of a piece with the rest of wartime baseball in that it exhibited inept and unthinking play in almost every game. But there was all-star pitching in this series too and some mighty slugging, much of it by Hank Greenberg.

The games were played under wartime travel restrictions, so the first three games took place in Detroit. Attendance was the greatest ever, as might have been expected in a country full of young men hungry to see good baseball, and well-heeled enough, thanks to service bonuses, to afford it.

The opening game was the worst disaster any team had suffered in a World Series opener. Hank Borowy, who could even have been a Tiger himself if Detroit had not waived on him, started off with a four-run cushion, created out of close decisions, misplays, and long hits. The first two batters to face Hal Newhouser, the twenty-five-game winner, beat out hits to the infield. One runner scored when catcher Paul Richards let a pitch get through him. Bill Nicholson's three-bagger scored two runs and a single brought in number four. In the third inning, Hal's troubles increased when Doc Cramer let a fly ball get away, giving Pep Johnson a double. Another double and single sent Hal back to the clubhouse and the Cubs ended the inning seven runs ahead. Borowy gave the Tigers six hits altogether but put five on base with walks and one more by hitting him. Yet nobody scored and Detroit left ten runners on base. Phil Cavarretta hit a homer in this game.

The second game featured Detroit's other famous returnee from the wars: Virgil Trucks, who had appeared in only one game that season (he was only a few days out of the Navy). Trucks was matched with Hank Wyse, a twenty-two-game winner who had not gone to war. The Cubs put Wyse a run ahead in the fourth when Doc Cramer again played a ball lazily, and the runner, Cavarretta, made two bases on what should have been a single. He came home on a hit by Nicholson. This made thirteen innings in a row that the Tigers had gone runless. And now they broke out all at once. With two out in their half of the fourth, Detroit got a man on when Skeeter Webb singled to left. Eddie Mayo, the second baseman, walked. Doc Cramer singled, scoring Webb. Then Hank Greenberg drove a ball into the bleachers, to make the score 4 to 1. After that Trucks allowed none of the Chicagos to get close to home.

The third game was one of the finest series games ever pitched—a one-hitter by Chicago's Claude Passeau, a thirty-four-year-old right-hander who was near the end of his career. Rain deprived the Tigers of batting practice and Passeau was not about to give them another chance. Rudy York made the only hit for Detroit, a single with two out in the second inning. Bob Swift, the catcher, reached first on a walk and got no farther. Nicholson, Hughes, and Passeau drove in all the Chicago runs.

Detroit's hero in the fourth game was Dizzy Trout, a big right-hander who won eighteen games in the regular season and had come up with a heavy cold when the series began. In Chicago, however, Dizzy was hot. He gave the Cubs only five hits, struck out six, and would not have allowed a run if Rudy York, in trying to nail a runner returning to third, had not fired the ball into the seats. The Tigers again got their runs all at once in a four-run fourth inning, featuring singles by Cramer, Greenberg, and Paul Richards.

The fifth game was supposed to be the one that decided the winner. The winner of the "rubber" game would have the edge and would be just one game from the Championship. So the Cubs sent Borowy back to make sure they took this one and the Tigers had to return with Newhouser, who had looked so hopeless the first time out. This turned out to be one of the worst-played games of the set, and if Borowy had been as sharp as before, the Cubs would have laughed their way to victory.

But Borowy had almost nothing. He did well until the third, when Skeeter Webb scored on a walk, a single, and a sacrifice. Borowy recovered that run next inning when he hit a double and scored on Stan Hack's single. In the sixth inning, however, Detroit, for the third time in the series, constructed a four-run inning. Cramer singled, and took an extra base when Andy Pafko fumbled the ball—the first of many misplays by both sides in this game. Greenberg doubled, scoring Cramer, and then Cullenbine and York both hit safely, sending Greenberg over the plate and Borowy back to the locker room. An intentional pass followed by an unintentional pass and then by a forceout scored two more runs. This was enough to win, but the Tigers scored three times more on two more doubles by Greenberg. Greenberg fell on his face on one of his dashes down the baseline and Mayo did the same. Cramer and Cullenbine let a fly ball drop between them and Mayo lost a pop fly in the sun, so the extra runs came in handy.

The Cubs did win the sixth game, to tie the series in one of the longest, sloppiest, and most heavily populated games in World Series history. It lasted twelve innings, with each side using nineteen players, with a total of nine pitchers. The winning run for Detroit, in the person of forty-year-old Charley Hostetler, who never played major league ball again, was on its way to the plate in the seventh when he took a headlong dive into the dirt and was tagged out. Then the game was won by the Cubs in the twelfth on a drive by Stan Hack that looked like a routine single. But it hit a bottle top, or a pebble, or a heel mark in the dirt in front of Greenberg and hopped crazily over his shoulder to score a run from first base. To make the whole silly business sillier still, the scorer gave Greenberg an error, then changed his mind four hours later. The Cubs had three errors of their own. Hank Borowy won this one by some sturdy relief pitching for the final four innings. Each club left twelve men on base. The game lasted three hours and twenty-eight minutes.

The series took one day off for the selling of more tickets and resumed with Hal Newhouser and Hank Borowy facing each other once more. This time Hank did not even have enough to get started on. Webb, Mayo, and Cramer, the first three batters in the game, all hit singles. Borowy then went back to the bench, and old Paul Derringer, veteran of so many World Series wars, came out to stem the tide. Derringer did better, but not well enough. Greenberg pushed the runners up with a sacrifice, Derringer put Cullenbine on the empty base, made Rudy York pop out, then walked Jim Outlaw to force in a run. Paul Richards, who had contributed to the hilarity of the first game by letting two pitches trickle past him, squared up all accounts by clearing the bases with a double. In the next inning Derringer set out to pass everyone in sight, after Cramer had singled. When he forced in Cramer by walking York, Derringer sat down and Hy Vandenberg took over. But Detroit was already six runs ahead and the cause was lost. The Cubs got three runs eventually but Newhouser then undertook to strike out anybody who came to the plate. And the Tigers added three more runs to make sure.

When everything was counted up after the series it turned out that Newhouser, in three appearances, had twenty-two strike-outs. And the Tigers had the biggest winners' share ever: $6443 each.

Leading hitters:

DETROIT TIGERS
Cramer: .379

CHICAGO CUBS
Cavarretta: .423

Winning pitchers:

DETROIT TIGERS
Trucks:	won 1,	lost 0
Trout:	won 1,	lost 1
Newhouser:	won 2,	lost 1

CHICAGO CUBS
Borowy:	won 2,	lost 2
Passeau:	won 1,	lost 0

1946

ST. LOUIS N.L. vs. BOSTON A.L.

WON BY ST. LOUIS, 4 GAMES TO 3

Game Scores:

Boston 3	St. Louis 2	October 6 at St. Louis
St. Louis 3	Boston 0	October 7 at St. Louis
Boston 4	St. Louis 0	October 9 at Boston
St. Louis 12	Boston 3	October 10 at Boston
Boston 6	St. Louis 3	October 11 at Boston
St. Louis 4	Boston 1	October 13 at St. Louis
St. Louis 4	Boston 3	October 15 at St. Louis

Only a veteran Red Sox fan could have understood what it meant to have Boston win a pennant after so many hungry years—and after so many millions spent and stars lured thither and managers shifted. On paper, the Red Sox had often been the best-looking club in the league. This season, with Ted Williams finally back from the war (no accelerated discharge for him) and hitting as hard as ever and with Dominic DiMaggio really looking, as the Boston song put it, "better than his brother Joe," the Red Sox finally did have the best-playing club too.

The St. Louis Cardinals had put together, out of back-from-service veterans and a few recruits, including a voluble twenty-year-old catcher named Garagiola, a fast, hard-driving, and well-knit club that clawed the pennant away from the Dodgers in the first play-off in major league history. The Cardinals won two straight from the Dodgers for the privilege of meeting the Red Sox.

Nearly everyone in the East favored Boston. For one thing, the Red Sox had never lost a World Series—although it was twenty-eight years since they had been in one. And Ted Williams was expected to rejoice in his first World Series by driving baseballs over the fence. Then the Cards had an untried manager, Eddie Dyer, a left-handed pitcher from twenty years before who had won hardly enough games to count. The Sox were managed by the great Joe Cronin, once the best shortstop in the league. But the Cardinals had a record of their own—they *always* won the World Series when it went the distance. They kept this record unbent.

In the first game, most of the Boston hitting was done by Dom DiMaggio and Pinky Higgins, while Ted Williams settled for a single that did not even help in the scoring. The only home run was made by Rudy York, heavyweight first baseman brought in from Detroit during the winter. (Higgins had been traded for during the season to join teammate York in providing the always desired "power at the corners.") Rudy hit an incredible home run on top of the left-field stand in to St. Louis to break up the ball game. So no one made much of the fact that lean Ted failed to rattle a fence-board. He had splashed National League pitching, including Rip Sewell's crazy eephus pitch, all over the fences in the All-Star game and it seemed a certainty that he would lead both clubs in batting.

In game number two, however, when some power from Williams would have saved the Red Sox, Ted was helpless against lean Harry Brecheen, now known as "the Cat." Ted did not excuse himself, but most people around the Red Sox realized that he had been injured in a foolish "all-star" series used by Manager Cronin to keep his club in shape while they waited for the National League play-offs to end. His elbow was actually still sore and he was unable to get his full power into his swing. But nobody else was getting distance out of Brecheen's pitches. The wiry left-hander allowed the Red Sox only four hits. An

188

error by Pinky Higgins on a sacrifice bunt in the fifth inning put two men on base who eventually scored. But these were extra. A run in the third, driven in by Brecheen himself, was all St. Louis really needed. Mickey Harris, the Red Sox left-hander, pitched nearly as well as Brecheen. But he found no runners on base for him to drive in.

The third game, played before a wildly rollicking crowd at Fenway Park, Boston, suddenly made all the smart bettors look good. The great Boo Ferriss, Boston's twenty-five-game winner, delivered a game nearly as good as Brecheen's, a six-hit shut-out with only a single base on balls. Rudy York won the game before the first inning was over, when, with two out and a runner on second, Manager Eddie Dyer decided to give Ted Williams a walk. Next at bat was Rudy, supposed to be less dangerous than Ted. He hung on to a count of three balls and two strikes. Then he settled the whole business by banging a line drive into the left-field screen for four bases. Rudy scored the extra run too, in the eighth inning. And Ted Williams amused himself and all the fans by taking advantage of the fantastic "Williams shift" with a bouncing bunt down the third-base line. Eddie Dyer had his third baseman playing on the wrong side of second base, with his shortstop slightly crowding second base too, so the only man who could field Ted's bunt was the Cardinal left-fielder.

The fourth game, however, left Boston fans aghast. Cronin had saved Tex Hughson for this one and Hughson, who had won twenty games in the season, was considered by many to be a better pitcher than Ferriss. But on this black day he could hardly have looked worse. The Cardinals waded into his pitches as if it were batting practice. The cannonading opened up in the second inning when Enos Slaughter hit a home run. After that it was indeed a slaughter. The Cards scored twice more in the second and three more times in the third. None of the pitchers Cronin scraped off the bench could hold the St. Louis hearties. Leading 8 to 3 going into the ninth, the Cardinals added four more runs just for fun, to sink the spirits of the Boston fans far out of reach. Every St. Louis player hit safely in this game.

Slaughter, Kurowski, and Garagiola got four hits each, while

Marion got three. Wally Moses of the Red Sox got four hits too and Bobby Doerr hit a home run, after which he had to quit because of a headache. A strange feature of this game was that three Cards hit two-baggers in a row and not one scored, as the Sox outfielders threw out two runners at the plate. But that was about the only part of the show the Boston fans could take any delight in.

Next day, however, the Red Sox once more pulled ahead in the series, when Joe Dobson, fourth-best of the strong Red Sox pitching staff, pitched a four-hitter, trimmed with eight strikeouts. The Cardinal pitcher, Howie Pollett, pitching with a pulled back muscle, gave up three singles in the first inning, one of them by Ted Williams, which gave Ted his only run batted in of the series. Harry Walker, with a single and a double, drove in all the runs for St. Louis.

The Red Sox took a plane to St. Louis to get an extra day of solid rest while the Cardinals came home on a sleeper. But it was the Cardinals who looked widest awake when play resumed. Harry Brecheen and Mickey Harris faced each other once more in the sixth game and once more Brecheen took over. He gave up seven hits and struck out six while Mickey Harris was bombed out by five hits in three innings. Lightning double plays and rifle throws from the outfield took Red Sox runs off base. Rudy York's triple in the seventh inning followed by Doerr's sacrifice fly gave the Sox their only run. Brecheen scored the first run for his own side when he ran home from third after a double by Schoendienst and a sacrifice by Terry Moore. Immediately thereafter, Musial, Kurowski, and Slaughter hit safely, and Harris was called home by his boss.

The final game, which the Sox were heavily favored to win, was talked about all winter, and part of the following year. It seemed to hinge on an accident to Dom DiMaggio, who came to bat in the eighth with his club two runs behind. Cronin had used two pinch-hitters in a row and both of them, Rip Russell and George Metkovich, had hit safely. Russell singled and Metkovich doubled, putting runners on second and third. But

Moses struck out and Johnny Pesky sent a short fly to Slaughter. At this point DiMaggio came up and cracked a double off the fence in right field, to tie the ball game. But Dom pulled a leg muscle as he turned first base and after reaching second he had to limp to the bench. As a result, Leon Culberson had to take Dom's place on the baselines and in the field. Apparently the only Cardinal who observed what this did to the Red Sox defense was Enos Slaughter, who soon got a chance to exhibit his knowledge. Enos opened up the home eighth with a single. Kurowski popped out while trying to advance Slaughter to second with a bunt, so Enos still stood on first base when Harry Walker came to bat. Harry drove a single into center, in front of the fielder. This was the sort of ball Dom DiMaggio loved to charge, and loved to rifle back to the diamond. But Culberson, "conceding" Enos third base, took the ball routinely. Johnny Pesky ran out on the grass to take the relay. Afterward it was said that Johnny held the ball too long. But a study of the film will show that Pesky spent most of his time waiting for the lazy throw to reach him. The mistake he made was common with major leaguers. He turned his back to the play and did not immediately pick up the runner. But he did let that ball fly home as soon as he had it. Slaughter, knowing that Culberson was no DiMaggio, had decided before he reached second base that he was going all the way home. Mike Gonzales, the third-base coach, who got some credit for "waving him home," merely waved him good-bye, for Enos was headed for home without regard for what the coach was doing. He beat the throw easily, in a showy slide. And that, it turned out, made the Cardinals Champions of the World.

Leading hitters:

ST. LOUIS CARDINALS
Walker: .412

BOSTON RED SOX
Doerr: .409

Winning pitchers:

ST. LOUIS CARDINALS
    Brecheen: won 3, lost 0
    Munger: won 1, lost 0

BOSTON RED SOX
    Johnson: won 1, lost 0
    Ferriss: won 1, lost 0
    Dobson: won 1, lost 0

1947

NEW YORK A.L. vs. BROOKLYN N.L.

WON BY NEW YORK, 4 GAMES TO 3

Game Scores:

New York 5	Brooklyn 3	September 30 at New York
New York 10	Brooklyn 3	October 1 at New York
Brooklyn 9	New York 8	October 2 at Brooklyn
Brooklyn 3	New York 2	October 3 at Brooklyn
New York 2	Brooklyn 1	October 4 at Brooklyn
Brooklyn 8	New York 6	October 5 at New York
New York 5	Brooklyn 2	October 6 at New York

The 1947 series was the first series to be televised, so naturally it brought the biggest take yet. It gave the eleventh World Championship to the Yankees, sent the Dodger fans once more into despair, and produced the nearest thing up to this point to a World Series no-hitter. The Dodgers were led into this series by soft-spoken Burt Shotton, a man almost the opposite of brash and brass-tongued Leo Durocher, who had been suspended for sitting down too close to a known gambler, or for something like that. The Yankee manager was Bucky Harris, former boy manager of Washington, a man beloved by the press, liked by most of his players, and barely tolerated by some of the Yankee brass, who thought him a "four-hour manager" who was too eager to get away from baseball in off hours.

But whatever Harris was, he was smart enough and determined enough to wrest the championship away from a scrappy, hungry, and talented gang from Brooklyn, who still ached over that game that got away when Henrich's third strike rolled past Mickey Owen away back before the war began.

Many of the same performers were back this year to try to drag the championship over to Brooklyn, where Hilda Chester and all her cohorts knew full well it had always belonged. And the Yankee roster too held several of the famous names who were there in 1941 to help do the poor Dodgers down. Tommy Henrich was here, and Joe DiMaggio, and Brooklyn's Hugh Casey and Pete Reiser. Pee Wee Reese was still at short for Brooklyn and Phil Rizzuto again played shortstop for the Yanks. Dixie Walker, the People's Choice, roamed the outfield as of old, and Cookie Lavagetto also made the scene, to the eventual dismay of the Yanks. But the man who drew most attention, many boos, and thunderous cheers, was the fellow who had replaced beloved Dolf Camilli at first base: Jackie Robinson, the first Negro to play in the big leagues and the first ever to reach the World Series.

There were heroes a-plenty in this series, and "unforgettable" plays of all sorts that have been long forgotten. But most famous of them all were a two-base hit by Lavagetto that turned Floyd Bevens' no-hitter into a defeat and a hair-raising, impossible catch by substitute outfielder, Albert Gionfriddo, who never played major league baseball again.

The series started off in a glorious manner for the New York contingent, giving immediate promise of turning into a rout of the Dodgers. Playing in the Stadium, where shadows, and distances, and cigarette smoke were all supposed to make enemy outfielders giddy in the head, the Yankees beat the Dodgers twice in a row and sent them reeling back over the bridge to snug Ebbets Field, apparently hopelessly out of it.

The first game saw the Yankee big-inning break Brooklyn hearts, as it had broken the hearts of so many other contenders. Ralph Branca, Brooklyn's ace, winner of twenty-one games that year, and a man who was only fifteen when the Dodgers last

194

played the Yanks, set down the first twelve Yankees to face him without allowing one to get on base. Then, in the fifth inning, it looked as though they might all get on base. The Yankees did not stop hitting Branca until they had made five runs and had sent him to the showers. The Yankees even had the gall to pinch-hit for their pitcher in that inning, sending up Bobby Brown, who walked with the bases loaded and forced in a run. Wallops by Lindell and Henrich drove in the rest. The final Brooklyn pitcher, who came in for the final two innings, with the Dodgers still two runs short, was Hugh Casey. Hugh gave only one hit but the Yankees by this time had relief pitcher Joe Page working and Joe, after allowing two runs, clamped down tight.

The second game was an even more cruel experience for the Dodgers. They had no real full-game pitchers on their staff and they had to piece out every game with an assortment of right- and left-handers. They began this one with Vic Lombardi, who had worked in thirty-six games that year and won twelve. Left-handed Lombardi was just what the Yankee sluggers had prayed for. They lit into him at once and before he was lifted in the fifth they had made nine hits and five runs, with Johnny Lindell, who hit a double and triple, doing most of the damage. Allie Reynolds, the Yankee Indian, lured east from Cleveland, meanwhile fed bad medicine to the Dodgers and coasted along on his growing lead. In the seventh inning, after piling up six runs along the way, including a home run by Tommy Henrich, the Yanks contributed their big inning—four runs—off relief pitcher Henry Behrman, who got only one man out. Stirnweiss wound up with three hits, including a run-scoring triple.

In Brooklyn, bloody, but still vengeful, the Dodgers turned on the Yankees at last. Their immediate victim was old Bobo Newsom, who had been a onetime teammate to almost everyone on the field. They gave old Bobo the big-inning treatment, with the lower end of the batting order teeing off to start a six-run inning. Bruce Edwards and Eddie Stanky helped drive Bobo to the showers and Carl Furillo, sent to bat in place of Pete Reiser, who had injured his ankle, drove in two runs with a double. This inning put the Dodgers ahead to stay, although they needed more runs to stay ahead. The Yankees kept getting two runs at a time off Joe Hatten and Ralph Branca. And when pinch-hitter Yogi Berra, the first pinch-hitter ever to do such a thing in the World Series, made a home run off Branca, Hugh Casey was sent in to blank the Yankees the rest of the way home.

The near no-hitter that Bevens pitched the next day did not exactly sparkle, for he gave ten walks and one of them turned into a run before anyone had made a hit, as Spider Jorgensen, after having walked, was pushed home by another walk, a sacrifice, and an infield out. The Yankees held a lead at that time, having scored a run on a bases-loaded walk and another on a triple by Bill Johnson and a double by Johnny Lindell, both off relief pitcher Hal Gregg. In the ninth inning Bevens kept his no-hitter alive when Bruce Edwards' long fly to right was tucked away by Tommy Henrich. Furillo got walk number nine, and Gionfriddo came in to run for him. Reiser, bad ankle and all, hit for Hugh Casey. Gionfriddo, after a stumbling start, stole second. Then Reiser was walked on purpose and Cookie Lavagetto came up to hit for Stanky. Bevens had no reason to be scared of Cookie, a .260 hitter who was finishing his final year in the majors. It might have been better if he had been a little scared, for after getting a strike on Cookie he threw the next ball high. Cookie hauled off and drove it right to the concrete wall, sending two pinch-runners home with runs enough to take the ball game.

The rejoicing in Brooklyn at seeing the series tied up died out quickly next day when Spec Shea finally threw the kind of game he was capable of. Shotton used eighteen players against him but Shea gave them only four hits to share. He struck out seven. Rex Barney, starting pitcher for Brooklyn, in less than five innings managed to give back nearly all the walks that Bevens had given away the day before. He walked nine batters. All the pinch-hitters worked well for Shotton in this game, except the one that counted most. Gionfriddo, batting for Hatten in the sixth, got a base on balls and scored a run. Arky Vaughan, batting for Behrman in the seventh, hit for two bases. Reiser, batting for Stanky in that inning, walked, or rather, limped to first. But Cookie Lavagetto, who batted for Casey in the ninth inning with the Dodgers only one run behind, struck out.

Game number six was the most hair-raising of all, the best attended, and the longest remembered. Over 74,000 people sat, stood, or draped themselves in the Stadium to see the Dodgers make the series even again. The pitching on both sides was uniformly haphazard. Allie Reynolds opened for the Yankees against left-handed Vic Lombardi but neither was able to complete the third inning. The Dodgers used three more pitchers and the Yanks another five. Altogether thirty-eight players got into the game, twenty-one of them for New York. Among the spare Yankees who took part was a rookie catcher, just finishing his first year in the majors, a twenty-eight-year-old service veteran named Ralph Houk. He hit a single when sent up to bat for Vic Raschi in the seventh inning, but his effort was in vain.

The Dodgers took the lead immediately with two runs in the first and another two in the third. The Yanks tied it then with a four-run inning. In the sixth, the score was 8 to 5 in favor of Brooklyn. Burt Shotton decided then to go on the defense and he placed deer-footed Al Gionfriddo in left field to replace slow-footed Gene Hermanski. It was his best move of the series. With two Yankee runners on base in the last of the sixth, Joe Di-Maggio, who had won the previous game with a home run, brought the tying run to the plate. And he quickly arranged to deliver it when he picked out one of Joe Hatten's best pitches and sent it whistling out toward the low bullpen fence in left field. It was obviously a home run. There was no one with a hope of reaching the ball. The Yankee contingent all rose up to roar their delight at seeing the score tied. But streaking from too far off, without a chance in the world of getting to the ball, came young Gionfriddo, obviously bent on breaking his neck against the wire fence. At the ultimate half-second, when the ball was the same as safely inside the barrier, and when Di-Maggio, running in that disdainful lope that men use when they know the ball is in the seats, was partway around the bases, Al leaped out, stretched his gloved hand a few inches farther than

197

it was humanly possible, and took the flying baseball in the very tips of the leather fingers. The screams that arose then, from Dodger and Yankee fans alike, could have stopped automobile engines on the parkway three miles off. It stopped all the runners on the base paths and they looked then at happy Al Gionfriddo, cavorting in with the baseball, and at each other in what was once described as wild surmise. Why hadn't they remembered the little badword Italian could run like a scared spider and wore his glove on his right hand?

But that unbelievable out, and the victory it insured, was all that Dodger fans could take home and snuggle up with. The next day the Yankees turned mean again, gave the Dodgers a head start, and then caught up with them and clubbed them about the head. All the same old pitchers showed up in this game, each contributing his tiny share to the accumulating disaster. Hal Gregg began and he lasted until the fourth, by which time he had given up three runs and put the Dodgers behind to stay. Pinch-hitting Bobby Brown's two-base hit, which drove in Johnson with the tying run, finished Gregg's day. Then Tommy Henrich, for the third time in the series, drove in the winning run. The Yanks added two more, but the victory was really insured by Joe Page, who came in to pitch the final five innings and did not give up a hit until the ninth, when Miksis singled and disappeared when Edwards hit into a double play. That won it for New York. And while the Dodgers trooped sadly home, the Yankee brass drove merrily downtown, took to fighting among themselves, and wound up with George Weiss being fired and rehired and Larry MacPhail first seizing control and then selling out. There was one black eye and many red faces after the evening had grown still.

Leading hitters:

NEW YORK YANKEES
Lindell: .500

BROOKLYN DODGERS
Furillo: .353

Winning pitchers:

NEW YORK YANKEES
Shea: won 2, lost 0
Reynolds: won 1, lost 0
Page: won 1, lost 1

BROOKLYN DODGERS
Casey: won 2, lost 0
Branca: won 1, lost 1

1948

CLEVELAND A.L. vs. BOSTON N.L.

WON BY CLEVELAND, 4 GAMES TO 2

Game Scores:

Boston 1	Cleveland 0	October 6 at Boston
Cleveland 4	Boston 1	October 7 at Boston
Cleveland 2	Boston 0	October 8 at Cleveland
Cleveland 2	Boston 1	October 9 at Cleveland
Boston 11	Cleveland 5	October 10 at Cleveland
Cleveland 4	Boston 3	October 11 at Boston

The 1948 World Series came close to becoming the only all-Boston series in history. The Red Sox ended the championship season in a tie with Cleveland and then engaged in the first play-off game the American League had ever known. Denny Galehouse, who had pitched for both Cleveland and Boston years before and had been a hero for the St. Louis Browns in 1944, tried to win it for the Red Sox. He was very near the end of his career and had been through the baseball wars. But the man who faced him, Gene Bearden, had been through the real wars and carried aluminum plates in leg and knee to remind him of it. He won the game for Cleveland, thanks to two home runs by Lou Boudreau, and put owner Bill Veeck into seventh heaven, and into the World Series.

It was a famous World Series in many ways. It was the climax

200

of a long and segregated career for valiant Satchel Paige, the Negro pitcher who had often been acknowledged the best pitcher alive—years before. He was now forty-two, but often accused of being sixty. He had been a winning pitcher for Cleveland and a mighty gate attraction. It was also the first series for the pitcher who was truly this era's best, strong Bob Feller, a Navy veteran and the strikeout king. It was the last World Series for the Boston Braves and their first in more than thirty years—since the "miracle" Braves of 1914. It was the first series in twenty-eight years for Cleveland, who had been "almost" winning for so long that Cleveland fans had developed a complex about it.

There were marvels in this series, as in all of them, but the one that caused most talk and stuck longest in memory was a call by an umpire, who declared a man safe who was so plainly out that even *he* was stunned by the call. It was the first instance in the World Series of the "count" play, used by pitcher and short-stop to pick off a runner on second. It worked perfectly too, and if they had remembered to tell the umpire about it, he'd have been ready for it and could have called it properly. Lou Boudreau, the shortstop manager, the man who dreamed up the Williams shift that had crimped Ted Williams' batting average for a time, cooked up this play and executed it. If the call had been correct, it might have won the game for Cleveland. It would at least have sent the game into extra innings. As it was, the Braves beat Feller in the first game, despite his having limited them to two hits.

The pick-off play came in the eighth inning. After catcher Bill Salkeld had drawn a walk, the second off Feller, Mike Mc-Cormick moved pinch-runner Phil Masi to second on a sacrifice and Eddie Stanky was passed on purpose. Then, with Masi tak-ing a wide lead off second, Boudreau signaled for the pick-off. Feller, watching the plate, counted to himself, then turned and threw blindly to the left of the base, knowing Boudreau would be there. Masi, half frozen with horror, dived back toward second and put his shoulder right into the glove that held the baseball, while his hand still groped vainly for the canvas bag. Umpire Stewart, caught completely out of position, could only

201

guess that the man had got back safely, as the runner does nine times out of ten. He signaled his decision and the Clevelanders, led by Boudreau, very nearly took leave of their senses. Feller, slightly shaken, went back to pitching, got the rival pitcher out, and then gave up a single to Tommy Holmes, which brought in Masi with the only run of the game.

The second game also got Masi into the ball game as a runner for Salkeld but this time Phil did Cleveland no damage. The Indians instead concentrated on mistreating Warren Spahn, who, according to some, represented half of the Boston pitching staff (Johnny Sain, who won the first game, being the other half). Spahn had actually had a somewhat off-year for him, with only fifteen victories, as against twenty-one the year before. Today Spahn lasted only until the fifth inning, while Bob Lemon went the distance for Cleveland. Joe Gordon, the old Yankee flash, played second base for Cleveland and drove in the first run off Spahn, tying the score in the fourth. Larry Doby then singled to send Gordon home and the Indians had the game won. They added runs in the fifth and ninth to make it certain.

In Cleveland, Gene Bearden, supported by the mighty Cleveland infield, suffocated the Braves on five hits in the third game. With Ken Keltner, Joe Gordon, and Lou Boudreau gobbling up ground balls behind him, Bearden soft-stuffed the Braves to death. He did not yield a walk, while the Indians got five from Vern Bickford in less than four innings, and used them to help manufacture their two runs.

Johnny Sain, who had squeezed out ahead of Bob Feller in the first game, just missed victory in the fourth game. He gave only five hits, while Steve Gromek gave the Braves seven. But Boudreau's blow in the first inning, which drove in Dale Mitchell, added to Larry Doby's third-inning home run, gave Cleveland the edge. A bases-empty home run by Marvin Rickert kept the Braves close. In this game, Masi was the catcher and Salkeld pinch-hit for him. He flied out in the ninth. As in the first game, there was another long argument between Lou Boudreau and Umpire Stewart, when Boudreau, trying to make a single into a double in the first inning, was called out at second base.

Bob Feller went after his long-sought World Series victory in game number five but this time he was no match for Warren Spahn. The Braves jumped on Feller at once for three runs, including a home run by Boston third baseman Bob Elliott. One of the runs came back promptly on Dale Mitchell's first-inning homer, but in the third inning Elliott hit another home run to hold on to the three-run lead. Cleveland in the fourth had a big inning that finished off starting pitcher Nelson Potter and brought in Spahn, who let them have only one hit the rest of the way. Jim Hegan drove in three of the four Cleveland runs with a home run. Right fielder Walt Judnich's single, scoring Joe Gordon, accounted for the other. The blow that finished Feller came in the Braves' seventh inning, after Bill Salkeld tied the score in the sixth with a home run. In the seventh, the top of the batting order let go on poor Bob. Two runs crossed the plate but the game did not seem lost, until Ed Klieman discovered he could not get anyone out. Two walks and a single sent three more runs across the plate. Then Russ Christopher tried it and he could not get a batter out either. Both the men he faced hit safely and the sixth run scored. Then Satchel Paige came in and got the last two men out. It was now 11 to 5 in favor of Boston, however, and that is how it ended.

The Braves, back in their own hunting grounds, went into the last game full of confidence and fight. Big Bill Voiselle, a thirteen-game winner, was their starting pitcher. But Warren Spahn, who had allowed only one hit the day before, while fanning seven, was in the bullpen ready to relieve if need be. Doubles by Dale Mitchell and Lou Boudreau put the Indians one run ahead in the third inning, but Boston caught up quickly in the fourth when Mike McCormick's single drove in a run. In the sixth a home run by Joe Gordon and an infield out by Jim Hegan added two runs to the Cleveland account and seemed to be almost enough to keep Bob Lemon safe, for Bob had kept the Braves' hits well apart. In the eighth inning, the Braves began to put hits together. They filled the bases with one out and Boudreau thought it was time Lemon sat down. Gene Bearden came back then to try to hang on. He faced a pinch-hitter, a part-time outfielder name Connie Conatser, who drove out a long fly, scoring Tommy Holmes. Phil Masi then hit for Salkeld, Phil being a right-handed batter, while Salkeld batted left. Masi doubled handsomely, bringing in a run from second base and the Braves needed only a run to tie. Mike McCormick, who had already driven in a run, came next to bat and he lashed fiercely at a pitch that rocketed straight back at the pitcher. Bearden, never flinching, grabbed the fiery ball and held it tight to end the Braves' bid for good—or until they should have moved to another city and wrapped Warren Spahn in a brand new ball club.

Leading hitters:

CLEVELAND INDIANS
Doby: .318

BOSTON BRAVES
Torgeson: .389

Winning pitchers:

CLEVELAND INDIANS
Lemon: won 2, lost 0
Bearden: won 1, lost 0
Gromek: won 1, lost 0

BOSTON BRAVES
Sain: won 1, lost 1
Spahn: won 1, lost 1

1949

NEW YORK A.L. vs. BROOKLYN N.L.

WON BY NEW YORK, 4 GAMES TO 1

Game Scores:

New York 1	Brooklyn 0	October 5 at New York
Brooklyn 1	New York 0	October 6 at New York
New York 4	Brooklyn 3	October 7 at Brooklyn
New York 6	Brooklyn 4	October 8 at Brooklyn
New York 10	Brooklyn 6	October 9 at Brooklyn

It seemed inevitable that if the Dodgers kept on meeting the Yankees in the World Series, they would eventually have to come out ahead. But this time they failed again, despite all sorts of favorable signs and portents. If anyone, for instance, had known that great pitching would decide the series and that the hitting would be feeble indeed, then the edge might have gone to the Dodgers, who had Newcombe and Roe and Branca. Who could have guessed that Tommy Byrne, one of the wildest pitchers ever to reach the majors, would pitch a fine game in the series, or that Don Newcombe, after pitching a five-hitter, would be clobbered cruelly on his next attempt? And who would have thought that, with no Yankee regular hitting close to .300 in the series, the Dodgers would not take them over? Well, nobody thought so but the Yankees. And they had two secret weapons in

Joe Page and Johnny Mize whom only they thoroughly knew the value of. And they also had Casey Stengel, who had been a Dodger manager himself once.

The first game, which must have marked the attainment of a life's ambition for big Don Newcombe of the Dodgers, nearly broke the big man's heart. Although his mates could get no more than two hits off Allie Reynolds, Don kept the Yankees far from the plate too, and struck out eleven of them, while giving not a single walk. Yet one stroke of the bat by strong-armed Tommy Henrich sent a ball into the friendly right-field seats and brought the game to a sudden and startling demise. Before the ball had got halfway to the stands Newcombe knew it was a home run. It was the last of the ninth, there had been no score, and nothing else was needed. Don just turned his back on the ball and trudged to the bench, so completely disconsolate that he was the very picture of the state of Brooklyn hearts and minds. Big glove hanging loose, head bent, mouth drawn down, he trudged glumly off, while Yankee throats screamed the cries of victory all around him.

The next day the game was turned right around. Preacher Roe, who eventually confessed to garnishing a pitch with saliva from time to time, in defiance of the rules, gave the Yankees only six hits and an inordinate number of pop flies. Vic Raschi, who gave only six hits in eight innings, and Joe Page, who gave only one, came just as close as Newcombe had. The one run they lost by came early in the game, when Jackie Robinson doubled and Gil Hodges singled in the second inning. Johnny Mize batted for Charley Silvera in the eighth inning and singled, but that was not enough to count, because the next pinch-hitter, Bobby Brown, batting for Raschi, struck out.

The Dodgers always felt they had the best chance in their home park but it had seldom turned out that way. It did not turn out that way this year either. Game number three was a tight one and it was not decided until the ninth inning. But when that moment came the Yanks had the bats and the pitching needed to get ahead of the Dodgers and keep them from catching up. Tommy Byrne, the wild man, was practically a master of control for the innings he worked. He walked only two and hit only one man with a pitch. And he hit a single in his only time at bat, to put the first run in scoring position. But after Pee Wee Reese hit a home run in the fourth (he was the man Byrne had hit with a pitch) Tommy was asked to sit down and Joe Page came in to pitch all the rest of the way. Ralph Branca, having given up that single run in the third inning, kept the Yankees well tamed until the ninth, allowing them only two hits. In the ninth he let them have two more hits, and they really hurt him. Yogi Berra started out with a walk. DiMaggio went out on a foul fly. Then Bobby Brown singled and Gene Woodling walked. This put three men on base, all there was room for. Johnny Mize then came up to pinch-hit again and this time, when he singled, it counted twice. Getting to first base left him nearly breathless, so rookie Hank Bauer ran for him. Burt Shotton decided that it was time for Branca to rest up too and he sent Jack Banta, a ten-game winner who had worked forty-eight games that season, to pitch in his stead. Jack threw a ball to Gerry Coleman which Gerry drilled into the outfield for a single and another run. Then Banta got the last man out.

In the Dodgers' ninth, the big guns wheeled up and let go. Luis Olmo, part-time outfielder from Puerto Rico and a .300 hitter, drove a home run into the seats. Roy Campanella, the Dodgers' prize catcher and probably the best in baseball at that time, came up after Snider made out and drove out another homer to bring victory closer still. Bruce Edwards was then sent up to bat for Banta. Bruce struck out and the Dodgers sank.

In the next game, the Dodgers had a big inning. But it came after the Yanks had had two medium-sized innings that put them six runs ahead, so the big inning did little to lift hearts in Flatbush. Newcombe, too eager to get back and show he could really do the job, started with only two days' rest and could not last through the fourth. He gave a base on balls and then delivered two-baggers to Brown, Mapes and, of all people, pitcher Eddie Lopat. That finished Newcombe and brought in Joe Hatten, who got out of that inning alive but then gave up a triple to Bobby Brown in the next inning. The bases were loaded at the time so this added three runs to the Yankee total and soon sent Hatten right back where he came from. The Dodger big inning came next, in the bottom of the sixth, and if it had not been for an annoying double play early in the proceedings, the Dodgers might still be hitting. Reese singled to open the inning, then Cox batted for Miksis and he singled too. But Duke Snider chose this moment to hit into a double play that left only one man on base. After that Robinson singled, and Hodges singled, and Olmo singled and Campanella singled and Hermanski singled. That accounted for four runs. Reynolds, replacing Eddie Lopat, struck out pinch-hitter Jorgensen and put a stop to Brooklyn hitting for the duration of the game. The Dodgers had counted on the fact that Reynolds, who had been ailing all season, would not be effective. They could not imagine what he'd have been like if he'd been well.

The last game was a typical Yankee barbecue, with extra-base hits scattered through the proceedings, lots of runs, and several crucial strikeouts. The Dodgers had another big inning too, but it came when they were eight runs down and it fell four runs short. The Yanks had made runs in the first, third, fourth, fifth, and sixth innings, on a couple of two-baggers by Gene Woodling, a double by Coleman, a triple by Bobby Brown, and a home run by Joe DiMaggio. It looked as if the Yankees might get a chance to prove that they could hit, as some said they could, in the middle of the night, for the game went on and on. And in the ninth inning, with the twilight deepening, the lights were turned on for the first time in a World Series game. The lights never went on in Brooklyn, however. In the seventh inning the Dodgers did finally get rid of Raschi, when Gil Hodges hit a home run with two on base and Jackie Robinson drove in another run with a long fly. But the Yankees merely sent in Joe Page, who always acted as if he did not want the Dodgers to get any hits at all. He let them have two hits to last them the last $2\frac{1}{3}$ innings, and then the Yankees were champions of the world once more. And Casey Stengel, once paid *not* to manage the Dodgers, had started on a long string of championships.

Leading hitters:

NEW YORK YANKEES
Brown: .500

BROOKLYN DODGERS
Reese: .316

Winning pitchers:

NEW YORK YANKEES
Reynolds: won 1, lost 0
Page: won 1, lost 0
Lopat: won 1, lost 0
Raschi: won 1, lost 1

BROOKLYN DODGERS
Roe: won 1, lost 0

1950

NEW YORK A.L. vs. PHILADELPHIA N.L.

WON BY NEW YORK, 4 GAMES TO 0

Game Scores:

New York 1	Philadelphia 0	October 4 at Philadelphia
New York 2	Philadelphia 1	October 5 at Philadelphia
(10 innings)		
New York 3	Philadelphia 2	October 6 at New York
New York 5	Philadelphia 2	October 7 at New York

Hardly any one outside of Philadelphia really believed the Phila-delphia Whiz Kids of 1950 would beat the Yankees in the World Series. But no one expected the series to be quite so dull and disastrous as it turned out to be. Despite the closeness of the scores, the Phillies never had a look-in. The Yankee sluggers actually went into a slump in the series, and still the Yankees won. The Phillies, who had to scramble for the flag right up to the final day, when they beat the Dodgers in ten innings, had no whiz left when they met the Yankees. Their top pitcher, Robin Roberts, was worn to the bone and could not open the series. In-stead, the best Phillie pitching effort was provided by Jim Konstanty, the four-eyed relief pitcher, who had set a new record by working in 74 games that season without starting one. He managed to finish a few, however, and got credit for sixteen

210

victories. Jim, in the first game, contrived to hold the Yankees to five hits. His mates, however, could collect only two small singles from Vic Raschi, and no runs at all. Indeed, all through the series they made only five runs, or 1.25 a game.

The Yankees had an easier time of it than the Phillies but they did not spread-eagle the field as of old. They were three games ahead of Detroit when the season closed.

The Yankees won the first game on a safe hit and a pair of outs. In the fourth inning, Bobby Brown doubled, went to third on a fly to the outfield by Hank Bauer, and scored on another fly by Gerry Coleman. The Phillie hitting was done by Willie Jones, sometimes called Puddin' Head, after a song that was popular then, and by catcher Andy Seminick, who had just posted the best batting average of his career (.288).

Robin Roberts felt rested enough to start the second game. He got a little more hitting behind him than Konstanty had, but still not enough to build more than a single run. That was one less than was needed. Allie Reynolds, still not supposed to be at the top of his form, worked for the Yankees and made it all look like a joke, even though he had to go ten innings before someone got around to winning the ball game for him. The Yanks scored in the second inning when Coleman's walk, Reynolds' single and Woodling's single made one run. In the fifth, Mike Goliat, the Phillie second baseman, now at the end of his only full season in the majors, singled, was pushed to third by Eddie Waitkus, and scored on a deep fly by Richie Ashburn, one of the two .300 hitters on the Phils (Del Ennis was the other). But in the tenth Joe DiMaggio brought it to a merciful end when he put one of Roberts' pitches out of the playing field.

In game number three, the Phillies took hold and outhit the Yankees, ten hits to seven, but they still could not come in ahead. This time they fumbled the ball game away in the final inning, after actually leading the Yankees for a while. Ken Heintzelman, a relief pitcher who had only three victories to his credit that year, pitched well for Philadelphia, giving only four hits in two outs more than seven innings. But one run scored on a walk and a stolen base by Rizzuto, an error, and Coleman's single.

211

Two more runs were scored on walks, fumbles, and poor infield play. In the eighth inning Heintzelman's skills suddenly disintegrated and he put three men on base on free passes after two were out. Eddie Sawyer, the Phillie manager, sent Jim Konstanty back to the mound then and Jim really did all a pitcher could do. He threw a good low pitch to Bobby Brown, which Bobby, who was hitting for Hank Bauer, bounced straight to the shortstop, Granny Hamner. But Granny had a sudden fit of nervousness, or something, and could not get his throwing hand around the ball. As a result, Gerry Coleman brought in the tying run.

In the ninth inning, Russ Meyer pitched for Philadelphia. Russ had lost more games than he had won that year and he was doomed to lose this one, although better support would have left him blameless. Gene Woodling, who had popped out when he batted for Eddie Lopat in the previous inning, drove a hard grounder into second-base territory. Jim Bloodworth, a veteran infielder who had played for five big league teams at four different positions, fought with the ball but could not make it behave. The next man up, Phil Rizzuto, also drove a ball hard at Bloodworth. Jim stopped this one in midair but could not hold it, and so two men were safe. Then Gerry Coleman, who choked his bat like a high school boy, slapped a nice clean single out on the left-field grass and the winning run raced home.

The final victory came easiest of all, although the Yanks had to struggle for it in the ninth inning. Whitey Ford, up from Kansas City that June, should have had a shutout, for he kept the hits scattered and could always make outs when there were runners on. The Yanks went into the lead at once with two runs in the first inning on hits by Woodling, Berra, and DiMaggio. This returned pitcher Bob Miller to the quiet of the dugout, where he probably gave thanks that he had not had to spend this season, his first full one in the majors, among the big boys in the American League. In the sixth inning the Yankees added three more runs off Jim Konstanty on a home run by Berra, a hit batsman (DiMaggio), a triple by Bobby Brown, and an out by Hank Bauer. This put Whitey Ford completely at ease and he should

212

have stayed that way. But in the ninth inning, Gene Woodling, usually as cool as Ford himself, dropped a long fly off the bat of Andy Seminick. Inasmuch as two men were already on base— Willie Jones had singled, and Del Ennis had been hit by a pitch —two runs quickly pattered across the plate. Mike Goliat then followed with a single and Casey Stengel decided his fair-haired rookie had had enough. He sent in the stolid Indian, Allie Reynolds, and Allie struck out pinch-hitter Stan Lopata.

That made it championship number two for Casey Stengel and the thirteenth for the Yankees. It was the sixth time they had scored a clean sweep in the World Series.

Leading hitters:

NEW YORK YANKEES
Woodling: .429

PHILADELPHIA PHILLIES
Hamner: .429

Winning pitchers:

NEW YORK YANKEES
Raschi: won 1, lost 0
Reynolds: won 1, lost 0
Ferrick: won 1, lost 0
Ford: won 1, lost 0

1951

NEW YORK A.L. vs. NEW YORK N.L.

WON BY YANKEES, 4 GAMES TO 2

Game Scores:

Giants 5	Yankees 1	October 4 at Yankee Stadium
Yankees 3	Giants 1	October 5 at Yankee Stadium
Giants 6	Yankees 2	October 6 at Polo Grounds
Yankees 6	Giants 2	October 8 at Polo Grounds
Yankees 13	Giants 1	October 9 at Polo Grounds
Yankees 4	Giants 3	October 10 at Yankee Stadium

Most of the excitement of this series took place before the series began, when the Giants, who should have been somewhere at the bottom of the league, roared up and stole the pennant from the confident Dodgers. It was really a greater miracle than that of the Braves in 1914, for the Giants were so dismally far down in midseason that their fans had already begun to wonder who would take over as manager next year. The manager of the moment was Leo Durocher, once the Giants' deadly enemy when he led the wild men from across the bridge, but now their own dandy leader, not beloved at all, but at least obeyed and believed in.

The Giants, before the season started, were supposed to be in contention. But they immediately dropped eleven games and

214

everyone gave up on them, except Durocher. In the middle of August, the Giants were 13½ games behind the Dodgers. (The Boston Braves in 1914 had been only 6½ games behind on August 10). Then a kid named Willie Mays, who had joined the club in May, began to develop confidence, to rob batters of base hits, to cut down runners from a furlong away, and to hit the ball steadily.

Of their final forty-four games, the Giants won thirty-seven, and climbed into a last-minute tie with the Dodgers. That was accomplishment enough for anyone. But the Giants went on and beat the Dodgers two out of three in a play-off, with the victory coming in the last eye-flutter, when Bobby Thomson, practically struck out, hit a just-too-good pitch by Ralph Branca out of the lot and brought in three runs, just enough to win.

Against the Yankees, however, the Giants found themselves thoroughly played out. Their top pitchers, Sal Maglie and Larry Jansen, who had won twenty-three games each during the season, were too tired to take the mound at the start. So Durocher sent in left-handed Dave Koslo to face tireless Allie Reynolds, who had appeared in forty-three games that season and had won seventeen of them, two of them no-hitters. Koslo, a ten-game winner, and seldom mentioned when people talked about pitching stars, did the Yankees up very nicely in the opener, with seven hits, and he never looked better than when he struck out two Yankee pinch-hitters in the eighth and ninth. The Giants took the lead immediately in this game, when Whitey Lockman's double scored Hank Thompson and sent Monte Irvin to third. Irvin then set everyone to screaming when he stole home to put the Giants two runs ahead. Irvin got four hits that day, including a three-bagger. The lone Yankee run came in the second inning when Mc-Dougald doubled and scored, on a hit and an error. In the sixth inning, with Westrum and Stanky on base, Al Dark drove a pitch into the seats. That practically ended Reynolds' labors and put the game out of the Yankees' reach. Not that they didn't try for it. They sent Bobby Brown up to bat for pitcher Bob Hogue in the eighth and Koslo struck him out. In the ninth, they used

Johnny Mize to bat for first baseman Joe Collins and Big John popped out. Then they put Woodling up in place of Tom Morgan, the plowboy pitcher, and Woodling struck out.

The second game would have belonged to the Giants too if they had had one more player named Irvin. Monte hit three singles in four times at bat. But all the rest of the Giants, among them, could manage only two hits off Steady Eddie Lopat, who was sometimes accused of warming up in a rocking chair. Larry Jansen, rested up now, gave the Yankees only four hits, but they bunched them a little better and scored in the first, second, and in the eighth inning against George Spencer. Joe Collins' home run in the second inning would have looked good the day before, when Johnny Mize hit for him. Ed Lopat needed no pinch-hitter. In the eighth, he singled to drive in pinch-runner Billy Martin with run number three.

The real feature of the second game, however, was not a play at all, but an outfield accident that put Mickey Mantle out of the series—his first. Mickey, running for a fly that DiMaggio caught, tripped and fell. When he hit the turf he lay absolutely motionless, and more than one spectator thought he might be dead. But he was actually paralyzed by pain and fear—pain from a badly twisted knee that was already damaged by disease, and fear that he might have brought his baseball career to an end. But he was sound and well when the next season began.

The Giants' pitcher for the third game was Jim Hearn, third-best on the staff but the only well-rested one now. Hearn worked just one out short of eight full innings and gave just four hits, not nearly what the Yanks needed even to stay in the game. The Giants in this game thoroughly outhit and outfoxed the enemy. When the game was still close, in the bottom of the fifth inning, the Giants having made the only run of the game when Bobby Thomson doubled in the second inning and Mays singled him home, Stanky introduced the Yankees to a scheme both devious and Dark. Dark, however, merely stood at the plate, committed to the hit and run, while slow-footed Stanky dug hard for second. Yogi had guessed the play and called for a pitchout. As a result

33. Al Smith, Chicago White Sox outfielder, obviously cannot believe his eyes when a Dodger fan in the fifth game of the 1959 World Series accidentally dumps a container of beer on Al's head. Fan was celebrating Charlie Neal's home run. *Wide World Photos.*

34. Miracle catch by Willie Mays close to bleacher wall in Polo Grounds robs Vic Wertz of Cleveland of a possible three-run homer in first game of 1954 World Series. *Wide World Photos.*

35. Two of the best at the top of their careers. Stengel and Durocher, enemy managers in the 1951 World Series, pose for traditional pre-Series picture. *Brown Brothers.*

36 and 37. Stride for stride: Whitey Ford in the opening game of the 1957 World Series pitched the Yankees to a 3 to 1 victory; Warren Spahn, greatest left-hander of all time, started the fourth game for the Milwaukee Braves but the pitch he is shown throwing here was belted for a home run by Elston Howard, tying the score. Still Braves won, 7 to 5. *Brown Brothers.*

38. Yogi Berra, out at first on a desperate play by Joe Black, who took throw from Jackie Robinson, makes an effort to influence the umpire. Opening game of 1952 World Series, Yankees vs. Brooklyn. *Wide World Photos.*

39. Wondering if his career is over, fallen hero Mickey Mantle is carried from the field after snapping his right knee on a drain pipe protruding from outfield grass in second game of 1951 World Series. This was Mickey's first World Series and he was just three weeks short of his twentieth birthday. *Wide World Photos.*

40. Celebrating Yankee winning of the World Championship in 1956 World Series, fans undertake to snatch the caps off the Yankee players. McDougald, in foreground, has already lost his. Behind him, also capless, are Johnny Kucks, winning pitcher, and Andy Carey, third baseman. Pitcher Tom Morgan, who did not do well in this series, engages in a fierce struggle to keep his cap. They cost about six dollars, new. *Brown Brothers.*

he was able to get his throw down to Rizzuto some three yards ahead of the runner. Rizzuto put his glove down and waited for Stanky to slide into a putout. But Stanky, while sliding, drew one foot back and kicked the ball clean out of Phil's glove into center field. Then he hopped to his feet and scuttled safely on to third base.

Dark then singled Stanky home and after Hank Thompson (the right fielder, not Bobby Thomson, the third baseman) had singled, and Irvin had brought Dark in with a ground ball that Bobby Brown misplayed, Whitey Lockman brought everybody else home with a home run, to make it 6 to 0, in favor of the Giants. In the eighth inning, Hearn, safe behind his fat lead, finally eased up a little. He hit Rizzuto with a pitch, then gave up a single to McDougald. He got rid of DiMaggio and Berra, but then walked the next two batters, forcing in a run. Available Jones came in then and got the side out. Woodling hit a home run in the ninth, but hardly anyone noticed.

The next day it rained, and for a long time afterward men insisted that it was the rain that saved the Yankees, or that cooled down the Giants. Whatever happened, the Giants never looked to be in the struggle again. Allie Reynolds needed that extra day off and on Monday he was the strongest man in the park. He allowed eight hits, but spread them out so that the Giants had one run in the first inning and one in the last. Al Dark doubled and Monte Irvin singled to make the first run. In the ninth inning, Bobby Thomson brought in the other Thompson with the other Giant run. In between times, the Yankees pecked away at Sal Maglie and Available Jones. The biggest hit was Joe DiMaggio's home run, which scored Yogi Berra ahead of him. Reynolds also drove in a run himself. Al Dark got three doubles in this game, and Willie Mays, who had made his first World Series hit in the previous game, got no hits at all, but hit into three double plays.

Game number five was one more of those Yankee sheep-killings, with everybody on the club except Eddie Lopat and Hank Bauer, who only got one at-bat, getting into the hitting or scoring. The Giants got the first run of the game, but after that they were out of it. When Gil McDougald, in the third inning, hit a home run with the bases full, the tone for the afternoon was set. Rizzuto got a home run too. Woodling got a triple. DiMaggio and Mize hit doubles. And the Giants, who had got their first run on an error by Woodling, kicked in with three errors to keep the score mounting. Eddie Lopat had the easiest time of his life, spreading his five hits thinner than boarding-house butter and walking only one man. The Giants used sixteen players, including five pitchers, with no pitcher lasting more than three innings.

In the deciding game, the Giants had their breath back and almost made a game out of it at the very end. Durocher put it up to Koslo this time but Dave, whose real first name was George, could not manage. In the sixth inning, Hank Bauer tripled with three runners on base and made the score 4 to 1. Vic Raschi had no trouble with the Giants until the fifth, when Stanky's fly brought Willie Mays home. In the seventh Vic let the first two batters get away from him and Casey sent in Johnny Sain, Boston's hero in 1948. Sain held everybody in line until the ninth. Opening that inning, Stanky singled. Al Dark bunted safely. Then Lockman put a short line drive into center to load up the bases. Stengel quickly sent Bob Kuzava in for Sain. Monte Irvin, making the first out, sent a long fly to Gene Woodling, on which Ed Stanky scored. Thomson's long fly also scored a run, and now the Giants were but one run behind. Sal Yvars, a part-time catcher who had seen very little work that season, came in to bat for Hank Thompson. Sal was a power hitter, right-handed too, and Kuzava was a lefty, so all the percentages were with Sal. He sized up his pitch and belted it with the fat part of the bat, hard, low, and long. Whitey Lockman headed for home. Bauer, in right field, was obviously too deep to catch a sinking drive like this. But he raced in toward it anyway, went to his knees and slid on the grass, and plucked that ball out of the air no more than six inches from the sod. It was the sort of desperation deed that Hank was noted for, and the sort of thing that the Yankees always came up with to break a fellow's heart. Thus ended successfully Casey Stengel's quest for his third world championship.

218

Leading hitters:

NEW YORK YANKEES
Brown: .357

NEW YORK GIANTS
Irvin: .458

Winning pitchers:

NEW YORK YANKEES
Lopat: won 2, lost 0
Reynolds: won 1, lost 1
Raschi: won 1, lost 1

NEW YORK GIANTS
Koslo: won 1, lost 1
Hearn: won 1, lost 0

1952

NEW YORK A.L. vs. BROOKLYN N.L.

WON BY NEW YORK, 4 GAMES TO 3

Game Scores:

Brooklyn 4	New York 2	October 1 at Brooklyn
New York 7	Brooklyn 1	October 2 at Brooklyn
Brooklyn 5	New York 3	October 3 at New York
New York 2	Brooklyn 0	October 4 at New York
Brooklyn 6	New York 5	October 5 at New York
(11 innings)		
New York 3	Brooklyn 2	October 6 at Brooklyn
New York 4	Brooklyn 2	October 7 at Brooklyn

After brooding a whole year over missing their chance to take revenge on the Yankees, the Dodgers came back to the World Series in 1952, convinced they had the moxie required to make hash of Stengel's minions. And the auspices seemed proper too, when the Dodgers, for the first time in their history, won the first game of a World Series. This, they told themselves, was perhaps the ingredient that had always heretofore been lacking. Drawing first blood had always been a Yankee privilege. But now . . .

The Dodgers had power in their lineup now and, as always, craft in their pitching. Duke Snider, Jackie Robinson, Gil Hodges, Roy Campanella, and Carl Furillo were all men who could break up a ball game on one swing. And there were few stronger pitchers than Joe Black and Clem Labine, or cleverer ones than Preacher Roe and Carl Erskine. And the Yankees seemed momentarily out of front-line heroes. There was no DiMaggio any more and while Mickey Mantle had been startling men and women everywhere with the power of his hits, he was still a freshman, and he had frequent lapses. Whitey Ford was in the Army and Ed Lopat had been laid up a good part of the season. The Yankees had just squeezed home ahead of Cleveland, and never seemed to use the same lineup twice. How could they hold off the Dodgers? No one knew how, but still they did.

The Dodgers put Joe Black, a freshman pitcher, on the mound in the first game, against the mighty Allie Reynolds, who had just completed the best season of his career. Joe was cool and strong and gave up only two extra-base hits—a triple to Woodling and a home run to McDougald. The Dodgers got three home runs. Robinson reached Reynolds for one in the second inning and Snider touched him for another in the sixth. Then when Rae Scarborough came in to relieve Allie, Pee Wee Reese hit a home run off *him*. Reese had been on base when Snider hit his, so this gave the Dodgers twice as many runs as the Yankees.

The Dodgers drew first blood in the next game too. But this time the Yankees came up with a brutal, big inning and reminded Brooklyn fans of other years. Carl Erskine started on the pitching mound for Brooklyn and lasted until the sixth inning when he filled the bases with no one out. Billy Loes then came in and Martin unloaded a home run on him and four runs scored before he could get more than one out. Billy Martin was something the Dodgers had not reckoned with. He was fairly new to the majors, and seemed merely a quarrelsome, .250-hitting second baseman who had just begun to play full time. The trouble was that he had a worrisome habit of hitting when it would hurt you most. And this he did to the Dodgers. Mantle made three hits in this game too and scored twice. The Dodgers could get only three hits off Vic Raschi.

But back in the Stadium next day, the Dodgers sent Preacher Roe out after the Yankees and he shot them with his little spitball, or something, and brought them home. Berra and Johnny Mize were the only men who could do anything with Preacher. Berra got a home run in the eighth inning and Mize got one in the ninth. But Berra gave his run back with another to spare when he let a pitch get through him in the ninth inning and two runs came rollicking home, just enough to win the game with. Jackie Robinson, Pee Wee Reese, and Andy Pafko had driven runs home earlier in the game to put the Dodgers ahead, and all Johnny Mize did was make it a little closer.

Joe Black was the choice to put the Dodgers two up on the Yankees. Joe was almost a match for Allie Reynolds this time. But Allie had too much help. First of all, Allie did what he had done so often before; struck out ten of the enemy and awarded them only four hits. Black gave only three hits in seven innings, but the first one he gave was a home run by Johnny Mize and that was enough to beat him. Mickey Mantle hit a triple to help with the other run. This was really one of the best games Joe Black ever pitched, in a career that did not have far to go. If only he had had Mize on his side!

Brooklyn really put up a scrap for the next game in which they outhit the Yankees 10 to 5. Erskine was all but beaten in the fifth inning when that insufferable Johnny Mize brought in three runs with his third home run of the series, and pinch-hitter Irv Noren and Gil McDougald brought in two more, to blast Brooklyn's four-run lead. But Erskine hung on and blew down the next nineteen batters who came his way, while his teammates undertook to rescue the ball game for him. Duke Snider, who had accounted for two runs with a homer in the fifth, brought in the tying run with a single in the seventh. And in the eleventh, with a run in scoring position, the Duke doubled and brought it home to put the Dodgers ahead in the series again.

Game number six was to be played back in Brooklyn and that, everyone conceded, gave Brooklyn the edge. Duke Snider was hitting them out into the streets again and Billy Loes, the third-best pitcher, was ready. Well, Snider did hit two out over his favorite fence and Billy Loes did his best, getting a hit and stealing a base. He gave up nine hits and for six innings kept the

222

Yankees away from the plate. In the seventh, he gave Berra a homer, gave Woodling a single, and then committed a balk and moved Woodling to second. Then Vic Raschi bounced a single off Billy's knee, to bring Woodling home, and Billy was lost. In the next inning Mantle drove a ball out of the park too. The Dodgers could not get that run back, so even though Preacher Roe got the last Yankee out with no harm done, the series was tied up.

Joe Black, the workhorse, came back to try for the deciding game but Mickey Mantle would not let him have it. The Dodgers stayed right even with the Yankees until the sixth, trading them blow for blow and run for run. Johnny Mize drove in the first Yankee run with a single in the fourth. The Dodgers, in their half of the inning, filled the bases on Lopat and Stengel took steady Eddie out. Allie Reynolds came back for still another stint and all the Dodgers could do with him was tie the score on Gil Hodges' long fly. Next inning Gene Woodling hit a home run and the Yanks were ahead again. In their half, the Dodgers made it 2-all when Billy Cox doubled and Pee Wee Reese drove him home. But in the sixth Mantle took over. His home run put the Yanks in front once more. Next time up he singled to bring in still another run. By this time, Reynolds had stepped out for a pinch-hitter and Vic Raschi had moved in. The Dodgers decided to wait this weary man out. Carl Furillo drew a walk. Rocky Nelson batted for Preacher Roe, who had taken over in the sixth inning, and all Rocky could do was pop up to the infield. Billy Cox made his second hit, a single. Pee Wee Reese waited and he too drew a walk. At this point Stengel removed Vic Raschi and sent in left-handed Bob Kuzava, to deal with left-handed-batting Duke Snider. Kuzava was the man who finished off the Giants in the deciding game of the previous World Series—but that had been in Yankee Stadium. In this park, Duke could drive a base-ball out of sight with his eyes closed. Perhaps that is just what he tried, for he flubbed a high pitch and popped it up in the air for the second out. Jackie Robinson came next. With a chance to put the Dodgers out in front, Jackie too may have been press-ing a little. Like Snider he took the count to three balls and two

223

strikes. The next pitch, a high one, looked good to him and he swung furiously. But he too popped it up. Only this time, no one seemed to want to catch it. First baseman Joe Collins looked up for it and could not find it. Pitcher Bob Kuzava, who was also within reach, stood still and stared in fascination. But second baseman Billy Martin, who would have been in on every play if he had his wish, refused to let it fall. Sprinting wildly in toward the plate with his gloved hand extended, he reached the ball just before it fell safely. And with that out he extinguished the final Dodger hope. Two potential runs had already come in by the time Martin rescued that ball and the third was well on its way. In the eighth and ninth Kuzava had no trouble with the Dodgers. He gave them no hits at all and struck out two.

This victory set more records for the Yankees: Four straight World Championships, to tie Joe McCarthy's record; fifteen Championships out of nineteen attempts; six championships in a row for the American League. And for Casey Stengel, number four.

Leading hitters:

NEW YORK YANKEES
Woodling: .348

BROOKLYN DODGERS
Reese and Snider: .345

Winning pitchers:

NEW YORK YANKEES
| Raschi: | won 2, lost 0 |
| Reynolds: | won 2, lost 1 |

BROOKLYN DODGERS
Black:	won 1, lost 2
Roe:	won 1, lost 0
Erskine:	won 1, lost 1

1953

NEW YORK A.L. vs. BROOKLYN N.L.

WON BY NEW YORK, 4 GAMES TO 2

Game Scores:

New York 9	Brooklyn 5	September 30 at New York
New York 4	Brooklyn 2	October 1 at New York
Brooklyn 3	New York 2	October 2 at Brooklyn
Brooklyn 7	New York 3	October 3 at Brooklyn
New York 11	Brooklyn 7	October 4 at Brooklyn
New York 4	Brooklyn 3	October 5 at New York

By 1953 it was getting tiresome: The Dodgers and the Yankees every fall and the Yankees always winning. But people still crowded in to see the games, even though the ticket prices all went up a dollar or two. This time at least there was something classic about the way the games worked out. The Yankees took the first two at the Stadium, then the Dodgers took the first two at their park. After that, the Yankees won them all.

This was the fiftieth anniversary of the opening of the annual World Series between the National and American Leagues. And it was the fiftieth series, there having been none played in 1904. It would have been fitting if it had been the best-played, but it was far from that. It did, however, provide one major thrill, with a new strikeout record by the Dodgers' Carl Erskine. The cast of characters was nearly the same as the year before, but, as so

225

often happens in the World Series, men who had been second-raters during the season became heroes in the six-game run for the roses. And heroes of the season floundered and flubbed their way through. Veterans found their youthful vigor again and relief pitchers outshone the starters. Billy Martin of the Yankees invoked memories of another Martin of some two decades earlier. Like the unquenchable Pepper, young Billy dominated the series at the plate, with twelve hits, a .500 batting average, twenty-three total bases, and eight runs driven in.

The Yankee pitcher for the first game was, naturally, Allie Reynolds. Allie had been a relief pitcher during the regular season, but it would not have been a Yankee World Series without Allie starting game number one. He had been doing it since 1949, missing only 1950, when he had taken game number two and won it. This time Allie was hardly his old self. Although he struck out six, he gave up seven hits, including three home runs, in less than six innings. Johnny Sain, who was thirty-six years old to Allie's thirty-eight, came in and got credit for the victory. The Dodgers had been bruising baseballs all season and they continued to do so. Their switch-hitting second baseman, a remarkably shrewd baseball man called Jim or Junior Gilliam, playing his first season in the majors, hit a home run in the fifth inning. Unhappily for the Dodgers, they had already spotted the Yankees four runs, in the opening inning, knocking Carl Erskine clean out of the box, so this run did not do much for them, especially as Yogi Berra got it right back with a home run in his half of the same inning. Erskine had wobbled almost at once. After getting McDougald out, he walked Collins and threw a three-base hit to Bauer. Then Erskine struck out Berra and immediately walked Mantle and Woodling, filling up all the empty bases. Billy Martin dutifully cleaned them all off with a three-base hit.

In the Dodger sixth, home runs by Hodges and by pinch-hitter George Shuba, who had Billy Cox on base ahead of him, added three runs to the haul and made it New York 5, Brooklyn 4. In the top of the seventh Brooklyn tied it up when Furillo drove in Campanella. The tie was broken right away by Joe Collins' homer, and in the eighth the Yanks poured in three more runs to make it certain, Johnny Sain himself supplying most of the power for these with a solid two-base hit with Martin and Rizzuto on base.

The second game was rather more of a dogfight. The Yanks took only a one-run start in this and Preacher Roe held them to five hits. But two of the hits were homers and they accounted for three runs. The Dodgers got two runs in the fourth when Cox hit a double with Hodges and Furillo on base and that was all the scoring Eddie Lopat allowed.

When they came to Brooklyn, the Dodgers sent Erskine back to work, for he had pitched only one inning two days before and had not really used up his strength. This game was the finest of his career, yet he barely pulled it out. In the eighth inning it was tied at 2 to 2, and Roy Campanella won it with a home run. Before that Jackie Robinson had kept the Dodgers even. Martin singled in the fifth for the Yankees, moved up a notch on Raschi's sacrifice, and scored on McDougald's single. But the Dodgers tied it up at once when Jackie Robinson doubled, took third on Raschi's balk, and scored when Billy Cox laid down a perfect squeeze bunt. This was the kind of baseball the Brooklyn fans doted on and the place nearly blew apart. Next inning, Jackie put his club ahead when he singled Snider home. Then Woodling drove in Bauer to tie it and Campanella saved the day. Meanwhile Erskine mowed down the Yankee sluggers, getting Joe Collins and Mantle four times each.

The following day the skies grew bright indeed over Flatbush as the Dodgers put the series into a tie. And they did it with their mighty bats, plus some good-enough pitching by Billy Loes and Clem Labine. This time it was the Dodgers who got the head start, with a three-run uprising in the bottom of the first inning, including a double by Gilliam, a single by Robinson, a walk to Campanella, and a double by Duke Snider that seemed to settle the issue then and there. But the Yankees stirred up trouble in the fifth inning when McDougald up and hit a home run after Billy Martin had tripled. But the Dodgers kept right on hammering at the baseball, as if they disliked having it in the park. Snider drove it clean out once, Gilliam got two more doubles, Snider got another, and Cox got one himself. In the ninth inning, however, a Yankee uprising began. Billy Loes put the first three batters on base, with two singles and a walk. Manager Dressen quickly sat him down and let Clem Labine take over. Clem struck out Rizzuto, got John Mize to pop up, and then threw one too good to Mickey Mantle, who pickled it to left field, where Don Thompson, in a defensive move, had taken over for Jackie Robinson. Whether Jackie could have fired the shot that Thompson did is uncertain. For Don, seeing Billy Martin scuttling for home from second base, fired the ball on a level line to Campanella and Campy had the ball waiting right there to lay on Martin's hide for the third out.

There was no more joy for the Dodgers after that. The fifth game was an act of brutality, with a five-run third inning by the Yankees putting Brooklyn out of business before they had had a good chance to size up the new pitcher, Hot Rod Jim McDonald, a nine-game winner for the Yankees and an affront to the Dodgers, who were used to the best. Johnny Podres filled the bases in the third inning while getting two men out. Russ Meyer came in to relieve him, pitched very carefully to Mickey Mantle, and Mantle very carefully hit the first pitch out of the park. It was no contest after that, although everybody seemed to be hitting home runs. Billy Cox and Jim Gilliam hit homers, and Campanella hit three singles. But this was all waste motion. Brooklyn's four-run eighth inning came when they were eight runs behind.

The final game really was a skin-tingler, chiefly because of Carl Furillo, who had come back out of a slump that year to lead the league in hitting. The Yankees took a three-run lead in the first two innings and Carl Erskine sat down in the fifth after giving up six hits. In the sixth inning Jackie Robinson doubled and then stole third while Whitey Ford was looking right at him and apparently not believing his eyes. Campanella brought Jackie home and the Dodgers were within reach. In the ninth inning, Allie Reynolds walked Duke Snider, and then Carl Furillo sent a twisting, stinging liner to his "opposite" field (right field) that just made it into the stands for a home run. The hysteria of the Brooklyn fans then was something to scare a tin monster. They

228

jumped up and down and beat each other's chests and shoulders and screamed all through Furillo's lazy circuit of the bases. Now the game was tied, but it was time to go out ahead, what with the Yankees having last bats. Billy Cox was up next and there were many at the park who felt sure Charlie Dressen would send in a pinch-hitter for Cox. But Billy had been having a good series, and was the best defensive third baseman. So Billy hit for himself and struck out. Then the relief pitcher, Clem Labine also struck out to end the inning and the Dodger fans muttered uneasily. Their forebodings were correct, for in the last inning, after Bauer had walked and Berra had lined out, Mantle scratched up a hit in the infield on his youthful speed. Now the Yankee desperado, tough Billy Martin, came up, ready to save another series. Sighting the pitch right down the bat, the way the coaches tell you to, Billy met one of Clem Labine's pitches squarely and drove it to the center-field grass for the game-winning single.

This of course set a new record for World Championships in a row and made Casey the most successful manager who had ever lived. But Charlie Dressen said: "If I'd had Don Newcombe, I'd have won this." Maybe he would have. Don had won twenty games in 1951 and now he was in the Army.

Leading hitters:

NEW YORK YANKEES
Martin: .500

BROOKLYN DODGERS
Hodges: .364

Winning pitchers:

NEW YORK YANKEES
Sain:	won 1, lost 0
Lopat:	won 1, lost 0
McDonald:	won 1, lost 0
Reynolds:	won 1, lost 0

BROOKLYN DODGERS
Erskine:	won 1, lost 0
Loes:	won 1, lost 0

1954

NEW YORK N.L. vs. CLEVELAND A.L.

WON BY NEW YORK, 4 GAMES TO 0

Game Scores:

New York 5 (10 innings)	Cleveland 2	September 29 at New York
New York 3	Cleveland 1	September 30 at New York
New York 6	Cleveland 2	October 1 at Cleveland
New York 7	Cleveland 4	October 2 at Cleveland

Probably the reason most people thought Cleveland was bound to win the 1954 series was that the American League had been winning the World Championship steadily for seven years. But even the most rabid Giant fans had not looked for a clean sweep, or expected that the Cleveland club would seem so completely outclassed in every game. The Polo Grounds and the spacious Cleveland park were jammed for every contest and the players involved saw the biggest payday any World Series participants had ever known: $11,150 to each winner and $6700 apiece to the losers. That was more than a year's salary to some of the members of the winning club.

The biggest thing in this series was Willie Mays, who had come back out of the Army stronger, faster, and more confident than ever. He had led the league in batting with a .345 average and had hit forty-one home runs. Willie indeed crushed the Cleveland hopes early in the series with a catch that can still hardly be believed even by men who saw it, a racing, reckless, straining, frantic gloving of a ball that would have been a long home run in any park in the world except the Polo Grounds, where the center-field fence was something just short of half a mile from home plate.

This desperation catch of a drive by Vic Wertz prevented a certain victory by Cleveland in the first game and actually threw the Cleveland club into such despair that they never stood a chance again. Until that catch the series had looked like a contest. After that it was a walkaway.

The first-game starting pitcher was Sal Maglie, the blue-jawed "barber" from Buffalo (who never shaved anyone except himself). Sal was not the top pitcher for the Giants that year. He had won only fourteen games to Antonelli's twenty-one. But he was Leo Durocher's idea of the right man to put a muffler on Cleveland's mighty right-hand batters—Bobby Avila and Al Rosen. Sal was murder on right-handers, whom he loved to brush back from the plate and then send fishing after his miraculous curve. But today he was not entirely flawless. In the first inning he brushed Al Smith a little too closely and put him on base. Then Bobby Avila singled and big bald Vic Wertz, the part-time first baseman, who batted left-handed and wore a leather guard over his instep to keep from mangling his own foot with foul tips—Vic hauled off on Sal's good pitch and smashed it almost as far as it would go, to make three bases and drive in two runs. Bob Lemon, Cleveland's twenty-three-game winner, was not giving a great deal away. But the Giants were able to pull up even in the third inning. Whitey Lockman and Al Dark hit singles, and Lockman scored as Dark was being forced at second by Don Mueller. Then Willie Mays walked and Hank Thompson brought Mueller in with a single. That is how the score remained, 2 to 2, until the eighth inning. Then, with two men on base, Vic Wertz found one of relief pitcher Don Liddle's pitches that suited him and he delivered his mightiest wallop. The ball went straight out over the diamond, high over everyone's head, headed for the wall, good for a sure 450 feet. Willie Mays, after one glance at its trajectory, turned his back on the ball and headed for the spot where he figured it would fall. He turned at the last second and saw it right at his shoulder. He stretched out his gloved hand, let the ball nestle there, then plucked it out with his bare hand, spun, and flung it fiercely back toward the diamond. As he did so he tumbled on the turf and lost his hat. But his confusion was nothing compared to the dismay of the runners who had started blithely home, ready to wait and shake Vic Wertz' hand as he came prancing over after them. They had to brake themselves, catch their balance, and scramble madly back to base lest they be doubled off. Leo Durocher had sent Liddle in to relieve Maglie on the theory that he could tie up these left-handers. But after this harrowing escape, he got Liddle right out of there.

The Indians, however, were done for. They never threatened again even though the game went ten innings. In the last of the tenth, Willie Mays walked and immediately stole second. Then Bob Lemon walked Hank Thompson on purpose. Dusty Rhodes, pinch-hitting for Monte Irvin, who had been unable to buy a hit all day, then popped a short fly into right field that just fell into the stands for one of those famous "Chinese" home runs for which the Polo Grounds was notorious. That added three runs and ended the game.

Durocher started his ace, Antonelli, in the second game and Antonelli had no trouble with the Indians. They made one run off him in the first inning when Al Smith hit the first pitch for a home run. But after that the Indians went hungry. Early Wynn, for the Indians, pitched a handsome game himself, allowing only four hits in seven innings. But in the fifth inning, he walked Willie Mays. Hank Thompson singled then and Dusty Rhodes, again substituting for Irvin, looped a soft liner into short center field for a single that brought Mays home and tied the score. Wynn struck out the next batter, and gave another walk, putting men on first and third. Antonelli grounded out, but Hank Thompson scored on the play. In the seventh inning, Dusty Rhodes got a good honest home run to make the game certain. This was a thoroughly frustrating game for the Indians, for they made eight hits and got six bases on balls. But every time they seemed to be getting somewhere Antonelli would strike a man out. He fanned nine altogether.

The third game was played in Cleveland, where there were no Chinese home runs. But the Indians were past help. The Giants had made six runs in this game before the Indians could score any. Ruben Gomez, a seventeen-game winner, did most of the pitching for the Giants with knuckle-baller Hoyt Wilhelm moving in in the eighth inning to hold the Indians hitless the rest of the way. Gomez gave up just four hits, one of them a home run by Vic Wertz in the seventh and another a double, that turned into a run, by pinch-hitter Bill Glynn in the eighth. The Giant runs came on two singles and an error in the first, Mays (who got three hits) driving in Lockman for the score. In the third inning another pinch-hit by Rhodes helped drive Cleveland pitcher Mike Garcia to the showers. With the bases full on singles by Dark and Mueller, a forceout by Mays and a walk to Thompson, Rhodes banged out a single to bring in two runs. Then second baseman Davey Williams put down a squeeze bunt and brought in a third run. The Giants scored runs they did not need in the fifth and sixth and they left nine men on base.

The final game also saw the Giants run off to a big lead before the Indians could score. Don Liddle started this game for New York and had a seven-run lead in the fifth inning. But then the Indians grew restive. Hank Majeski, pinch-hitting for relief pitcher Narleski in the fifth, hit a home run with two men on base. The Indians scored again in the seventh and Hoyt Wilhelm came in to pitch. The Indians got a hit off him and Durocher, thirsting to close the series now, sent Johnny Antonelli back. Antonelli gave no hits and walked only one, while he struck out three of the five men he faced. Monte Irvin came to life in this game after going hitless in the other three, and got two hits, a single and a double, and drove in two runs. Al Dark and Don Mueller made three singles each, while Wes Westrum brought in two runs with sacrifice flies. More than seventy-eight thousand people saw this final game. It was only the second time in history

233

that the National League had taken the series with four straight victories and no ties. The last time had been in 1914.

Leading hitters:

NEW YORK GIANTS
Dark: .412

CLEVELAND INDIANS
Wertz: .500

Winning pitchers:

NEW YORK GIANTS
Grissom: won 1, lost 0
Antonelli: won 1, lost 0
Gomez: won 1, lost 0
Liddle: won 1, lost 0

1955

BROOKLYN N.L. vs. NEW YORK A.L.

WON BY BROOKLYN, 4 GAMES TO 3

Game Scores:

New York 6	Brooklyn 5	September 28 at New York
New York 4	Brooklyn 2	September 29 at New York
Brooklyn 8	New York 3	September 30 at Brooklyn
Brooklyn 8	New York 5	October 1 at Brooklyn
Brooklyn 5	New York 3	October 2 at Brooklyn
New York 5	Brooklyn 1	October 3 at New York
Brooklyn 2	New York 0	October 4 at New York

It turned out at last that 1955 was the year so long awaited, when Brooklyn would win the Championship from the Yankees. And the Brooklyns won it the way a set of heroes should, coming from behind, winning everything in the home park, then carrying the fight to the enemy and beating him where he lives.

Too bad that all of the original Yankee-fighters could not have been in this crowd that finally brought the shield home, with the Yankee corpse laid out upon it. But all the dandy managers were gone. And many of the original darlings of Flatbush were off somewhere growing fat. The Duke was still here, and Pee Wee and Gil Hodges. Jackie Robinson was winding it up. Jim Gilliam was no junior any longer. Roy Campanella was at the height of a distinguished career. Carl Furillo still plodded the outfield, no faster than he had ever been, but just as strong. The new boys were Sandy Amoros in the outfield—and what a lucky day it was when they put him there!—and a scattering of brand-new pitchers. Carl Erskine, and Billy Loes, and John Podres and Clem Labine had been here before. But where were Hugh Casey and Freddy Fitzsimmons and Whitlow Wyatt and Preacher Roe? Perhaps not melted like the snows of yesteryear, but far off and nearly as forgotten.

The hero of this series was not Don Newcombe, as Charlie Dressen might have forecast. It was Johnny Podres, who had won only nine games that year, against Newcombe's twenty. Or it was Sandy Amoros, who was a weak-hitting outfielder. Or maybe it was Walter Alston, the soft-spoken countryman from Ohio, spending his second season as a big-league manager. He was the man who put the players where they were needed, and who kept his team's spirits high despite the quick losses in the first two games.

The near-hero of the series, the man who would have been a big name if the Yankees had won, was Joe Collins—another weak bat that became a power when the big money was at stake. He won the opener with two home runs. Don Newcombe was the victim of both home runs and the loser of the game. He was never given another chance in the World Series until 1956, when he was bombed out in two innings.

Whitey Ford won the first game, although he gave up runs enough to frighten his teammates. But Joe Collins' two home runs and one by rookie Elston Howard, made in his first World Series at-bat, made difference enough to bring Ford in ahead. In the second and third innings, the teams ran neck-and-neck—two runs for Brooklyn, then two for the Yankees; one run for Brooklyn, then another one for the Yanks. Furillo's home run following Zimmer's single started the Brooklyns off and the Yanks caught up on a home run by Howard with Collins on base. Collins' first home run just evened up for a home run by Duke Snider. The Yanks went ahead when Ford scored on Noren's out and Collins got all the extra runs in the sixth inning by knocking the ball into the seats while Berra was on base. The

236

Yanks needed both those runs. They even tried for another when Billy Martin, still imbued with the spirit of that earlier Martin who had run off with a World Series in the depression days, tried to steal home and missed. In the eighth inning, Jackie Robinson *did* steal home for Brooklyn, but Don Zimmer could produce only one more run and that was not quite enough.

Game number two was a triumph for Tommy Byrne, who had been fired off the Yanks four seasons earlier when Dan Topping got sick of seeing him walk so many men. Tommy now had good control, and he could hit. He gave Brooklyn five hits, only one for extra bases, while Tommy himself drove in two runs with a ringing one-base hit in the fourth, when the Yankees got all their runs. Except for that inning, when Berra, Collins, Howard, Martin, and Byrne all got on base, Brooklyn had good pitching from Billy Loes, rookies Fred Bessent and Karl Spooner, and veteran Clem Labine. Billy hit two batters, however, and was batted hard in the fourth inning. He struck out five while he was in there.

The third game found most of the Brooklyn fans glumly expecting the worst. Since 1921, no club had ever lost the first two games of a World Series and then won the series. And Johnny Podres had been wild all year. Besides, he threw a high fast ball such as the Yankee sluggers grew fat on. But in the series Johnny, in celebration of his twenty-third birthday, conquered all his faults. His change-of-pace, which he could throw into the strike zone again and again, had the Yankees overstriding and popping up. He struck out six and gave only two bases on balls. Mantle, playing with a bad leg, made a home run but the Yankees never drew close. Mantle's homer tied up the game at 2-all in the second inning but the Brooks kept getting runs two at a time. Campanella, who made more hits than anyone else, started the scoring with a home run into the left-center-field stands, with Reese on base. He drove in another run in the next inning. Furillo's double scored another while Gilliam, Reese, and Amoros drove in the rest. A triple by Andy Carey drove in the final run for the Yankees.

It seemed too good to be true, that the Dodgers should keep right on hitting in the fourth game, but they did. Indeed, they hit harder than ever, with every man in the lineup determined to drive the ball out of the park. The Yankees started off as if they meant to have the game to themselves, with a home run by McDougald, a run-scoring single by Phil Rizzuto, and a two-base blow by Martin, while the Dodgers were just able to get one across on Gilliam's double. But in the fourth inning, behind 3 to 1, the Dodgers started to fire the fieldpieces. Campanella, Hodges, and Snider all put perfectly good baseballs completely out of the field and they had made it 7 to 3 before the Yankees could find a pitcher who would make the Dodgers hold still. The Dodgers had started Erskine and he lasted until the fourth, when he was unable to get the side out. Bessent kept the Yanks from scoring any extra, and Clem Labine, although he gave up two runs, was able to coast in with a three-run lead.

The fifth game found the Yanks gritting their teeth. They *had* to take one of these games in Brooklyn, to hold to their battle plan. But the Dodgers had a long slim rookie named Roger Craig, who would one day grow famous with another New York team (then unthought of) because of the number of games he lost. Roger limited the Yanks to three hits until the seventh when pinch-hitter Bob Cerv hit a home run and Elston Howard walked. Then Labine had to rescue Roger. But the Dodgers by that time were well ahead, thanks to a home run by Sandy Amoros and two by Duke Snider plus a single by Jackie Robinson that scored one run. Yogi Berra's home run off Labine kept things interesting but did not save the Yankees, who went back to Yankee Stadium a game behind.

The sixth game was all over in the first inning. Karl Spooner, a mysterious young pitcher who had struck out fifteen batters his first time out but had never quite realized his potential, started for Brooklyn and lasted a very short time indeed. He got only one of the first six batters out and when he had two on base and two runs already in, young Bill Skowron (called Moose because he looked like Mussolini) hit a good pitch into the seats. That made five runs for New York and they needed no more. In the fourth inning, Furillo, who got one of the four hits Whitey

Ford gave away, drove Reese across the plate for the only Brooklyn score.

But then came the seventh game and for the first time in Flatbush memory, the wayward darlings of New York's most populous borough were named the Champions of the World. This was one of the closest and most thrilling games of all the Yankees and the Brooklyns ever played, and doubly thrilling to the long-frustrated Brooklyn fans because it all came out right. Johnny Podres pitched this game for Brooklyn against Tommy Byrne, the re-educated pitcher, Bob Grim, and hard-throwing Bob Turley, one of the smartest pitchers the Yankees ever owned. The three of them together could not match the craft and determination of John Podres, who again mixed his change-up with his whistling speed, to keep the Yanks off balance. He gave up eight hits, but always managed to put a Yankee down when there was a runner in scoring position. The Brooklyn fielders welcomed many an easy fly. The Dodgers collected only five hits altogether, one each for Gilliam, Reese, Campanella, Hodges, and Hoak. But with a walk, an error, and three sacrifices (one safe on the error), they managed to add these hits up to two runs. The first run came in honestly enough when Campanella hit a two-bagger in the fourth inning and promptly scored on a single by Hodges. The extra run came in the sixth, after a single by Reese and a sacrifice bunt by Snider, which Snider knocked out of Skowron's glove when Moose tried to put the tag on. Then Campanella sacrificed the runners to second and third, Furillo walked, and Hodges drove a fly deep enough to bring Reese home. In an effort to keep the inning alive, Alston sent George Shuba to bat for Don Zimmer. And even though George grounded out to end the inning, the strategy saved the ball game. For it led to the moving of Jim Gilliam from left field to second base to replace Zimmer, and the insertion of wing-footed Sandy Amoros in left field. Sandy became the game's hero on the first play he made. Martin walked to start the inning, then McDougald bunted for a base hit. With men on first and second, Yogi Berra came to bat. Amoros cheated toward center field with a left-handed batter up, but Yogi sliced a pitch that looped up

239

just inside the foul line. It was obvious to Martin and McDougald, and to coach Frank Crosetti, that the ball would drop safely, and both runners set out at top speed to get as far away from first base as they could. Both would surely score. But Amoros, after the manner of one Gionfriddo, set his eye on the ball and set his heart on having it. Moving like a hungry hound, he sped toward the foul line and reached there just in time to seize the ball before it hit the grass. As if that were not enough, he cocked his arm quickly and fired the ball to Reese, who wheeled and rifled it down to Hodges, who got his foot on first base to make McDougald out before the frantic runner could scramble back. That was as close as the Yankees ever came to turning the Brooklyn applecart upside down.

Leading hitters:

BROOKLYN DODGERS
Snider: .320

NEW YORK YANKEES
Bauer: .428

Winning pitchers:

BROOKLYN DODGERS
Podres: won 2, lost 0
Labine: won 1, lost 0
Craig: won 1, lost 0

NEW YORK YANKEES
Ford: won 2, lost 0
Byrne: won 1, lost 1

1956

NEW YORK A.L. vs. BROOKLYN N.L.

WON BY NEW YORK, 4 GAMES TO 3

Game Scores:

Brooklyn 6	New York 3	October 3 at Brooklyn
Brooklyn 13	New York 8	October 5 at Brooklyn
New York 5	Brooklyn 3	October 6 at New York
New York 6	Brooklyn 2	October 7 at New York
New York 2	Brooklyn 0	October 8 at New York
Brooklyn 1	New York 0	October 9 at Brooklyn
(10 innings)		
New York 9	Brooklyn 0	October 10 at Brooklyn

The mystery about this series to Brooklyn fans is how any game could be called "poifect" when the Dodgers lost it. For a truly poifect game now, you could go back to the seventh game in the previous World Series, the one Sandy Amoros rescued. But the record-keepers all insist that the game pitched by Don Larsen in Yankee Stadium on Monday, October 8 was a perfect one because no opposing batter reached first base. So even though the Dodgers blew this one—and the series too—it is still celebrated as the one and only World Series no-hitter, and the only World Series perfect game.

    You could ask a few prejudiced spectators who sat behind home plate in this game and they might grumble that on the last pitch of the game, the third strike to pinch-hitter Dale Mitchell, the pitcher received a generous assist from the umpire, who by this time was perhaps as eager as most of the spectators were to see the game end without a flaw. That last pitch *was* pretty high—say about opposite the batter's nose. But even Dale Mitchell did not growl about it more than briefly. It would have been a shame to ruin the effort on that last pitch. And anyway, a seasoned pro like Mitchell, with two strikes on him, should have known better than to trust the umpire.

The Dodgers started out in this series exactly as if they were not satisfied to have won a series the year before but wanted to go right on playing on a level with the Yankees. Who did they think they were? U.S. Steel?

They looked like the class of both leagues in the first two games, both of which they came from behind to win comfortably, responding each time to a Yankee assault by a vicious and overwhelming counterattack that took all the enemy's forward positions and held on to them. President Eisenhower himself came to see the opening game in Brooklyn, the first time that had happened, outside Washington, since the days of Franklin Roosevelt. The Dodgers simply could not lose with Ike looking on.

Sal Maglie, whom the Dodgers had hated to death for many seasons, worked for Brooklyn in this game and after a nervous start, settled down to shave the Yankees real close, and to send them fishing after his retread curve ball which, now that he was thirty-nine, really should have lost its snap. In the very first inning, Enos Slaughter, who was a year older than Maglie, belted out a single and was brought in on a home run by Mickey Mantle. But wiry Sal settled down then and struck out ten Yankees while his mates started collecting runs in every way imaginable. Whitey Ford, a left-hander, should have known what was going to happen to him. What *always* happened to left-handers in Ebbets Field? They got *rooned,* that's what. In the second inning, Jackie Robinson (who had once numbered Sal Maglie one of his most-hated opponents) hit a home run to

242

show Ford what was around the corner. Then, the next man up, Gil Hodges, singled and Furillo, the man after that, brought him in with the tying run, on a double. In the third inning, Reese singled and so did Duke Snider. Then another right-handed batter, Hodges, laid into the ball once more and this time hit it into the seats, to make it five runs for the Dodgers. The Yankees got a spare run in the fourth when Billy Martin hit a home run. But the Dodgers matched that quickly on a double by Campanella and a single by Sandy Amoros.

In game number two the Dodgers acted like the Yankees, and gave their iron-throated devotees one of the greatest thrills of their many seasons at Ebbets Field. The Yankees treated Don Newcombe most cruelly in this game. In the first inning, Joe Collins drove in a run with his only hit of the day. And in the second inning, while Don was laboring to get two men out, the Yankees landed on him for five runs, the first one sent home by pitcher Larsen's single and all the rest on a grand slam home run by Yogi Berra. That put the Dodgers six runs behind and apparently lost them the ball game. Ed Roebuck managed to get the side out in that inning but no one believed the Yanks were through scoring. As it happened, they were not. But what else they scored mattered little. For the Dodgers, in the home half of the inning, smote three Yankee pitchers—Don Larsen, Johnny Kucks, and Tommy Byrne—for six runs. The amazing part of all this was that Larsen had two men out when the ax fell. Indeed, he had three men out, but Joe Collins, usually errorless, bobbled a ground ball and that left the gate open, through which all those runs flowed. A sacrifice fly by Campanella, a walk by Gilliam, and a single by Reese, plus a home run by Snider, put the Brooklyn mob back even. Two doubles by Gil Hodges put them so far ahead it hardly mattered what the Yankees did. They used seven pitchers, for one thing, and they kept the game going for three hours and twenty-six minutes, the longest World Series game ever heard of.

The next day the Yankees took an hour and nine minutes less to take one from Brooklyn. Whitey Ford pitched this one for

243

the Yankees, while young Roger Craig tried to win for Brooklyn. Craig gave up seven hits while Ford gave eight, but one of those Craig surrendered was a home run by Enos Slaughter, with Bauer and Berra on base.

The fourth game left the Dodgers panting far behind. Tom Sturdivant permitted them only six hits among fourteen players. The Yanks got seven, but again they chose long ones. Mantle hit a home run in the sixth, and in the next inning, Hank Bauer hit his first World Series home run. The pitcher who threw the ball that Bauer turned into a homer was a great big twenty-year-old right-hander from California, just up from Montreal that year to win five and lose five for Brooklyn. His name was Don Drysdale. He pitched two innings, gave up two hits, and was charged with two runs. But Erskine had already lost the game.

The fifth game was the one they called perfect. Like all no-hitters, this was short of action, but before it was very old, the fans had forgotten that this big Larsen fellow, who pitched without any windup, just as if he had men on base all the time, was the very one who gave up four runs in less than two innings in the second game. This day he let only one man get as many as three balls. He struck out seven and had only two close calls. In the second inning, while Brooklyn fans awaited the explosion, Jackie Robinson drove a shrieking liner at Andy Carey, who just managed to throw up his glove and hit the ball. It bounced high, but had lost its fire and Gil McDougald, alertly backing up the play, snatched up the ball and gunned it to first base to beat Robbie by the length of his shoe. In the fifth inning, Gil Hodges hit a ball a long way and Mickey Mantle had to sprint and reach for it backhanded. But it stuck in his glove. Sandy Amoros then hit a long long foul that was about a foot out of fair territory. After that no one really tagged the ball at all and Larsen seemed to grow stronger and stronger while just about everyone began to cheer his every out.

Brooklyn had a long way to come but they kept on coming. Back in Ebbets Field they may have thought for a moment that they were up against the same impossible pitcher they had just

244

got away from, for Bob Turley, a strong man who could make a baseball hum, and who also pitched without a windup, began to treat them just as meanly as Larsen had. He struck out eleven Dodgers and would not let anybody get across the plate. Meanwhile Clem Labine was pitching his heart out to stay even. At the end of nine innings, Brooklyn had made three hits while the Yankees had made four. The wire finally snapped in the tenth, when Bob Turley's luck gave out. He had walked seven men but had never been in real danger until now. This time he walked Jim Gilliam and saw him move to second on a sacrifice. Then he walked Duke Snider to get a chance at a right-handed batter. That happened to be Jackie Robinson and Jackie had done very poorly so far. This time he caught an inside pitch on the nose and drove it about clothesline high into the outfield. Enos Slaughter moved in to tuck it away and then suddenly realized it was hit too hard to sink. He leaped for it but could not reach it and it rattled off the wall to bring the winning run in.

There were no more such thrills for the Brooklyns. In the last game, the Yanks turned in a laugher. They scored immediately when Yogi Berra slammed out a home run with a runner ahead of him. Then Yogi came up in the third inning with a runner on and he did the same thing. This put the Yankees much farther ahead than they needed to be, because Johnny Kucks was giving the Dodgers only three hits that day. But Elston Howard decided he needed a home run too, and he drove Don Newcombe out of the box with a four-bagger in the fourth inning. Bill Skowron topped them all with a grand-slam homer in the seventh, to give him something extra to celebrate, besides winning another World Championship, Casey Stengel's sixth.

Leading hitters:

NEW YORK YANKEES
Berra: .360

BROOKLYN DODGERS
Snider and Hodges: .304

Winning pitchers:

NEW YORK YANKEES

Ford:	won 1, lost 1
Sturdivant:	won 1, lost 0
Larsen:	won 1, lost 0
Kucks:	won 1, lost 0

BROOKLYN DODGERS

Maglie:	won 1, lost 1
Bessent:	won 1, lost 0
Labine:	won 1, lost 0

1957

MILWAUKEE N.L. vs. NEW YORK A.L.

WON BY MILWAUKEE, 4 GAMES TO 3

Game Scores:

New York 3	Milwaukee 1	October 2 at New York
Milwaukee 4	New York 2	October 3 at New York
New York 12	Milwaukee 3	October 5 at Milwaukee
Milwaukee 7	New York 5	October 6 at Milwaukee
(10 innings)		
Milwaukee 1	New York 0	October 7 at Milwaukee
New York 3	Milwaukee 2	October 9 at New York
Milwaukee 5	New York 0	October 10 at New York

Having a baseball club in Milwaukee was one thing. But having it win a World Championship, well that was getting a little ridiculous. These after all were just the Braves, transferred from Boston, and everybody knew that the Braves were the last stop on the downhill slide after you could not make it any longer with the Yankees.

These Braves, however, looked less like the tired old Boston club than anyone could imagine. Of the pennant winners of 1948, only Warren Spahn remained. The other hero of that season, Johnny Sain, had been swapped off to the Yankees for $50,-000 cash and a rookie pitcher named Lew Burdette, who had pitched in two games for the Yankees and allowed one run in

1950. No one expected *him* to amount to much. But here it was seven years later and Lew had already been top pitcher in the league one year (1956) with an earned-run average of 2.71. In this series he was the unrivaled hero, outpitching even his ageless teammate Warren Spahn. For Lew won three of the seven games played and worked twenty-four innings in which no runs were made. The other Milwaukee victory was won, naturally, by Spahn. Before Lew Burdette nobody had won this many ball games in a series since 1920, when Stan Coveleski of Cleveland did it.

Spahn pitched the first game against Whitey Ford and lost it by giving up seven hits in less than six innings. Coleman's single and Bauer's double put the Yankees ahead in the fifth inning. In the sixth inning a solid hit by Andy Carey scored Elston Howard, and Coleman brought in another run to make it 3 to 0, Yankees. The Braves scored in the seventh on a double by Wes Covington and a single by Red Schoendienst.

But the next game was Lew Burdette's and he was bound not to let anyone get it away from him. Bobby Shantz tried it but Bobby had been too often to the well this season and he did not have quite the strength that was needed. In the second inning, the Braves jumped ahead on a triple by Hank Aaron and a single by Joe Adcock. The Yankees took that right back when Slaughter walked, Kubek singled, and Coleman drove Slaughter home. Next inning Johnny Logan hit a home run to put Milwaukee in front; then Hank Bauer homered to make it even once more. After that Lew Burdette clamped down tight. His side got ahead in the fourth inning when Wes Covington, a man to whom bunting did not come naturally, failed to lay down a sacrifice with Adcock on second and Andy Pafko on first. So Wes hit a single to left-center instead, bringing Adcock home. And when Tony Kubek missed Enos Slaughter's throw at third, Pafko kept on coming with the fourth run. Two pinch-hitters singled off Burdette in the seventh and the ninth but no one else could do anything.

The Yankees always have to have one big game, one laugher where everybody gets a base hit, and they had it this time in the third game, the first at Milwaukee, when Bob Buhl tried to beat them and could not last an inning. They then roundly clubbed pitchers Pizarro and Conley, eased up on Ernie Johnson, and really assassinated a youngster named Trowbridge, who was charged with five runs in one inning, for an earned-run average of 45.00. The man who enjoyed himself most in this game was young Tony Kubek, playing his first year in the big leagues. Tony lit the first bomb by hitting a home run his first time up, batting second in the first inning. He hit another in the seventh inning, with a single in between, to account for four runs. Mickey Mantle also hit a home run and so did Hank Aaron, but his hardly made a dent. By that time the Yankees were six runs ahead and after Hank closed the gap by two runs, the Yankees added five more. Bob Turley and Don Larsen, the no-windup boys, both worked in this one, and they allowed eight hits and eight walks between them.

The Braves came back in the next game, regardless of the clubbing, and pulled it out of the jaws of disaster at the final moment. Spahn pitched this and he stayed in there even when the roof began to crumble in upon him. He had a lead of 4 to 1 in the ninth inning, his lead having been furnished him in the fourth inning when Hank Aaron and Frank Torre both hit home runs, Aaron's coming with two men on base. Spahn practically had the side out in the ninth, although two batters had got away from him. There were two outs and two strikes on Elston Howard when big Elston drove a pitch right out of the park to tie the score. Then in the tenth, with Spahn still clinging grimly to his job, Kubek scratched up an infield hit and Bauer put the Yanks in front with a triple. The Braves won the game in their half of the tenth, with an argument. The argument was presented by pinch-hitter Nippy Jones, who insisted he had been hit by a pitch. And when the umpire said no, Nippy got the ball away from Berra and showed the umpire where it was marked with shoe blacking. The ump said, okay, you're right. Berra said oh no, he's wrong. But the ump then showed the ball to Berra, who did not have time to think of any other explanation of how that black mark got there.

So Nippy went to first for free and Felix Mantilla, whose shoes were probably unshined, came in to run for him. Johnny Logan then delivered a double that tied the score up again. Then Edwin Mathews hit a home run and won the game with it.

Lew Burdette, all nicely warmed up now from his efforts in the second game, engaged in a fierce duel with Bob Turley and Whitey Ford and outlasted them both. He scattered seven hits among the starving Yankees and Slaughter grabbed two of them. All of them were singles and none turned into runs. Three hits in the sixth off Whitey Ford gave the Braves one run and made Ford the losing pitcher.

When they returned to New York to settle the thing, it was Turley again and Bob this time was strong and sharp. He allowed only four hits and struck out eight. Two of the hits were home runs by Frank Torre and Hank Aaron, else Bob would have had a shutout. The Yanks supplied two home runs themselves, by Berra and Bauer. Berra's came with Enos Slaughter on base and that extra run was the difference. Buhl and Ernie Johnson struck out nine Yanks between them, but the home run Ernie gave Bauer in the last of the seventh cost him the game.

It really was not right to ask Lew Burdette to pitch another game in the series, with only two days' rest since he pitched the shutout, but Spahn was sick in bed and who else could Manager Fred Haney call on? It was all right with Lew, who sailed right into the Yankees again and treated them just as he had before. He gave them seven hits this time but he was working with a four-run cushion from the third inning on, so he was able to relax a little. At that, only Hank Bauer, with a two-bagger, got more than a single and only one Yankee got a base on balls. The Yankees used five pitchers, but what they needed most of all was men who could hit. The Braves got their four runs when Ed Mathews hit a double with Hazle and Logan on base. Hank Aaron drove Mathews home and Wes Covington put Hank on third, whence he scored on a forceout. In the eighth inning Del Crandall made it fancy by hitting a home run off Tommy Byrne. Then the Braves all went back to Milwaukee to

250

help the town (still irked at being called "bush-league" by the haughty Yankees) break loose.

Leading hitters:

MILWAUKEE BRAVES
Aaron: .393

NEW YORK YANKEES
Coleman: .364

Winning pitchers:

MILWAUKEE BRAVES
Burdette: won 3, lost 0
Spahn: won 1, lost 1

NEW YORK YANKEES
Ford: won 1, lost 1
Larsen: won 1, lost 1
Turley: won 1, lost 0

1958

NEW YORK A.L. vs. MILWAUKEE N.L.

WON BY NEW YORK, 4 GAMES TO 3

Game Scores:

Milwaukee 4 (10 innings)	New York 3	October 1 at Milwaukee
Milwaukee 13	New York 5	October 2 at Milwaukee
New York 4	Milwaukee 0	October 4 at New York
Milwaukee 3	New York 0	October 5 at New York
New York 7	Milwaukee 0	October 6 at New York
New York 4 (10 innings)	Milwaukee 3	October 8 at Milwaukee
New York 6	Milwaukee 2	October 9 at Milwaukee

This was one time when even Casey Stengel's detractors had to admit the old man made the difference between victory and defeat. The 1958 series was as good as gone, and the Yanks had not even dared to order any victory champagne, when Casey reached back into his bursting memory for the tricks he needed to outwit the wily enemy. It had been years, almost half of Stengel's life, since any club down three games to one had had to play sudden death through the last three games of a World Series and had then won out. Pittsburgh did it against Washington in 1925. But they did have a hand from the weather. The

252

deciding game in 1925 was played in a steady downpour, the only World Series game ever played under such conditions.

Casey had neither snow nor rain nor gloom of night to help him cook up his wizardry. He just had craft and self-confidence, and a baseball memory that never let go of a fact, even if it seldom held on to a name. Like Connie Mack, to whom Lou Boudreau was always Boordee, Casey often had his own version of players' patronymics. But he could remember the time a kid screwball pitcher struck out a right-handed power hitter, and if you doubted it you were free to look it up. If you knew where to look.

At this point in Casey's career, the Milwaukee Braves were the only club in either circuit from whom the Yankees had never won a series. Casey probably had that fact in mind too as he moved grimly into a replay of the previous year's meeting.

The Milwaukee pitchers reversed their roles in this series, with Spahn coming out the big winner and Burdette the loser. Spahn pitched the first game against strong Whitey Ford, who had a good year with the Yankees (fourteen wins) but not by any means his best. Nor did he pitch his best game today, even though he struck out eight, and was not charged with the loss. Spahn struggled through the whole game, grim as ever, and never losing heart, even when the Yankees jumped ahead of him in the fifth inning on a home run by Hank Bauer with a man on base. In the previous inning, Bill Skowron had homered, but the Braves had recovered and gone ahead on a walk to Aaron, and blows by Crandall and Spahn himself. Spahn made two hits in the game and drove in the second run. In the eighth inning, a walk to Ed Mathews and a double by Hank Aaron, putting runners on second and third, prompted Stengel to call back Whitey Ford and send in his four-eyed reliever, Ryne Duren, who threw the scariest fast ball in the majors. But Wes Covington managed to meet one of Duren's pitches well enough to send it high and far into the outfield for a sacrifice fly that brought in the tying run. Then, in the tenth, singles by Adcock, Crandall, and Billy Bruton won the game.

Lew Burdette tried for the second game, as he had the previous year. This time he looked like a loser, for half an inning—or until the Milwaukee batters in the first inning put him so far ahead he could have finished on one leg. The first three Yankees at bat in the game reached base and Howard came to bat with the bases full. All Elston could provide, however, was a force-out that brought in a run, before Yogi Berra ended everything by grounding into a double play. Then the Braves decided to make things safe for Burdette, who had just missed a chance to extend his scoreless-inning streak (he had twenty-four left over from the previous series). Bob Turley pitched for the Yanks in this one. He had just completed the best season of his career, and his last really good year in baseball. The tragedy that befell him before he could get more than one man out would have sent a less stout-hearted player out seeking a job in a filling station. But Bob came back to be the series hero.

The first man to face Turley, Billy Bruton, hit a home run. After that it got worse. Turley managed to strike out one, and one got away with a free walk to first, but everybody else hit, and Turley left the mound with the count 2 to 1 against the Yankees. Duke Maas, brought from Kansas City that year to work in twenty-two games as a "middle" pitcher for the Yankees, tried it then and tried in vain. He had two on base, and two men out when Lew Burdette, the pitcher, came up. One more run had scored on a sacrifice. And Lew, contrary to World Series and baseball tradition, delivered a three-run home run that made it 7 to 1. Johnny Kucks got the last man out. But in the next inning the Braves nicked him for the eighth run. By the seventh Burdette had allowed a home run to Mickey Mantle, and one additional hit. Then the Braves gave him two more runs to play with, and in the eighth presented him with three more. This caused him to relax a little in the ninth when home runs by Bauer and Mantle, plus a single by McDougald, added three runs to the Yankee total and brought them within eight runs of a tie.

Perfect-Game Don Larsen pitched the third game, the first in New York. Facing him was Bob Rush, a ten-game winner, something less than perfect. Don had no trouble with anybody.

254

While Hank Bauer, with three hits, including another home run, drove in all four of the Yankee runs, Larsen sprinkled six singles among the Braves and struck out eight. In the eighth inning, when Larsen, who had seen little action since July, began to grow arm-weary, Ryne Duren came in to help him and gave no hits at all. Poor Bob Rush pitched one of the best games of his life too, giving only three hits in six innings. But he gave five walks and could not keep Hank Bauer from dumping a single into center field with the bases full.

The next game seemed to put the series on ice. Spahn in this one was his invincible best, crafty, intense, completely centered on his job, twisting those low pitches in where no one could get them into the outfield, yielding only one extra-base hit (a triple by Mantle), and one single, then knocking in a run on his own. He struck out seven, including two pinch-hitters. And Norm Siebern of the Yankees matched Hack Wilson's 1929 experience of losing two flies in the sun. That put the Braves ahead three games to one.

Hardly anyone believed then that the Yanks could make it, even after they took the final New York game. Bob Turley won this one with a five-hit shutout, and he had occasion to give thanks for Elston Howard, playing left field, whose diving, sliding catch of a drooping line drive was turned into a double play in the sixth inning, just as Turley was giving signs of slipping. After that play, the Yanks came up and murdered Lew Burdette. It had been 1 to 0, in favor of New York, up to then, because of a home run by Gil McDougald. A double by Berra, a single by Skowron, and another double by McDougald set matters rolling, and Bob Turley singled to send a couple of runs home too. The Yanks had five more runs before Juan Pizarro could stop them. Juan was charged with one more run, but that was of no account. Turley from then on was untouchable. He struck out ten.

The Milwaukee fans had already forgotten this defeat and were savoring the championship when the clubs flew back to Milwaukee. But the Yankees scratched, clawed, and scrambled to a ten-inning victory in the sixth game. This was the really crucial game, the one that the Braves *had* to win—because they used up Spahn in trying for it—and the one that Stengel took away from them by shifting his troops about in a manner that perhaps no other manager would have quite dared to attempt.

Although Whitey Ford had pitched only three days before, Casey felt he had to send him after this one. There was no point in trying to save your best when there might be nothing to save him for. But Whitey could not restrain the Braves. Hank Bauer gave him a home run to start on but the Braves tied the score when Hank Aaron drove Red Schoendienst across the plate in the last of the first. Then in the second inning, Warren Spahn spoiled things for Whitey by hitting a single to bring home Wes Covington, with the second run. When Whitey put Red Schoendienst on base, Casey decided to use Art Ditmar. Art was nobody's choice for league's leading pitcher that season. But he was strong, never grew rattled, and (you could look it up) had shut out Milwaukee for six innings of relief in the previous World Series, striking out three and not giving a single base on balls.

Ditmar was the man of the hour, or of that particular moment. But he received some unlooked-for aid from Coach Billy Herman of the Braves. With Schoendienst on first and Andy Pafko on third, Ditmar induced Johnny Logan to pop a fly to left field, where Elston Howard awaited it. Howard, with his catcher's strong and accurate arm, was no man to take chances with. But Billy Herman, regardless of the shallowness of the fly, decided to send Andy Pafko home. Andy could run. But he could not outrun a thrown baseball and the ball was waiting for him a second or two before he got to the plate. Yogi Berra did not hesitate to tag Andy out.

Ditmar pitched through the fifth inning without letting Milwaukee get close. Then Stengel sent Jerry Lumpe in to hit for Ditmar in the sixth and Jerry struck out. There was no Johnny Mize on the bench this year. So the rally produced only one run, Berra having driven Mantle home to tie the score. The new pitcher was Ryne Duren, who was told just to go in and throw until he grew tired. He threw so hard for 4⅔ innings that he struck out eight men. The Yankees put him ahead in the tenth, with a home run by McDougald and successive singles by Howard, Berra, and Skowron. In the home half of the tenth, Ryne's arm began to give out. He got one man out, then could not get the ball over the plate to Johnny Logan. With Logan on first, Hank Aaron and Joe Adcock hit singles to bring Logan across the plate and put the tying run within easy reach. Frank Torre stepped in to pinch-hit and Casey Stengel strode in to take Duren out. Who was left? Why, tomorrow's pitcher, Bob Turley. There would be no tomorrow, however, if Torre brought those runs in, and Turley was a man who could bear down in the clutch. So Bob came in and threw hard to Torre. Torre swung hard at what seemed a good pitch, misjudged the speed of it, and just boosted it out across the diamond into McDougald's glove. That was the out that made the series even.

Casey had to use Larsen then in the final game and Larsen had not had rest enough. He filled the bases at once. But the Braves could not find the formula for bringing in those runs. One came in when Covington made out, and that was all the Braves could do until the third, when three Braves came to bat and two of them hit singles. The Yanks were leading then, 2 to 1, thanks to two wild throws by first baseman Frank Torre, who tossed away a bunt by Howard and a ground ball by Jerry Lumpe. Howard had been trying to move Yogi Berra up with his bunt so the errors filled the bases. A forceout and a sacrifice fly scored two runs. So the threat in the third might have put the Braves ahead. If there was any one pitcher who had worked hard in this series it was Bob Turley. But Stengel needed just one look to tell when Bob was throwing well. And Bob, since his Baltimore days, had always been a man who could reach way down and find that reserve strength. He found it today. After silencing the Milwaukee threat in the third he gave up only two hits, including a home run to Crandall. And the Yankees, in the eighth, iced the championship by suddenly lowering the boom on Lew Burdette. A two-out double by Berra, singles by Howard and Carey, and a booming home run by Bill Skowron gave Turley all the edge he required.

The sudden turning of the tables caught everyone unprepared.

Even the Yankee office staff had not been looking for victory and when the time came for celebration, there was only domestic champagne to wallow in. "Why not imported?" demanded George Weiss, who believed in traveling first class. Well, that's all they had hereabouts. "You could have had some flown in," George growled. He and Stengel had never doubted.

Leading hitters:

NEW YORK YANKEES
Bauer: .323

MILWAUKEE BRAVES
Aaron: .333

Winning pitchers:

NEW YORK YANKEES
Larsen:	won 1, lost 0
Turley:	won 2, lost 1
Duren:	won 1, lost 1

MILWAUKEE BRAVES
| Spahn: | won 2, lost 1 |
| Burdette: | won 1, lost 2 |

1959

LOS ANGELES N.L. vs. CHICAGO A.L.

WON BY LOS ANGELES, 4 GAMES TO 2

Game Scores:

Chicago 11	Los Angeles 0	October 1 at Chicago
Los Angeles 4	Chicago 3	October 2 at Chicago
Los Angeles 3	Chicago 1	October 4 at Los Angeles
Los Angeles 5	Chicago 4	October 5 at Los Angeles
Chicago 1	Los Angeles 0	October 6 at Los Angeles
Los Angeles 9	Chicago 3	October 8 at Chicago

In 1959, there were still forlorn Brooklyn fans who would sit up until their eyes grew red-rimmed, just to listen to the night games of the club that used to play in Brooklyn, and to root still for the Duke, and Carl Furillo, and Gil Hodges, and Jim Gilliam. And most of them used to dwell unhappily on what might have been if only the Dodgers could have stayed on and could have kept on bringing those pennants to Brooklyn.

Of course playing the Chicago White Sox was not the same as playing the Yankees, especially when the White Sox were owned now by that most virulent of Yankee-haters, Bill Veeck. But just the same, it was another World Championship, only the second one that any Brooklyn fan could remember. And it was won by a collection of the old familiars, with just a few kids

259

added who had never played at Ebbets Field. Snider was just a part-time performer now, as Carl Furillo was. Poor Roy Campanella had been permanently crippled in an auto accident. Jackie Robinson was a businessman going gray. Don Newcombe had gone to Cincinnati. Pee Wee Reese had called it off after just one season in Los Angeles. Pete Reiser was a manager in the Texas League. Sandy Amoros hung on as a pinch-hitter.

But Clem Labine was still ready to ride in to the rescue. Johnny Podres still threw the high hard one. And Johnny Roseboro, Campanella's substitute, held the number one job now.

Veeck's White Sox, while not so exciting nor so solid a club as the 1948 Cleveland Indians, outran and outfought the Yankees and Cleveland and thrilled their hometown with their speed on the bases and their magical defense. If Veeck had had his way, he'd have added old Satchel Paige to the roster too, despite his fifty-three years. But soft-spoken manager Al Lopez allowed that when Paige flew in, Lopez would fly out. He could put up with musical scoreboards and other spectacular gags. But he was serious about winning baseball games.

Los Angeles had to win a playoff with Milwaukee to earn the pennant, so they came into the series either worn out or full of momentum, depending on which sports-page seer you favored. And the White Sox, closing with a five-game lead, may have lost momentum. Or perhaps they were rested and ready.

Whatever the contributing factors, both clubs looked very different from what they had seemed in the regular season. The White Sox, who had featured speed and tight defense, came up with some mighty work with the bat. And the Dodgers cut down base stealers as if they had armed their catcher with a .30-.30 Winchester.

The opening game turned all the forecasts upside down. In it the White Sox hit two home runs and four doubles, stole no bases at all, and choked off the Dodgers with eight singles and no runs. The big man in this game was the biggest man on the field, a retread from Cincinnati named Ted Kluszewski, whose mighty arms were too muscular to suffer the restraint of sleeves. Ted, at thirty-five, was nearing the end of the row. But he did most of the heavy hitting in the series. In this game he hit two home runs and batted in five of the eleven Chicago runs. The Dodgers, in a vain effort to halt the march of the Chicago monsters, used five pitchers, starting with Roger Craig, and including a wild youngster named Koufax who had won only eight games that year. Koufax pitched two hitless innings, but by that time Chicago was eleven runs ahead.

The second game brought Johnny Podres into action against eighteen-game winner Bob Shaw. Podres had won only fourteen games in the regular season. But he won this one, even though he had to get out in the seventh inning to allow pinch-hitter Chuck Essegian to come up and hit a home run that tied the score. After that, Charley Neal, who had already hit one home run, hit another with a man on base and made the score 4 to 2 in favor of Los Angeles. Chicago had scored twice in the first, on blows by Kluszewski and Sherm Lollar. They scored again against relief pitcher Larry Sherry, when Klu and Lollar again hit safely. Lopez put in a runner for Klu. But he should also have put one in for Lollar, because when Al Smith drove a double to deep center field one run scored and slow-footed Sherm was cut down on a streaking relay, Moon to Wills to Roseboro. And that cost the ball game.

Larry Sherry, tired or not, had to put the fire out in the third game too, when Don Drysdale began to wobble in the eighth. Don had really been kept alive by Chicago ineptness at the plate and on the bases. He gave eleven hits, yet only one runner crossed the plate. Poor Dick Donovan, the Chicago pitcher, worked like a champion for six innings, giving the Dodgers only one hit and no walks. But in the seventh the strain grew too great and his control cracked. A single and two walks filled the bases, and Donovan was out of there. Gerry Staley came in. But so did Carl Furillo, and Carl had the better of the contest. His pinch-single drove in two runs and really won the game. Sherry rescued Drysdale in the eighth, after big Klu and Lollar had cut loose again. Sherry let Klu score but no one else did.

In the next game, who should show up but Larry Sherry once

261

more, to pitch the last two innings after Roger Craig had allowed the White Sox to build four runs and tie the score? And of course the men who built the runs were that same outrageous pair, Kluszewski and Lollar. Klu drove Landis in with a single. With two out and two on, Lollar cleaned off the bases with a home run. The Dodgers had scored all their runs too after two were out, in the third inning, with Hodges and Roseboro doing most of the work. Sherry gave no hits in the two innings he worked and when Hodges contributed a home run of his own in the eighth, Sherry got credit for the victory.

In the fifth game, the White Sox got the pitching they had been bragging about when Bob Shaw and Dick Donovan combined to shut the Dodgers out. Billy Pierce, the wily left-hander, got into this game too but all he managed to do was walk a man. Then Dick Donovan stepped in and pitched hitless ball the rest of the way. Pierce came in when Walt Alston sent in a left-handed batter to hit for right-handed Don Demeter. Then when Lefty Bill came to the mound, Alston called back the pinch-hitter, Ron Fairly, and sent up right-handed Rip Repulski instead. And to make the whole maneuver thoroughly ridiculous, Pierce walked Repulski on purpose and immediately left the game. The lone Chicago run came in on successive singles by Nellie Fox and Jim Landis, followed by a double play that permitted Fox to score. A minor feature of this game was the appearance of Larry Sherry as a pinch-hitter in the ninth inning.

Having squeaked this one out, the White Sox dragged the series back to Chicago and looked at first as if they were going to give up without any further struggle. Johnny Podres was at his crackling best in the first three innings, and the White Sox looked like the hitless wonders of old. Early Wynn, the Chicago pitcher, was but a shadow of his best. In the third the Dodgers made two runs on a walk to Neal and a home run by Snider. In the fourth, Wynn cracked up completely. Before he could get two men out the Dodgers had scored twice on blows by Larker, Wills, and Podres. Neal, who made three hits in the game, drove in two runs with a double off relief-pitcher Donovan. Moon's homer scored two more. Johnny was set to coast the rest of the way, but the road suddenly turned uphill. In the last of the fourth inning Podres hit Landis with a pitch and then, as so often happens, began to grow tense. He walked the next man, Sherm Lollar. Big Kluszewski, Chicago's old reliable, then drove another home run into the seats and set the scoreboard banging and whistling. Podres then walked Al Smith. It had obviously become a case for Superman. So Larry Sherry was returned to the mound and he stopped all further scoring by Chicago. In the ninth inning, with the score 8 to 3 for his side, Walt Alston amused himself by sending in a pinch-hitter for his weary home run hitter, Duke Snider. Chuck Essegian, the pinch-hitter, thereupon hit a home run, his second of the series. That was a pinch-hitting record. And it was the only way to justify sending up a hitter for the Duke. To the Chicago fans it looked like rubbing it in and they all went home to wait glumly until next year, or until some year soon after that.

Leading hitters:

LOS ANGELES DODGERS
Hodges: .391

CHICAGO WHITE SOX
Kluszewski: .391

Winning pitchers:

LOS ANGELES DODGERS
Podres: won 1, lost 0
Drysdale: won 1, lost 0
Sherry: won 2, lost 0

CHICAGO WHITE SOX
Wynn: won 1, lost 1
Shaw: won 1, lost 1

1960

PITTSBURGH N.L. vs. NEW YORK A.L.

WON BY PITTSBURGH, 4 GAMES TO 3

Game Scores:

Pittsburgh 6	New York 4	October 5 at Pittsburgh
New York 16	Pittsburgh 3	October 6 at Pittsburgh
New York 10	Pittsburgh 0	October 8 at New York
Pittsburgh 3	New York 2	October 9 at New York
Pittsburgh 5	New York 2	October 10 at New York
New York 12	Pittsburgh 0	October 12 at Pittsburgh
Pittsburgh 10	New York 9	October 13 at Pittsburgh

What did a club have to do, the 1960 Yankees must have asked themselves, to make the Pirates realize they were licked? The Yankees gave them a head start, caught up with them and clobbered them unmercifully, did it all over again the next day when they got them into the Stadium, and then, after the Pirates had pulled even, the Yanks took them home and gave them one more fearsome clubbing before the home fans. It was all no use. Seizing on a wild bit of luck here and a crazy bounce there, the Pirates finally caught the Yankees and beat them in the most hair-raising finish the series had seen to that day. And in that way they ruined Casey Stengel's last World Series, made the Yankee brass go home muttering about trading off Whitey Ford,

264

The Sixties

41. There goes the championship! Joe Pepitone, unable to get a line on a throw from Third Baseman Clete Boyer, because the ball was lost in the background of white shirts, desperately digs after the ball as Jim Gilliam runs all the way to third. A sacrifice fly brought Gilliam in with the run that took the 1963 World Series for the Dodgers. *Wide World Photos*.

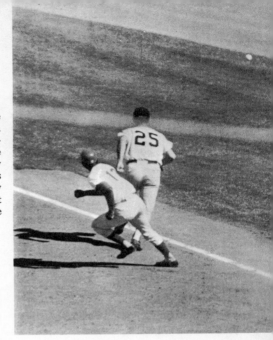

42. Pittsburgh's greatest moment. Bill Mazeroski, Pirate third baseman, who has just hit a ninth-inning home run to win the World Championship for Pittsburgh, brings the celebration with him as he comes in to score in seventh game of 1960 series. *Wide World Photos*.

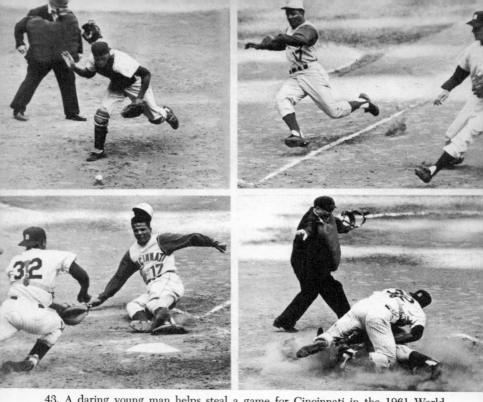

43. A daring young man helps steal a game for Cincinnati in the 1961 World Series. Elio Chacon, Red second baseman, ran home when Elston Howard let a pitch get by. He slid right under Howard's desperate diving tag. This was in the second game, only game the Reds won. *Wide World Photos.*

44. St. Louis catcher Tim McCarver is a picture of righteous outrage as he protests Umpire Bill McKinley's decision that Joe Pepitone, Yankee first baseman, was hit by a pitch in the second game of the 1964 World Series. *Wide World Photos.*

45. Cincinnati managed to look hopelessly inept on this play in the third game of the 1961 World Series. Frank Robinson, the right fielder, and Elio Chacon, the second baseman, knocked each other right out of action for a few seconds when they collided while chasing Yogi Berra's pop fly. *Wide World Photos.*

46. Sandy Koufax, best pitcher in baseball at the time and the hero of the 1963 World Series, in which the Dodgers took four straight from the Yankees, modestly accepts the adoration of Los Angeles fans after winning the first game. *Wide World Photos.*

47. Willie Davis, Los Angeles outfielder, roars his disagreement with the man who called him out at second base in the first game of the 1966 World Series. Next day he had more to brood about as he dropped two fly balls and threw wild to third, all in the same inning. *Wide World Photos.*

48. A portent of things to come was this first-inning home run by Frank Robinson of the Baltimore Orioles, in the first game of the 1966 World Series. Everyone, including Dodger Left Fielder Tommy Davis, hopes to catch the ball. *Wide World Photos.*

and even provided an excuse for getting rid of George Weiss, the man who had built pennant winners year after year.

This was in a sense a turning point in baseball. Had the Yankees won and had Stengel thus been rendered immune from "retirement" for another year or two, would there have been any Mets? Or if there had been would they have found available the baseball brains, the showmanship, the shrewd sense of how to ignite the fervor of the young fans that George Weiss and Casey Stengel provided? It hardly bears thinking about.

Reading the statistics of the 1960 series, a fan might at first believe that the Yankees had won every game. For they set new World Series batting records of every hue. They scored fifty-five runs, against only twenty-seven for the Pirates, for a new top mark. They made ninety-one hits, against the Pirates' total of sixty, and ninety-one was a new record too. The Yankees' team batting average of .338 was the highest ever set for a seven-game series. They even set a record "slugging average" (whatever that is) of .528. They made ten home runs and seventeen other extra-base hits. And Bobby Richardson, who had hit a fat .252 in the regular season, set a new World Series record for runs batted in: twelve. And by driving in six in one game, he set a new World Series game record too. His mightiest blow was a bases-loaded home run in the third game.

Spectacular fielding by both infield and outfield helped save ball games for the Pirates. And other matters that do not show in the statistics, such as drive, courage, team spirit, and dogged refusal to roll over, all helped bring Pittsburgh her first World Championship in thirty-five years. One of her heroes was her incredible relief pitcher, Elroy Face, who came close, in 1959, to winning every game he tried for. Elroy did not get credit for any victories, but he worked in every game the Pirates won and he saved three of them. In the final game he was just too tired to be of much use. But the Pirates won that one anyway after it looked as if Face might be tagged with the defeat.

The first game, pitched by Vernon Law, who was concealing a limp, needed strong pitching by Face to pull it out. In the very first inning, Roger Maris, the man who would break Babe Ruth's record, hit a home run to start the Yankees in front. But the Pirates corrected that imbalance right away. Bill Virdon walked to start things, tried for second and kept on going when Kubek let Berra's throw get by into center field. A double and a single meant two runs. Then Bob Skinner stole second and scored on Clemente's single. This meant Ditmar had to sit down. Then Vernon Law kept the pot from boiling over, although there was violent activity from time to time. In the fourth inning, Maris and Mantle both got on base, on a single and a walk, and both of them nearly scored when Yogi Berra drove a high pitch almost as far as it would go, out toward the center-field fence. Fleet Bill Virdon took after the ball, however, and managed to nail it in the fingers of his glove just when it seemed sure to escape. Skowron singled after that and one run scored. But the Pirates quickly made two and increased their lead when Bill Mazeroski, with Don Hoak on base, hit a home run. There may have been an omen in the fact that Bill, batting eighth in the order, hit the only Pittsburgh home run in the first six games and hit safely in every game but one. Mazeroski also scored on Virdon's double in the sixth inning, to make the score Pirates 6, Yankees 2.

In the eighth inning, lame Vernon Law began to lose his sharpness. Hector Lopez and Roger Maris both hit to open the inning and Elroy Face, who always seemed ready, hurried in to blank the Yankees' big men. In the ninth, pinch-hitter Elston Howard, with Bobby Richardson on base after a forceout, added two runs to the Yankee total with a home run. But Face stayed on the job and after Kubek had singled, he got Lopez to hit into a double play.

The next game was the inevitable laugher that the Yankees could not do without. It had been a long time since any World Series crowd had seen such an apparent mismatch, so many runs scored, and so many hits collected. Bob Turley, the Yankee pitcher, was no Christy Mathewson this day but he did not need to be. He gave up thirteen hits, including three two-baggers. But the Pirates had a hard time scoring all the same. For the Yankees, scoring was about all they did. After treating the Pirate pitcher, Bob Friend, with great gentleness for the first two in-

266

nings, the Yankees went to work on him. Richardson walked, Turley bunted him on to second, and Kubek's single sent him home. Then McDougald's double scored Kubek. And when it came Bob Friend's turn to hit next inning Manager Murtaugh deemed him expendable and used a pinch-hitter in his place. The new pitcher, Fred Green, was welcomed by Mickey Mantle, who sent one of his choice pitches into the stands in right-center field to score Roger Maris ahead of him.

In the sixth inning, Green was still there when the bomb exploded. Elston Howard led off with a triple. Then came a double by Richardson and a quick retreat by Green. The new pitcher was a familiar face: the old Dodger laborer, Clem Labine. Clem at this stage had not too much left. What he had was soon distributed among the hungry Yankees. Labine threw out Bob Turley and fed a low pitch to Kubek for an easy grounder. But Dick Groat could not decide how to hold it so Kubek reached base. Then McDougald singled and Maris walked to force in an extra run. Labine did strike out Mantle. But Berra's single then scored two runs and Skowron's single scored one. That was enough for Labine and too much for the Pirates. Not for the Yankees, however. They got two more runs that inning and more in the seventh, on a mighty three-run home run by Mantle that was estimated at over 475 feet. And they scored still another run on a double and a wild pitch. The Pirates did get the satisfaction of driving Bob Turley into the dugout, when Bob hit a batter and was then hit for three singles, adding up to three runs, just thirteen short of a tie.

All good ball clubs come back fighting after a brutal defeat. And the Pirates did too. But what about two such defeats? In the third game, the Yankees again beat the Pirates all around the head and ears, for a total of ten runs. Meanwhile, Whitey Ford, who had not had a really strong year, tossed just four hits to the Pirates, one of them by Mazeroski. The Yankee scoring came in two large chunks: Six runs in the first inning and four in the fourth. Clem Labine, relieving Vinegar Bend Mizell in the very first inning, after three singles and a walk had scored a run and left the bases loaded, was the victim of gross indignities. While he was getting one man out, Elston Howard singled, and Bobby Richardson hit a grand slam home run. After that Kubek singled and Bob Cerv singled. It took over half an hour to get the Yankees out. In the fourth, Mantle's two-run homer and Richardson's two-run single scored the runs.

The next day the Pirates were just as ready for a fight as ever. A good thing too because it was a tight struggle and it is doubtful if anyone but Elroy Face could have managed it. Skowron's home run gave the Yanks an early lead that Ralph Terry seemed bound to hang on to. But in the fifth inning, Gino Cimoli hit the ball for one base. The next blow, a grounder by Smokey Burgess, should have been a double play, or at least a forceout. But Skowron was a step too slow and both runners were safe. Terry got the next two men out. He got two strikes on Vernon Law. But then Vernon cut loose and drove a two-base hit to left field that scored a run. Bill Virdon then drove the two runners home with a single and gave Law a lead that he never quite relinquished. In the seventh, the Yankees scored one more run on a double by Skowron, a single by McDougald that Bill could not score on, and a just-missed double play that he did score on. When pinch-hitter John Blanchard singled, it was time to send for little Elroy. He came in and stamped out every last spark of flame, with the help of another bone-rattling circus catch by Virdon some four hundred feet from the plate, right against the fence.

The Pirates were glad to see Art Ditmar again, in game number five and they treated him much as they had before, scoring three runs in the top of the second on a single, two doubles, a missed double play, an error, and some hard running and sliding. In the third inning they added another run on Groat's double and Clemente's single, and still another in the ninth on a single, an outfield error (by Bob Cerv), a wild pitch (by Ryne Duren), and another single. The Yanks could gather only two runs. One came in the second on Howard's double and singles by Richardson and Kubek. The other came in the third on Maris' home run. But soon after, it became a job for Elroy again. A scary hard drive by Richardson that was caught for an out indicated that the Yanks were going to start to hit Haddix' pitches on the nose. Two quick singles made it sure. So Elroy came in, took the ball in his fingertips, and dared the Yanks to hit it. McDougald tried and hit into a double play. Maris tried and missed three times.

In the sixth game the Yankees turned ugly again. Without Face to tame them, they tore into five Pirate pitchers for seventeen hits and twelve runs. Whitey Ford strung out nine more scoreless innings, to get a good start on his way to break Babe Ruth's pitching record. The Yankee runs came in smaller lots this time, and they did not all derive from power hitting. In the second inning, a walk, a single, a hit batsman, and another single meant one run. In the third inning, there was another hit batsman, then a double, a single, a single, a sacrifice fly, a single, and a triple. The three-bagger was provided by the mighty Richardson, who looked like a combination of Mantle and Maris in this series. Bobby got another triple later that sent home a run and he scored himself on a squeeze play. Blanchard got two doubles and a single.

So then it had to go to the seventh to be settled. And in the final game the Yanks were hitting the ball as hard as ever. Pittsburgh took a four-run lead with two runs each in the first and second innings. Rocky Nelson's two-run homer brought the first runs home. Bill Virdon's single with men on second and third scored the next two. The Yankees started to strain at the leash in the fifth when Moose Skowron drove a ball into the seats. Next inning, a single and a walk suggested it was time for Face again. But this time Elroy had nothing left. After he got Roger Maris on a foul he gave a single to Mantle and a home run to Yogi Berra. He got the next two out, went through the seventh unscathed, and started the eighth inning. He threw out Maris at first and Mantle lined out. But Skowron bounced a single in the infield, then Blanchard hit safely to score a run, and Boyer's double scored another. That made it 7 to 4 in favor of New York and when it came Face's turn to bat next inning, Gino Cimoli appeared in his place. Gino singled. Then Bill Virdon hit a ball that, as it turned out, really cost the ball game. The ball skipped sharply straight at Kubek, for an easy double play. But just as it reached him it found a pebble, or a hard spot, and took a sudden wild bound. The ball struck Kubek in the Adam's apple and sent him crumpling to the ground. Both men were safe and Kubek had to leave the game. After that, while Bobby Shantz and Jim Coates were getting two men out, there were two singles and a home run, to put five runs across the plate and give the Pirates a two-run lead.

They lost the lead in the very next inning on singles by Richardson and pinch-hitter Dale Long, a single by Mantle, and a near-double play that allowed McDougald to score the tying run.

The game ended in a satisfactorily spectacular manner. Bill Mazerozki, the "weak" end of the Pirate batting order, opened the last of the ninth. He watched the first pitch go by. The second one came in a little higher and it suited him just right. With a clean and easy swing he met it head on and sent it sailing over the scoreboard, where the score said 9 to 9. Only this made it 10 to 9 and the Pirates were champions. The crowd broke loose then and some of them trotted down the third-base line with Maz. The celebration lasted all night, filling the streets with torn-up paper, unearthly noise, stalled trolleys, dancing fans of all ages and both sexes, weary policemen, and bewildered dogs and cats.

Leading hitters:

PITTSBURGH PIRATES
Burgess: .333

NEW YORK YANKEES
Mantle: .400

Winning pitchers:

PITTSBURGH PIRATES
Law: won 2, lost 0
Haddix: won 2, lost 0

NEW YORK YANKEES
Ford: won 2, lost 0
Turley: won 1, lost 0

1961

NEW YORK A.L. vs. CINCINNATI N.L.

WON BY NEW YORK, 4 GAMES TO 1

Game Scores:

New York 2	Cincinnati 0	October 4 at New York
Cincinnati 6	New York 2	October 5 at New York
New York 3	Cincinnati 2	October 7 at Cincinnati
New York 7	Cincinnati 0	October 8 at Cincinnati
New York 13	Cincinnati 5	October 9 at Cincinnati

By the time the Cincinnati Reds won the pennant in 1961, there was half a parkful of ardent fans who could not remember the last time the Reds had been in a World Series. Just twenty-one years had gone by since the days of Paul Derringer and Ernie Lombardi and Bucky Walters. In that series Fred Hutchinson had been a rookie pitcher for Detroit. Now he was leading the Cincinnati club in what nearly everyone agreed was a pretty hopeless assault upon the Yankees.

Baseball interest in 1961 centered largely on Roger Maris' breaking of the home run record and on the fact that the Yankees could win the pennant even without Casey Stengel to guide them and George Weiss to recruit their strength. It was a fact of course that all the first-string Yankees this season and most of the bench had been Weiss's projects from years back. Even

271

Roger Maris had been brought to New York after Weiss had stayed on his trail from the time he was a Cleveland property and playing for Reading. But this year it was Ralph Houk's club and Weiss and Stengel sat in the stands in seats they had paid for.

Whitey Ford of the Yankees had completed the finest season of his career, with twenty-five wins against only four losses, and the Yankee owners probably counted themselves shrewd indeed for not having followed their first impulse, which was to trade Ford off on the strength of his fine showing against Pittsburgh in the 1960 World Series. Because he did even better in the 1961 World Series and, without Ford, the Yankees would not have been there.

The Reds had a hero of their own in Joey Jay, a dropout from the Braves who suddenly found himself and pitched the Reds into the pennant. Joey won the only game the Reds could get away with in the series. The Cincinnati batting hero, as usual, was a hitter unheard of during the regular season, Johnny Edwards, who had a season average of .186. Edwards made two hits in the second game and both hits drove in runs. The base-running hero was another almost-unknown, Elio Chacon, the merry South American, who ran home on a short passed ball to break a tie in game number two.

The first game added nine scoreless innings to Whitey Ford's string, to bring him really close to the other Babe Ruth record that would "never be broken": 29⅔ consecutive scoreless World Series innings. Ford gave the Reds only two hits, while Jim Brosnan, the pitcher who wanted to be an author (and got his wish), combined with starter Jim O'Toole to give the Yankees only six. The only runs of the game were made Yankee style, on home runs by Elston Howard and Bill Skowron.

The second game stayed even until the fifth inning, when young Elio, son of a former "Cuban Giant," took alert advantage of one of the few passed balls Elston Howard ever committed. But Ralph Terry was pitching at the time and Ralph was continually surprising his catchers with new pitches. In the fourth inning the Reds had scored two runs on a single and a

272

home run. Then the Yanks scored two, in their half, on a walk to Maris and a home run by Berra. Elio made it 3 to 2, and in the next inning a double by Wally Post and a single by Johnny Edwards made it 4 to 2. Terry had walked Gene Freese to get at Edwards, and even when Edwards singled home the run, the Yanks did not believe it. In the eighth inning, with Luis Arroyo pitching, they walked Freese again to get still another crack at Edwards, and this time Edwards hit a two-bagger to make the score 6 to 2.

The Reds put up a mighty struggle in the third game. But after Maris hit his only homer of the series to put the Yanks ahead, the Reds seemed to lie down and roll over. Bob Purkey pitched the third game, and pitched as if he thought he was Joey Jay. He gave the Yankees only six hits. But two of them, alas, were home runs, one a pinch-hit homer by John Blanchard, who was trying out for the role of Johnny Mize, and the other by Maris, who had just this lone homer left in his bat after a nerve-racking race that had his hair coming out in clumps. Manager Hutchinson had the wheels spinning as he tried to maneuver the Yankees out of this one, but who can think of a good answer for a home run—except another home run? Hutch removed both men who scored for him—sending up in the seventh inning a pinch-hitter for Elio Chacon, who had bunted safely, and got around to third on an error and an out, then scored on a double. He used a pinch-runner for the pinch-hitter, to no avail, and in the ninth inning he sent Cardenas up to bat for Edwards, who had doubled and then scored on Eddie Kasko's single. This move paid off, for Cardenas hit a two-bagger. But no one could bring him home. There was one ominous feature of this game which seemed to indicate the clubs still tended to choke up a little when they faced the Yankees. In the seventh inning, both Elio Chacon and Frank Robinson headed full speed for Berra's short fly and hit each other full speed, bouncing apart and dropping limply to the ground, while the ball popped out of Robinson's glove and Tony Kubek scampered home.

Up to this point, the Yankees, except for those home runs, had been comparatively feeble at bat. Maris had gone hitless in ten trips to the plate and Mickey Mantle had gone hitless in only four at-bats. He was suffering from a late-season injury. But the other Yanks were just suffering from bashfulness. In the fourth game they lost every trace of diffidence and cut loose like the old-time Yankee clubs. While Ford was sturdily picking up the scoreless innings that would make him the record-holder, the Yankees made ready for an uprising. Jim O'Toole could not match Whitey Ford but his pitching was far from feeble. He gave five hits in five innings and yielded two runs. But then Manager Hutchinson got tired of waiting for someone to break through on Whitey Ford and he sent Dick Gernert up to bat for O'Toole. The best Dick could do was ground into a force play. Soon after that, Whitey Ford hurt his foot and left the game. But Jim Coates was every bit as miserable to the Reds. He gave them only one hit in four innings. The Yankees happily piled into Jim Brosnan after one man was out in the sixth. Howard started with a double. Berra was walked to fill the empty base. Then Skowron supplied the desired ground ball, but it rolled oh so slowly down the third-base line and big Bill was able to foot it out to first. That put three on base. Boyer hit a double and took two of them off. In the next inning, Brosnan seemed to have a severe attack of writer's cramp. Maris was walked on purpose after Richardson had singled and gone to second on an error. But after a wild pitch, the next man, Hector Lopez, spoiled everything by belting a single that scored two runs. Then Berra was walked on purpose and Skowron slammed the ball straight back at Brosnan. It rapped the author on the shinbone, and bounced far enough away so Lopez was able to score. This added up to seven runs. The Reds got none. And Ford had pitched thirty-two consecutive scoreless innings in World Series play, for a record that seemed very likely to last forever.

Of course the Yankees had to have one game when they annihilated pitchers and lost a box of baseballs. That came in the final game of the series. And the first victim was the best pitcher the Reds owned, Joey Jay, who could never win ball games for anyone but the Reds. In game number five, everyone, even the Yankee second-stringers, unloaded on poor Joe. Mantle and

Berra had been benched by injuries, but they were never missed. The second-string outfielders, Blanchard and Hector Lopez, contributed a homer apiece. Blanchard also hit a double and a single, while Lopez added a triple. Hector drove in five runs altogether while Skowron pushed over three, with timely singles. The Yankee total was fifteen hits. Ralph Terry, despite his bulging lead, could not get by the third inning, and Bud Daley, the man with the crippled arm, replaced him and gave out only five hits in almost seven innings.

The Reds hit hard in this final game but they never drew close to the Yankees. Frank Robinson hit a double and a home run, while Gene Freese, who had hardly hit at all in other games, hit a two-bagger. Wally Post, another major disappointment, drove in two Cincinnati runs with a homer and a single. The Reds used eight pitchers in the fifth game. That was a World Series record, too, but one that is likely to be matched before long.

Leading hitters:

NEW YORK YANKEES
    Richardson: .391

CINCINNATI REDS
    Post: .333

Winning pitchers:

NEW YORK YANKEES
    Ford: won 2, lost 0
    Arroyo: won 1, lost 0
    Daley: won 1, lost 0

CINCINNATI REDS
    Jay: won 1, lost 1

1962

NEW YORK A.L. vs. SAN FRANCISCO N.L.

WON BY NEW YORK, 4 GAMES TO 3

Game Scores:

New York 6	San Francisco 2	October 4 at San Francisco
San Francisco 2	New York 0	October 5 at San Francisco
New York 3	San Francisco 2	October 7 at New York
San Francisco 7	New York 3	October 8 at New York
New York 5	San Francisco 3	October 10 at New York
San Francisco 5	New York 2	October 15 at San Francisco
New York 1	San Francisco 0	October 16 at San Francisco

How the Yankees managed to win the 1962 World Series, when outscored and outpitched, will always remain a mystery in San Francisco. In the seven games, the Giants scored twenty-one times while the Yankees scored twenty. The Yanks made forty-four hits while the Giants made fifty-one. Yankee pitchers struck out thirty-nine, and Giant pitchers struck out the same number. The Giants made five home runs to the Yankees' three. But still the Yankees won more ball games.

It may have been the weather. For the first time in the memory of many fans, the series was completely disrupted by rain. It rained on both sides of the continent. The fifth game, scheduled for Yankee Stadium, was put off a day by rain. The sixth game, scheduled for San Francisco's Candlestick Park, started three

276

days late and was played under conditions so sloppy their like had not been seen since Walter Johnson had to wallow about on the pitching mound in the final game of the series of 1925.

It might be assumed that the delay, enabling the Yankees to start Whitey Ford three times, made all the difference—except that the Yankees lost two of the games that Ford started. The player who really grew strong on the delay was Ralph Terry, the man with a million pitches. He lost the second game, although he gave only five hits. Then he won the fifth game and the seventh game. His masterpiece was the finale, in which he allowed the Giants but four hits.

The Yankees had no big innings in this series and delivered no base-hit barrage. Maris and Mantle, for the most part, hit like second-string infielders. The big man at the plate was a switch-hitting converted shortstop playing his first year in the Yankee outfield—Tom Tresh, son of a former White Sox catcher, who in his twelve seasons in the majors had never got into a World Series. Tom's series average was .321. But the top batter of the series was a Giant—José Pagan, with an average of .368. José hit .259 in the regular season.

Whitey Ford, starting the first game, was able to add only 1⅔ scoreless innings to his record string, and the villain who brought the string to an end was José Pagan. In the second inning, Willie Mays singled, went to third on Jim Davenport's single, and scored on a bunt-base hit by José. The Yankees had already counted two runs on a double by Roger Maris, which followed a pair of singles by Richardson and Tresh. Roger made a practice in this series of hitting only when it would hurt. In the third inning, the Giants hung on when a single by Felipe Alou and another by Mays brought in the tying run. Cletis Boyer's home run in the seventh inning gave the lead back to the Yankees and they clenched their teeth on it in the eighth when Maris singled, moved up when Elston Howard was hit by a pitch, and scored on Dale Long's single. At this point, "Perfect-Game" Don Larsen came in to hold off the boys he used to play with. Howard scored on Clete Boyer's high and wandering fly, which José Pagan followed clear out into left field. Out of position, and out of reach, José could not catch slow-moving Elston at the plate. The Yankees added one final run in the ninth inning when Howard brought Tom Tresh home with run number six.

In the second game both pitchers seemed in top form. Ralph Terry gave no enemy batter more than one hit. But the one he gave to Willie McCovey went all the way over the fence—and that was more than all the Yanks together could produce off Fred Sanford. Sanford, a hard-working pitcher who never seemed to let down, pitched one of his finest games. He gave a double to Mickey Mantle and gave Tom Tresh and Clete Boyer a single each. He struck out six.

The Giants got all they really needed to win in the very first inning when Roger Maris, racing in to make what would have been a headline play on a sinking line drive by Chuck Hiller, dropped the ball an instant after he took hold of it. It rolled on to deep right field and Chuck made two bases. Felipe Alou put him on third with a bunt and brother Matty Alou brought him in on an infield out to second base. McCovey's additional run just made it certain. A mighty blow that cleared the right-field fence by several yards, it seemed, to Giant fans, to augur blue skies and happy days at Candlestick.

At Yankee Stadium skies were indeed blue for the third game, but not for the Giant fans. Almost seventy-two thousand people, including thousands of Giant fans left behind when the club went west, piled into the ball park to create the biggest crowd since Milwaukee played here in 1958. Again both pitchers looked nearly indomitable. Billy Pierce, who used to give Casey Stengel fits when he pitched for the White Sox a few seasons earlier, granted only two hits in the first six innings, allowing Kubek and Howard each a non-scoring two-bagger. But aging Billy (going on thirty-six) weakened in the seventh inning. Tom Tresh opened the inning with a single and went to third when Mantle singled and Felipe Alou was handcuffed for a few moments by the sizzling jump of the ball. Mantle also took an extra base while Alou was trying to subdue the baseball. This put both runners in a position to score on Maris' single. This ball too bounced weirdly in the outfield and McCovey could not secure it, so Maris had two bases. Pierce was asked to sit down then while Don Larsen was given another chance to do his old comrades down. Don came close to winning, too. The only run he gave up came after a long fly by Howard had allowed Maris to advance to third. Then Don hit Skowron with a pitch. Don hadn't meant it that way but this dark deed set up a double play with a forceout at second as well as first. And the double play was right there to be plucked when the next batter, Clete Boyer, grounded neatly to Chuck Hiller at second base. But Chuck chose this moment to get the ball wedged in the webbing of his glove. He got it out in time to put Boyer out at first. But meanwhile Maris had scored with the run that made the difference. And the out that would have ended the inning remained in Hiller's glove, or some such place.

In the eighth the Giants hit another man with a baseball. But this time it was Bill Stafford, the pitcher, who was struck by a ball that came whistling off the bat of Felipe Alou and nearly removed Bill's leg at the knee joint. Bill scrambled for the ball, picked it up, nailed Alou at first, then rolled on the ground in pain. But he was damned if he would leave the ball game. The trainer took several minutes to mutter the incantations that stopped the leg from hurting and to okay Bill's ability to pitch with his proper motion. Bill was not quite himself when he resumed. Willie Mays drove one of Bill's pitches to deep left field for a double to open the ninth and moved to third on an infield out to the right side. He might just as well have held his ground, for the next safe hit was a home run by Ed Bailey. The Giant fans were all up and screaming for Jim Davenport to keep the action alive. But Stafford, steadying down, fed a fast ball to Davenport and Jim popped it to Tom Tresh for the final out.

Game number four saw a record set but it was not one that most fans remembered needed setting. It was instead one of those statistical oddities that only the true fanatic draws any juice from. In this game, Chuck Hiller, who was not one of the league's top hitters (he hit three home runs all season), slammed a home run into the lower right-field stands, the

Johnny Mize preserve, while three mates were on base. This was all the cause for celebration the Giant fans needed. It won the game for San Francisco. But the figure-fanatics cherished it because it was the first grand-slam home run ever hit by a National League batter in a World Series. Before Chuck hit this one, with Davenport, Matty Alou, and Bowman on base ahead of him, the score was tied 2 to 2. Each team got one more run in the ninth. Whitey Ford tried for this one but was taken out when the Yanks got a rally started in the sixth. Berra batted for him and Don Larsen came in to pitch to Yogi. He walked Yogi, and then completed his pitching for the day by throwing the next batter, Tony Kubek, out at first. But Don got credit for the victory because Hiller's four-run homer came in the next Giant inning.

In the fifth game, Ralph Terry scored the first World Series victory of his life, after four misses. The extra day off was apparently all he needed. Of course he needed the assistance of the batters too. Most of that was supplied by Tom Tresh, who made the first extra-base hit of the game and scored the first run. Tresh doubled to open the fourth, advanced on an infield forceout, then trotted home on a wild pitch. Workhorse Sanford, pitching strongly and grimly, saw another run get away when his catcher, Tom Haller, allowed a pitched ball to get adrift while Bobby Richardson was on third. Bobby gratefully accepted the opportunity to bring in the tying run. The Giant scores had been earned by the sweat of their own brows. In the third inning José Pagan singled, moved to second on a sacrifice, and scored on Chuck Hiller's two-bagger. In the fifth, José made the other score with a long, low home run into the seats in left field. But in the eighth inning Sanford began to show wear. He struck out Ralph Terry to begin with but the next three men turned tough on him. Kubek hit to right for one base. Richardson hit to left for another. Then Tom Tresh hit into the seats for four bases and three runs. A single and a double in the ninth put the Giants one run nearer but Terry stopped them right there.

When the Yanks got to San Francisco it was raining. It kept on raining for three days. Tarpaulins, prayers, optimistic forecasts, letters to Santa Claus, and even swirling helicopters turned loose over the wet sod by Horace Stoneham all availed nothing. The field became a sinkhole. When the rain stopped on October 15, the latest date for a World Series game since 1946, the outfield was like a newly dipped sponge and the infield was two degrees drier than a pig wallow. None of this troubled Billy Pierce, however. He had almost gone the distance last time. Now he was rested up enough for the full route. The long rest and the slow track made him a nine-inning pitcher once more. He gave only three hits, a home run, a double and a single, while his playmates reached an assortment of Yankee pitchers for ten. Ford made another start in this one but went down under a Giant broadside in the fifth inning. He gave seven walks, nine hits, and five runs. The wet field played a part in Ford's downfall. In the fourth, Felipe Alou singled. Willie Mays walked. Then Whitey tried a pick-off play on Alou, but he forgot he was handling a spitter. The wet ball slipped out of his hand and sailed out into center field, where it plopped into a puddle of mud. While Mantle was excavating to find the ball, Alou ran all the way home. Next up was Orlando Cepeda, who had never in his life, before this game, made a hit off an American League pitcher, despite appearances in three All-Star games and in three games of this series. Orlando had broken the spell with a lucky-bounce hit in the second inning. Now he got a real on-the-line two-bagger that brought home Mays and left Orlando where he could score on Davenport's single. In the fifth, three Giants hit singles to make one run. Then Orlando added another sure-enough hit to provide another run. And that was more than all the nine little Yankees could do.

The final game was the latest in the season of any World Series game in fifty years. In 1912, the final game had been played on the sixteenth of October too. This game at Candlestick Park was as tight a game as anyone could dream up, for not a single run was batted in. The Yankee run, the one that won the game, scored on a double play. And then the Giants came within an inch or two of tying it up in the ninth. Matty Alou bunted safely. The next two batters struck out. Willie Mays blasted a double to right, where Roger Maris, by a running pickup and cannonball throw, held Alou at third base. Next was big Willie McCovey, a man who was given to putting permanent dents in baseballs. McCovey drove the home fans to near hysteria by sending up a high, rocketing foul that had the smell, the sound, and the distance of a home run. Then he hit a good pitch right between the eyes and drove it ten feet high out over the infield—a solid single or even an extra-base blow. The stands rose up as one. The crowd roared. Ralph Terry's heart sank. But Bobby Richardson leaped high, high into the air, stabbed at the ball, and brought it down dead. With it of course he brought down the World Championship.

Leading hitters:

NEW YORK YANKEES
Tresh: .321

SAN FRANCISCO GIANTS
Pagan: .368

Winning pitchers:

NEW YORK YANKEES
Ford: won 1, lost 1
Terry: won 2, lost 1
Stafford: won 1, lost 0

SAN FRANCISCO GIANTS
Larsen: won 1, lost 0
Sanford: won 1, lost 2
Pierce: won 1, lost 1

1963

LOS ANGELES N.L. vs. NEW YORK A.L.

WON BY LOS ANGELES, 4 GAMES TO 0

Game Scores:

Los Angeles 5	New York 2	October 2 at New York
Los Angeles 4	New York 1	October 3 at New York
Los Angeles 1	New York 0	October 5 at Los Angeles
Los Angeles 2	New York 1	October 6 at Los Angeles

The Yankees did not begrudge, or hardly begrudged, the hapless Dodgers a victory in the World Series after so many misses. But there really was no need for the Dodgers to rub it in by taking four games in a row. It was enough to make a man wonder if perhaps old man Stengel did know something about the Dodgers that he forgot to tell the people when they fired him. It hardly seems as if any Stengel club would have fallen down and rolled over the way the Yankees of 1963 did in New York and in Los Angeles.

Not that there was not a struggle. But this time the Dodgers acted the part of the rich relatives and looked from the beginning like the club that was sure to win. What hardly anyone (except several thousand people in Los Angeles) expected was a complete shutout for the Yankees. The wise money, as usual, was on the Yankees and they remained favorites until the first

283

game was over. They had won the pennant easily while the Dodgers had saved it only by a last-minute set of three victories over a St. Louis team that seemed about to sweep on to complete victory. But once the Dodgers and Yanks met on the field, the boys from Los Angeles became everyone's favorite.

This was another series in which new records of every sort were set. Sandy Koufax—and the best part about Sandy was that, like the club itself, he was *born* in Brooklyn—broke Carl Erskine's World Series strikeout record by striking out fifteen Yankees. Whitey Ford, who already owned the World Series win record for pitchers, also set a new record for World Series losses by a pitcher—seven. Towering Frank Howard, Los Angeles' favorite monster movie, hit the first home run ever put into the upper left-field deck in the Dodgers' new park. The Yankees set a club World Series batting mark—.171—that was *almost* a record low. Walter Alston, Dodger manager, used only thirteen players altogether to win the series, the fewest ever employed since Connie Mack won the 1913 series with only twelve. The starting pitchers in the first two games were left-handers. And Sandy Koufax tied a record by striking out the first five batters to face him in the series. The winner's share of loot was a new high, $12,794. The loser's share was a record too, $7874.

Whitey Ford, as always, started for New York in the Stadium. It did not take him long to get the word on who was going to wind up on top. In the second inning, with one out, Frank Howard drove a ball on a line out to the most distant wall—a 460-foot double that would have gone right through an old-fashioned board fence and would have been a home run in many parks. Then Moose Skowron, a notorious "streak hitter" who had been dumped by the Yankees, made the first move in the drama called "The Moose's Revenge" by rifling a single over second base, sending Howard home. Dick Tracewski, Dodger substitute second baseman who was strictly a glove man, bounced a safe hit over the middle base. Then John Roseboro, the catcher, who owned a .236 season batting average, hit a hump-backed home run into the right-field seats that put the Dodgers four runs ahead. In the next inning, Jim Gilliam and Tommy Davis, the National League batting champ, both singled, and the vengeful Moose drove in a run with another sharp single. Ford got out of the game in the fifth inning when Hector Lopez went to bat for him and struck out. The rest of the Yankees were never *in* the game, it seemed. They were five runs down in the eighth when Tony Kubek outran a throw to first to scratch up an infield hit, and Tom Tresh, last year's hero, drove a home run into the stands, batting right-handed. At this point, Sandy Koufax already had struck out fourteen batters, the fourteenth being Bobby Richardson, who came up just before Tresh hit his homer. In the ninth, with two men out, Harry Bright, a utility man who had played most of the season in Washington, came to bat and nearly everyone in the park, with the Yankees pretty clearly out of it, was cheering for Harry to strike out. He did, too. And this guaranteed him a place in World Series records. In this game, everyone had centered so on Koufax' strikeouts that no one noticed that the Dodgers had put in a good part of the day hitting the polluted air themselves. They made ten strikeouts.

The second game brought out another brace of left-handers: John Podres and Al Downing. Podres had faced the Yankees four times in World Series play, since 1953, and he had beaten them twice. Al Downing was just completing his first full year with the Yankees. But Downing did well all the same and was beaten as much by the inept play of his teammates as by the batting of the enemy. Podres was the old master, however, and kept the Yankees without any runs until the final inning. Then he began to grow tired and Alston quickly replaced him with Ron Perranoski, best relief pitcher in the league.

Maury Wills opened the ball game with a single to center and went on to second when Joe Pepitone apparently missed the pick-off sign and moved in for a bunt when Downing snapped the ball to first. Joe grabbed the ball about a stone's throw off first base and turned to see little Maury hotfooting it on to second. Frantically Pepitone heaved the ball to second and wildly Bobby Richardson leaped for it. Maury dived in headfirst before Richardson came down with the ball. That play seemed to unsettle all the Yankees. This was like another session with Jackie

285

Robinson, when no one knew what he might not try to pull next. Jim Gilliam singled to right field and a fine throw by Roger Maris kept Wills from scoring. Then Willie Davis popped a fly to right and Maris got all twisted up trying to figure out how to reach it. He started in, then turned to run out, and promptly fell down. The ball fell safely and was called a double. Two runs scored.

In the fourth inning, the first man up was Moose Skowron, still bent on showing the Yankees what a mistake they had made in cutting him loose. There was no one on base this time for Moose to drive in, so he drove the first pitch into the stands and scored the third run himself. Soon afterward, Al Downing was recalled and Ralph Terry went out to keep the score where it was. In the eighth inning, Willie Davis hit a two-bagger and Tommy Davis rather overdid it by hitting a triple to bring him home. That put Los Angeles ahead 4 to 0. The Yanks got a minor look-in at the very end, when Mickey Mantle softened up Johnny Podres with a stinging line drive that sent Tom Davis nearly to the wall before he caught it. Then Hector Lopez bounced a fair ball into the left-field stands for a ground-rule double. Walter Alston at this point sent Perranoski to the rescue. Elston Howard hit Ron for a single, bringing in the only Yankee run. Then Perranoski got one out on Pepitone's ground ball and struck out Cletis Boyer.

Out in Los Angeles an adoring mob awaited their heroes. Only about fifty-six thousand people could get into the park there but more people were watching on television than had ever watched any World Series before. In the home opener, the Dodgers used their big right-hander, Don Drysdale, a native Californian, bigger than Koufax, although not quite the pitcher that Sandy had become, and like Koufax a member of the Dodgers staff since Ebbets Field days. Don was the best pitcher in the league in 1962, with twenty-five victories. This year it had been Koufax, with twenty-five wins, and Don had won just nineteen, with seventeen losses. But this World Series game was probably Don's best effort of the year. He gave the Yankees only three hits, two of them by Tony Kubek. The Dodgers made only four hits themselves, off Jim Bouton and Hal Reniff. But Bouton walked five of the Dodgers and that helped develop the game's only run.

In the first inning, with one out, Bouton walked Jim Gilliam. Willie Davis was out on an outfield fly. And then Bouton, one of the hardest throwers ever seen, threw a ball a bit too hard and it sailed to the backstop. Gilliam reached second on that and from there Tom Davis brought him home with a sizzling drive that bounced off the pitcher's mound and off Richardson's shins. That ended the day's scoring. Drysdale struck out nine and gave only one base on balls.

The tension in the final game had everyone screaming, for of course it was generally accepted that a four-straight beating by the Dodgers would constitute revenge enough for all the humiliations the ex-Brooklyn club had known at Yankee hands over the past two decades. It was Koufax and Ford again and this time they were much closer to being even. Sandy set no strikeout records—only eight in this game. But he was as good as he needed to be and allowed the Yanks only six hits. Still the Yanks were in the ball game right along and had a good chance to win it right up to the end, when an unbelievable error by Joe Pepitone sank their ship. It was ironical that Pepitone almost won the game for New York too, with a powerful drive that was hauled in by Ron Fairly just a few feet short of the fence.

Whitey Ford could hardly have done better than he did in this game. He allowed only two hits. Unhappily for him one of them had to be a two-block drive by Frank Howard that was the first batted ball ever to land safely in the upper tier of the left-field stands. Mickey Mantle, who had been nearly helpless at the plate this series, matched this blow with a home run every inch as long. But then the Dodgers got their other run when Pepitone lost Clete Boyer's long throw, after Boyer had stabbed a high-bounding ball by Gilliam. The ball, said Joe, disappeared in the background of white shirts and he could not find it. It hit his wrists and rolled off into foul ground, with Joe pounding after it. Gilliam made it all the way to third and Willie Davis brought him in from there with a long fly to Mickey Mantle, who was too far away to throw Gilliam out.

287

Hearts stopped in the Yankee ninth when young Dick Tracewski, who had played like a champion, almost did a Joe Pepitone
on an easy throw to second base. The throw was in Dick's glove,
the umpire had called the man out, Sandy Koufax had leaped
three feet into the air with a howl of triumph, when the ball
showed up, rolling foolishly away in the dirt. Dick had forgotten
to squeeze it. Now Bobby Richardson was safe at second and
Elston Howard was safe at first. Koufax had already struck out
the two switch-hitters, Tresh and Mantle, on changeups, but that
final out was still missing. Hector Lopez came to bat. Koufax
threw one pitch. Lopez topped it on the handle of his bat and
rolled it feebly to short, where Maury Wills ate it up and fired it
hard to first. This time when Koufax leaped up everybody else
leaped with him and even the Dodger brass counted the extra
cash well lost in this abbreviated triumph. They did point out
wistfully, later on, that, had it gone the distance, as Yankee series usually did, it would have grossed seven million dollars.

Leading hitters:

LOS ANGELES DODGERS
T. Davis: .400

NEW YORK YANKEES
Howard: .333

Winning pitchers:

LOS ANGELES DODGERS
Koufax: won 2, lost 0
Podres: won 1, lost 0
Drysdale: won 1, lost 0

1964

ST. LOUIS N.L. vs. NEW YORK A.L.

WON BY ST. LOUIS, 4 GAMES TO 3

Game Scores:

St. Louis 9	New York 5	October 7 at St. Louis
New York 8	St. Louis 3	October 8 at St. Louis
New York 2	St. Louis 1	October 10 at New York
St. Louis 4	New York 3	October 11 at New York
St. Louis 5	New York 2	October 12 at New York
New York 8	St. Louis 3	October 14 at St. Louis
St. Louis 7	New York 5	October 15 at St. Louis

In 1964, the series went the limit again, as it so often did when the Yankees were in it. And it wound up in the wildest switch of personnel that ever took place outside of musical comedy, with the Yankee manager being fired, the St. Louis manager resigning, and the Yankees then hiring the St. Louis manager to replace the man they just fired.

All this came about really because, long past midseason, both clubs looked as if they had lost the pennant and it took a series of losses by the enemy and unexpected triumphs by the Cards and Yanks to get them both into the World Series. In both leagues the pennant races were decided by one-game margins. Long before they were settled, the brass of both clubs had made up their minds that the managers would have to go. The Cards moved first, firing their general manager, Bing Devine, who promptly signed with the New York Mets. This move prompted their manager, Johnny Keane, to type out his own resignation, which he saved until after the series was over. Of course no big league club owner would offer a job to the leader of a rival club when he was still on the rival club's payroll. That would be tampering, and baseball club owners, all being honorable men, would hardly stoop so low. Still Keane might have had a suspicion there would be an opening on the Yankees—or somewhere—by the time the season was over. The only man who seems not to have had a suspicion was Lawrence Berra, who had won the pennant in his first year as manager, but had won it too slow, and had failed to live up to the caricature of himself the sportswriters had created. Yogi, called into a conference with the Yankee leaders, thought he was going to discuss a new contract. Instead he discussed a new job—a nothing job that would keep his name on the payroll and pay him twenty-five thousand dollars a year. How badly jolted he was by this development, only his friends ever knew.

But next thing anyone knew, Yogi was with the Mets. This was managed without any tampering, for George Weiss of the Mets, owning an old-fashioned conscience, studiously steered clear of Yogi, despite his own eagerness to add Yogi's name to the roster. But a friend stepped in, carried the word to Yogi, and Yogi up and asked what the outlook was at the Mets. He wound up with a better job, and with the Yankee salary still in his pocket.

As for the World Series, that was old-fashioned in its suspense and high excitement. Injured men tottered to the plate and worked wonders. Heroes struck out. Decisions were angrily protested. New records for home runs were made. Creaking veterans outstripped the younger men and turned into heroes again.

The worst thing that happened to the Yankees in the first game was not merely losing the game but losing their best pitcher, the old reliable Whitey Ford. Whitey's arm went bad in this game and laid him up for the series. He would require a fantastic operation before he ever recovered his skill.

The St. Louis hero of the series was pitcher Bob Gibson, a

long lean and powerful young man who struck out more batters in the series than anyone had ever struck out before in a seven-game World Series. But there was a movement afoot also to name Tim McCarver, the St. Louis catcher, President of the United States, or at least Dictator of St. Louis, for all the mighty batting feats he performed. Hero of the pennant drive had been Barney Schultz, the grizzled knuckle-baller, who, some said, had escaped alive from the battle of the Little Big Horn, or some affray not much more recent, and who had worn the uniform of over sixteen different ball clubs. Barney tried to be a hero in the series but made it only once. Back in New York there were those sourpusses who growled that if Bobby Richardson had been able to get some of those double-play balls out of his glove in time, the Yanks would have triumphed. But Bobby, brooding over his failures, bravely quoted the Bible to prove that almost any man was likely to commit a sin or bobble a baseball.

The first game blew up in the sixth inning, when the Yankees were ahead 4 to 2. Up to this point Ford had allowed five hits and had struck out four. The Yanks had made their runs on hard wallops off Ray Sadecki. In the second inning, Howard singled and Tom Tresh hit a home run. Clete Boyer singled and stole a base. Ford singled, scoring Boyer. Linz walked. Bobby Richardson hit a long, long single into left field on which Ford tried to score. But Lou Brock, the prize package brought in from Chicago in a trade that prompted the St. Louis club owner to fire the general manager, cut Ford down with a trolley-wire throw from deep left field.

In the sixth, St. Louis unloaded their bombs. Brother Ken Boyer opened with a single. Rookie Mike Shannon, a local boy, then hit one of the mightiest home runs ever seen in the park—a 450-foot drive that boomed off the wall. McCarver then hit for two bases and Ford knew he had nothing left. Al Downing came in to pitch but was immediately set upon by pinch-hitter Carl Warwick, who hit a single, and center fielder Curt Flood, who hit for three bases and sent pinch-runner Javier home. That accounted for four runs. St. Louis scored three more times while

291

the Yanks could score only once. Barney Schultz gave only four hits the rest of the way.

The second game turned matters around. Rookie pitcher Mel Stottlemyre, who had started that season in Richmond, went the whole nine innings for New York and once having been given a lead managed to cling to it. The Yankees, with a lead of 4 to 2, put the game on ice in the ninth inning, but the game was really won in the sixth when a disputed call by the plate umpire seemed to take the starch out of the St. Louis pitcher Bob Gibson. Gibson had looked stronger even than Stottlemyre from the beginning. He had struck out six batters in the first four innings and allowed one run. In the sixth, he fired one of his smoke balls close to Joe Pepitone and Umpire McKinley ruled that Joe, who had pulled away from the pitch, and seemed to have fouled it off, had been nicked on the uniform. Joe did not seem to believe it himself but he gladly accepted the free base while all the Cardinals roared a protest. Mickey Mantle, his ailing leg wrapped in bandages, had already walked, so this pushed him to second base. A single by Tom Tresh brought him home. In the next inning, Gibson wobbled even more. The first three batters, Linz, Richardson, and Maris, all hit singles to add two runs, with the help of a groundout by Mantle. And in the ninth the Yankees got to Barney Schultz, who had permitted only one home run in the regular season. Phil Linz started him toward the bench with a home run and Maris finished him with a single. But the Yankees took to relief pitcher George Richardson just as heartily and kept right on hitting until they had more runs than they needed.

The third game was played in New York and the home fans were relieved to see that their heroes looked as unbeatable as ever. This was the tightest of all the games, and the best-pitched, with Jim Bouton giving only six hits and Curt Simmons giving only four. But Simmons pitched only eight innings. Barney Schultz gave up the hit that lost the ball game. New York scored first, on a single by Howard, a walk to Pepitone, and a double by Boyer. St. Louis got the run back in the fifth inning on McCarver's single that was good for two bases when Mantle mishan-

292

dled the ball in the outfield. McCarver got to third on an infield out and scored when Curt Simmons, the pitcher, powered a hot drive directly at Clete Boyer, who fought it off but could not field it. Still, if McCarver had been on second, or on first, he would never have made it home.

In the ninth inning, the manager lost the ball game by taking out his pitcher to use a pinch-hitter to bring the winning run home. McCarver reached first on an error, and was sacrificed to second. Then Johnny Keane sent veteran Bob Skinner up to hit for Simmons. Skinner hit a fly ball to Maris and the next batter, Curt Flood, popped one to Mickey Mantle. When the Yanks came up, they finished it in a rush. Barney Schultz threw one pitch to Mickey Mantle, and Mickey drove it back three times as fast as it had been thrown and six times as far. It was Mickey's sixteenth World Series home run, a World Series record, and it was the winning run too.

The Cardinals evened up the game count next day, in another tight ball game. The man who won this game had been trying for a long long time to win a ball game in New York. He was Roger Craig, who had lost twenty-four games for the Mets in 1962 and twenty-two in 1963. He had beat the Yankees before in a World Series, in 1955. The starting pitcher for St. Louis was Ray Sadecki, and Ray should have remained in bed on this bitter cold day. The first four men to face him hit safely. Before he could get more than one man out there were three runs charged against him. But then Craig came in, looking more like Slim Summerville than ever, and amazed the Yankees and their fans by striking out eight New York batters in 4⅔ innings. By the sixth inning, the St. Louis batters had got their breaths back and were ready to commit a mass assault upon Yankee pitcher Al Downing. Pinch-hitter Warwick started with a single. Curt Flood followed with another single. An error by Bobby Richardson filled the bases. Then Ken Boyer cleaned them all off with a blow that sailed right inside the left-field foul line into the stands. That was all the scoring of the game and Yankee fans went home sulking over Richardson's ball-caught-in-the-webbing bit that led to a hurried throw and error, and at Roger Craig's amazing pick-off of Mantle on second base. But New York fans had often seen that miraculous pick-off move of Craig's. It had been all the Met fans had to cheer about in many games.

In the fifth game, St. Louis went ahead once more in a ten-inning hair-raiser that set the New York fans to moaning over the errors their heroes committed, and the victory that might have been. But no one had any right to take this ball game away from Bob Gibson, who struck out thirteen Yankees, and himself pulled off a fast-thinking play that unquestionably saved the ball game. With the Cardinals ahead 2 to 0, in the ninth inning, Mantle reached first on an error. Gibson struck out Elston Howard. Then Joe Pepitone drove a pitch directly back at Gibson. It struck the big pitcher on the hip and bounced off toward the third-base line. Gibson was after it like an aroused spider. He snatched it up off the grass, turned awkwardly, and snapped the ball off-balance to first. It just nipped Pepitone, who threw a public tantrum when the umpire signaled him out. But for one reason or another the umpire stuck to his decision, letting Pepitone and Berra howl and stamp. Bob Gibson, limping ever so slightly, tried to get a fast ball by the next batter, Tom Tresh, but Tresh drove it far over the wire screen in right-center field. That tied the score. If Pepitone had been on base it would have won the ball game. But the Cards did that in the next inning when the Yanks began to misuse the baseball. White walked at the start. Then Ken Boyer, trying to lay down a sacrifice bunt, put one down that the Yanks could not get to, and he reached first safely. Groat then tried to sacrifice and missed the ball completely, leaving the lead runner Bill White completely at sea off second base. Elston Howard got the ball down there to pick him off by three yards, but White chose to run on to third and Phil Linz, unsettled by this improper move, bounced his throw to third baseman Gonzalez and White was safe. Groat then hit into a forceout. Then up strode young Tim McCarver, hottest of all batters in this series. He looked at many different pitches. With the count three and two, he swung at a good one and put

294

the ball into the right-field stands for a three-run homer. The Yanks could do nothing more.

When the clubs returned to St. Louis, the home fans never doubted that the series was as good as won. But the Yanks conceded nothing. To lose two World Series in a row! That would be too much. So they bided their time against pitcher Curt Simmons, then clouted him in the fifth and sixth innings. The Cards were ahead 1 to 0 at this time, when Tom Tresh opened the fifth inning with a two-base hit. After Simmons struck a man out and got another one on an infield roller, Jim Bouton, the pitcher, hit an honest single to center and Tresh scored. In the next inning, Maris and Mantle, in single file, hit home runs to right field. Mantle was batting right-handed, too. This convinced Johnny Keane that Simmons was a loser and he lifted him in the next inning. But Schultz and Richardson looked even better to the Yankees. They got a run off Schultz in the eighth and then filled the bases on him. At this point George Richardson came in to pitch to Pepitone, and Pepitone, sick of being hooted at by the St. Louis fans, hit a grand slam home run to make the score 8 to 2.

The Yanks went into the final game, confident they could pull the thing out of the fire. They had done this any number of times before. And they did come frighteningly close, leaving the St. Louis fans limp. Both Gibson and Stottlemyre seemed strong and confident as they faced off for the finale. And possibly if the Yanks had been able to complete a double play Stottlemyre would have lasted. He was working with only two days off; but so was Gibson. In the fourth inning, Ken Boyer, who except for his fourth-game home run, had not accomplished much with his bat up to now, opened the inning with a single. Groat received a walk. Stottlemyre, who specialized in forcing batters to hit into the dirt, fed a nice low pitch to the next man, Tim McCarver. Tim hit it hard into the turf and it streaked straight for Pepitone's glove. Joe got off a fine throw to Phil Linz to make the out at second, but when Linz undertook to snap the ball back to Stottlemyre, who covered first, the ball bounced on the base path and rolled to the stands. Boyer kept right on going to cross the plate with the first run.

Mike Shannon singled then to push McCarver over to third. Then the two youngsters staged a double steal, just as their daddies used to do. Howard powered the ball to Richardson, who ran in to grab it short and fire it back. But the play had really caught him unawares and he threw into the dirt. The ball got by and McCarver was safe at the plate. Maxvill then singled to send Shannon home and this put the Cards three runs ahead and finished Stottlemyre. Al Downing took over for the Yanks in the fifth inning. He threw just one pitch to Lou Brock and merry Lou drove it on a line into the cheap seats for a home run. Al's second pitch was turned into a single by Bill White. Then Ken Boyer banged a two-base hit to right field and Berra decided he needed a right-handed pitcher, or at least a different one. He tried Roland Sheldon, who got the side out for him. Now it was St. Louis 6, New York 0. But the home fans were not permitted to rest easy. In the sixth inning, Gibson, who had every right to be tired, eased up a bit too much on the Yanks. Richardson beat out an infield hit. Maris laced a single to right. Then Mickey Mantle, whose aches and pains had not held him back much at the plate, landed on a Gibson fast ball and hit another right-field home run, good for three runs. In the seventh Ken Boyer hastened to make the lead a little bit longer by hitting a bases-empty homer off Sheldon. Then in the ninth both Phil Linz and Clete Boyer hit home runs, to make it four home runs in a row, counting the work of both clubs. Johnny Keane refused to give up on Gibson just because he had let the Yanks draw within two runs. And the determined right-hander struck out two of the last three batters to win the championship like a champion.

Leading hitters:

ST. LOUIS CARDINALS
McCarver: .478

NEW YORK YANKEES
Richardson: .406

Winning pitchers:

ST. LOUIS CARDINALS
Sadecki:	won 1, lost 0
Gibson:	won 2, lost 1
Craig:	won 1, lost 0

NEW YORK YANKEES
Stottlemyre:	won 1, lost 1
Bouton:	won 2, lost 0

1965

LOS ANGELES N.L. vs. MINNESOTA A.L.

WON BY LOS ANGELES, 4 GAMES TO 3

Game Scores:

Minnesota 8	Los Angeles 3	October 6 at Twin Cities
Minnesota 5	Los Angeles 1	October 7 at Twin Cities
Los Angeles 4	Minnesota 0	October 9 at Los Angeles
Los Angeles 7	Minnesota 2	October 10 at Los Angeles
Los Angeles 7	Minnesota 0	October 11 at Los Angeles
Minnesota 5	Los Angeles 1	October 13 at Twin Cities
Los Angeles 2	Minnesota 0	October 14 at Twin Cities

Anyone with any sense at all could have told you in advance that if the Minnesota Twins could take a game from Drysdale and one from Koufax they were a cinch to beat the Dodgers in the 1965 World Series. The trouble was that nobody with any sense figured the Twins could beat either of those pitchers. Nor did anybody suspect that Claude Osteen would be the pitcher to win the Dodgers' first victory.

But that is always the way in a World Series. It's always a Claude Osteen or a Cookie Lavagetto or a Lou Johnson or a Pepper Martin who turns out to be a hero, while the season heroes too often evolve into World Series busts. It is not that either of the mighty Dodger pitchers turned into a bust. But each man did lose his first start. And the heroes were men who had earned only the narrowest fame before these seven games were played.

There was Lou Johnson, for instance. Lou practically epitomized the Dodgers' winning spirit and the ineffable joy of competition. Yet before the World Series games were played, Lou was just a permanent minor leaguer who had had his two or three shots at the big time and never made it. Lou had played for sixteen or more different minor league clubs, all the way from the Pony League to the Pacific Coast League, and including the Three-I and the Mountain States. His best hitting had been done for Paris of the Midwest League. He had played thirty-four games for the Cubs in 1960 and had batted .206. But he was alive with the desire to get to the top in baseball and to hang on there. He had the effervescence of a Willie Mays, even if only half the skills, and he rejoiced openly in every success, so that the fans made him their favorite.

The man who drew first blood for the Dodgers was a journeyman pitcher who had been traded back and forth between the leagues. The chief advantage he had was his proven ability to beat the Minnesota Twins. While he worked for Washington, Claude beat Minnesota five straight times. And in spite of an unspectacular won-lost record (15 and 15) he owned a handsome earned-run average of 2.79.

The Minnesota hero was a man who had once been fined for not trying hard enough. He tried hard enough in the series and if the Twins had won he would have been the man largely responsible. He was Zoilo Versalles, Minnesota shortstop, one of the fastest men in the game, and a scrappy, never-say-die performer, who was almost the whole show in the first game. He hit a home run and a single, batted in four runs and stole a base, besides performing his usual miracles in the field. Another recordmaker was Minnesota rookie Frank Quilici, a .208 batter during the season who made two hits in the third inning of the first game.

Everybody knew the Twins had the hitting and the Dodgers had the speed and the pitching. Everything depended on the ability of the Dodger pitchers to hold down the score. In the first game, Don Drysdale felt lucky to hold the Twins to seven runs. The Twins got one run away from him in the second inning, just after the Dodgers had scored. Twin first baseman Don Mincher hit a home run to tie the score. In the third inning, Quilici rolled the ball down over third base. It hopped into left field and trickled on and on, while he ran to second base. Then Mudcat Grant, the pitcher, laid down a bunt to push the man to third. Don Drysdale, scurrying to field the ball, slipped on the sod and found himself sitting on his duff with the ball in his hand. From this non-recommended position he tried to flip the ball to Jim Lefebvre, who was covering first. Jim scooped the ball up and tried desperately to get it tight in his glove. The umpire stabbed his fist in the out sign, then swept out both hands to indicate Grant was safe. That was when Zoilo came up and fired his home run into the left-field bleachers. Sandy Valdespino, next up, hit for two bases. It was obvious that Drysdale's trip to the sod had cost him his effectiveness. His knee had taken a twist and his stride was not the same. He did get Tony Oliva out on a ground ball. But Harmon Killebrew then singled and Don Mincher walked. Earl Battey, next at bat, looped a single into short right field, bringing two runs home. Then Quilici came up for the second time in the inning and hit a single. At this point Manager Alston took Drysdale out. But the horse had been stolen long before. The Dodgers got a lone run in the ninth but the Twins had already made eight, so this availed very little.

Game number two brought Sandy Koufax out to get even. But the Twins were no more awed by him than they had been by Drysdale. Again it was Zoilo Versalles who delivered the best blow, a three-base hit on which he soon came in to score. Koufax in six innings in this game gave up six hits and two runs. The extra runs were made off reliever Ron Perranoski. Jim Kaat, the Minnesota pitcher, gave up seven well-scattered hits.

The play that set Koufax to wobbling was an error by Jim Gilliam. He booted a ground ball, hit hard by Zoilo Versalles, and Zoilo, who could outrun his shadow, made it all the way to second base. Joe Nossek moved him to third with a bunt and Tony Oliva, leading batter in the American League, made sure he got

300

home by hitting a double. Then Harmon Killebrew brought Oliva home with a single and the Twins had all the runs they needed. But the Dodgers scored a run in the seventh inning on a single by John Roseboro that brought Ron Fairly home, so the Twins went out and got a few more. The game had already been saved by Bob Allison, the Minnesota left fielder, who pursued a sliced drive off the bat of Jim Lefebvre and caught up with it just as everyone had decided the ball would fall safe. If it had it would have been good for at least two bases and maybe three, would have driven in a run and put the tying run in scoring position. Bob's catch was one worthy of the series, a reckless drive toward the wire fence that ended with a shoetop catch and a tumbling slide along the grass. As soon as he had coasted to a stop, Bob lifted his glove high to show the umpire he still held the ball.

With all this championship fielding and batting, teamed with tight pitching, and added to the fact that the Dodgers had used up their best pitchers in vain, the Minnesota fans settled down to await the coming triumph and the wild celebration. But right away they were reminded that they were not playing with kids. When they moved to Los Angeles, Claude Osteen came out to play with them and he was one man they just loathed seeing on the mound. Claude gave their big ugly batsmen just five hits, with only Versalles getting more than a single. The Dodgers meanwhile teed off happily on Camilo Pascual. They could not get their hits close enough together to score, however, until the fourth inning, when Ron Fairly doubled and Lou Johnson, to everyone's amazement, bunted him on to third. Lefebvre singled. Then Wes Parker walked and the next man, John Roseboro, drove two runners home with a good long single to right field. A single by Willie Davis and a double by suddenly rejuvenated Lou Johnson added another run in the fifth and persuaded Manager Sam Mele that he had better use a pinch-hitter for Pascual. The pinch-hitter grounded out. Rookie Jim Merritt then tried getting the Dodgers out but they worked him for another run, on a single by Wes Parker and a double by Maury Wills, who was not supposed to hit—just run. To show how completely out of kilter all advance dope could be, Wills was quickly picked off second base by the new pitcher. Both sides lost men through painful injuries in this game. Jim Lefebvre hurt his foot while crossing the plate with the second run and catcher Earl Battey of Minnesota, running for a high foul that was falling at the edge of the stands, nearly decapitated himself on a neck-high railing. Dazed and unable to speak, he had to leave the game.

In the next game, Don Drysdale came back, determined he was not going to slip and fall down again. He had a tough opponent in Mudcat Grant, but this time Don had big hitters on his side. Lou Johnson and Wes Parker hit home runs to match those hit by Killebrew and Oliva. And the Twins committed errors of judgment and performance, only two of which showed up in the score. In the first inning, the Dodgers played Dodger baseball, running and taking advantage of the breaks. Maury Wills hit a feeble roller toward Don Mincher, the Minnesota first baseman. Don got hold of the ball but had to wait for pitcher Grant to get to first base. Then he let the ball go half-heartedly, so it arrived along with the runner, who piled into Grant, who knocked into the umpire, who staggered a bit and called Maury Wills safe. Then Willie Davis tried the same bit. He chopped a ball to Mincher. Again Mudcat Grant was slow in making the scene, and again Mincher, after starting to outrace Davis, tossed the ball in late and everybody went down in a heap. Davis was safe and Wills was discovered perched on third. The irony of it all was that these two clown acts were scored as hits. And then, when Ron Fairly hit a slow ground ball to Quilici, the Twins missed the double play and Maury Wills scored.

In the second inning, the Dodgers started that play-for-the-break system all over again. Wes Parker bunted and made it to first. He stole second and when Mudcat Grant's pitch flew right past the catcher, he kept going to third. John Roseboro grounded to Quilici and Quilici let the ball go through his legs, so Parker came in with run number two, and nothing yet that really looked like a hit. But when the Twins started to get tough, the Dodgers responded in kind. Killebrew's fourth-inning home run was immediately matched by Wes Parker. Then Oliva hit a home run in the sixth and the Dodgers quickly staged another track meet.

Willie Davis hit a single to Tony Oliva, with Gilliam on first. Oliva made a useless effort to catch Gilliam at third and the ball went on by the relay man, allowing Davis to reach second. Al Worthington came in to pitch then and Ron Fairly welcomed him with a single. Again a futile effort to hold the lead runner missed the cut-off man and gave Fairly an extra base. Then Lou Johnson bunted. Worthington pounced on the ball—but everyone else had wanted to field it too, so there was nobody to cover the base. Quilici scurried toward first at the last minute, Worthington flipped a hasty throw at him, Quilici missed it, and Fairly just kept on running until he crossed the plate. The Twins tried hard to catch up, but the Dodger fielding was just too strong for them. And a home run by Lou Johnson made it certain. Don Drysdale had eleven strikeouts.

Now that Drysdale had done it, Sandy Koufax decided he could too. And naturally he did. The game he pitched the following day did not even have the Twins in it, as far as scoring threats were concerned. The Twins got four singles and Koufax struck out ten. The Dodgers hit hard, ran fast, and grabbed every advantage, just as if the Twins were keeping it close. Willie Davis stole three bases and Maury Wills stole one. Altogether the Dodgers made fourteen hits, three of them by Ron Fairly and four by Wills. At one point, Frank Quilici had a chance to discover that Joe Pepitone was right about the way throws from third to first disappeared against the white-shirt background. It was a warm day and when Frank ran to cover first in the opening inning, on Jim Gilliam's sacrifice bunt, the throw from Harmon Killebrew just went right through Quilici. Not that this affected the game. Any one of the Dodgers' seven runs would have been enough. Koufax went through the first twelve Minnesota batters without allowing a man to reach first.

The sixth game was a triumph for a man who won the first game and had deserved to win the fourth—Mudcat Grant, the courageous and hardworking Minnesota pitcher. Mudcat applied his own bat to the job of beating the Dodgers, back home in Minnesota, and he batted in three juicy runs on a handsome homer into the left-field seats. The Dodgers scored only once, on

Ron Fairly's home run in the seventh inning. By that time Mudcat had a five-run lead and he could afford to let one get away.

Mudcat's home run came in the sixth inning. Bob Allison walked with one out and stole second base as Don Mincher was striking out. This left an open base, where the Dodgers decided to put Frank Quilici, who was bound to be a tougher man than the pitcher, who would be next at bat. But Mudcat came up ready to hit. He did not even look at a pitch but jumped on the first ball and sent it out of the park, to his own loud delight.

The Twins tried to slow the Dodgers down by loading their diamond with loose sand, part of which they were ordered to remove. But even after they had taken off a wheelbarrow load or two there was still enough left to cut down on those stolen bases and to slow down the baseline choppers. "That's what a diamond is supposed to be like!" said Minnesota Coach Billy Martin. The umpires did not quite agree.

It was obvious that Sandy Koufax would be called on to put the championship on ice. Even Don Drysdale, whose "turn" it was, agreed that if he had been manager he'd have sent Sandy out after this one. Sandy was as sharp as ever in this game. But Jim Kaat was sharp too and there was no fat lead for Sandy to work with. He needed none, however. He allowed only three hits, one a double by Quilici, and struck out ten. He wound up the game with two sizzling strikeouts and only once seemed in danger of yielding a run. That was in the fifth inning, when Quilici hit his two-bagger. Pinch-hitter Rich Rollins walked. Then Zoilo Versalles pounded a ball down the third-base line, a sure two-bagger or triple if it got by. But Jim Gilliam, the third baseman, dived hard to his right, snagged the ball backhanded, and scurried to third to make a forceout on the approaching runner. After that, the Twins had no chance.

Lou Johnson celebrated the finest week of his career by hitting the foul pole with a home run drive in the fourth inning. And Ron Fairly got another double to lead all the hitters with an average of .379. Versalles and Killebrew, with .286, were the best Minnesota hitters. And that was not the way it was supposed to be at all. But then, in a World Series, it seldom is.

Leading hitters:

LOS ANGELES DODGERS
Fairly: .379

MINNESOTA TWINS
Versalles and Killebrew: .286

Winning pitchers:

LOS ANGELES DODGERS
Drysdale: won 1, lost 1
Koufax: won 2, lost 1
Osteen: won 1, lost 1

MINNESOTA TWINS
Grant: won 2, lost 1
Kaat: won 1, lost 2

1966

BALTIMORE A.L. vs. LOS ANGELES N.L.

WON BY BALTIMORE, 4 GAMES TO 0

Game Scores:

Baltimore 5	Los Angeles 2	October 5 at Los Angeles
Baltimore 6	Los Angeles 0	October 6 at Los Angeles
Baltimore 1	Los Angeles 0	October 8 at Baltimore
Baltimore 1	Los Angeles 0	October 9 at Baltimore

Before the 1966 World Series began, and experts all over the country propounded that the Dodgers would most likely win on their pitching, Hank Bauer, the battle-scarred ex-Yankee who managed the Orioles, kept urging that his pitchers were "not all that bad." When the series was over, and the Baltimore pitchers had set new records for depriving the other side of runs, he was heard to murmur: "I didn't think our pitchers were all that good."

Whether they were all that good or the Dodgers, at bat, were all that bad would never be known. But the records were plain to read. The Dodgers had set a new low in batting for a World Series: a team average of .142. The strength of their own pitching was indicated by a new low batting average for a *winning* club in a World Series: the Oriole team average of .200. The Oriole bats, however, and especially the bats of Frank and Brooks Rob-

306

inson and Paul Blair, were those that would be remembered and memorialized, while the sensational pitching of a forgotten man named Moe Drabowsky, who had been passed around the other league like an unwanted relative, perhaps best symbolized the Oriole triumph. Moe had not been analyzed by the experts before the series and had not figured to do more than plod in to toil a few vain innings against the Dodgers' matchless Sandy Koufax or their nearly matchless Don Drysdale.

Every World Series has to turn some near-nobody into a hero, however. The Brooklyn Dodgers had had their Sandy Amoros and their Al Gionfriddo. The Philadelphia Athletics had Howard Ehmke. The Cardinals had Pepper Martin. The Giants had Dusty Rhodes. And now the Orioles contributed this Polish-born, aging (thirty-one), undistinguished right-hander, who came into the first game in the third inning, struck out eleven (a new record for a World Series reliever), allowed only one hit, and gave up not a single earned run. His mates had provided him with runs enough to win on, chiefly through home runs by the two Robinsons—Frank, also an exile from the other league, and Brooks, a slightly built young man who did not look strong enough to push a bunt past the pitcher. In the first three innings, the Dodgers had given up more runs than they had yielded in five previous home World Series games in 1964 and 1965. But they did set one record that helped bring the gleam back to the eyes of their owners: Despite a less-than-capacity crowd and thanks to a capacity price (twelve dollars for a box seat), they established a new record for one-game gate receipts: $557,336.

Losing the first game did not dismay the Dodgers in the least. They had almost always come from behind to win (when they did win) the World Series. But the second game all but destroyed them. This one—the one they were *sure* to win because the great Koufax would pitch—was quickly kicked into the depths of Chavez Ravine when Willie Davis, a thoroughly experienced outfielder, dropped two fly balls in a row, and threw one ball nearly into the stands. The autumn sun did blind him, for it shone straight into his face. But still—three errors in a row! He could have caught both flies and it might not have done much good, however, for the Orioles had produced another non-famous pitcher, who did not permit a single Dodger to cross the plate. Jim Palmer, a twenty-year-old who would have gladly agreed he was lucky to be in the same park with Sandy Koufax, out-pitched old sore-arm Sandy from first to last. He gave up three singles and a double, walked three, and struck out six. Sandy allowed six hits, including a triple by Frank Robinson, and Willie Davis let in three unearned runs. Jim Gilliam, Ron Fairly, and Ron Perranoski each supplied an error in this game to help the Dodgers tie the World Series record of six in a game. If the official scorer had been a touch less soft-hearted he might have made it seven, for Jim Gilliam butchered the very first batted ball of the game and let it become a base hit.

When the teams went to Baltimore to play the games shrewdly scheduled by the new commissioner to take place on a weekend, the Oriole fans were convinced their boys would make it four in a row; and some of the Dodger fans had begun to believe it too. Where would they ever find the pitching they needed to become invincible again, now that Drysdale and Koufax were obviously worn down to the handle?

They very nearly found it in Claude Osteen, who pitched the third game. Claude gave up only three hits, walked one, and struck out three. But one of the hits was a home run by still another National League reject, center fielder Paul Blair. And the Dodgers, for all their determination, could not match it. The Orioles had sent in their own sore-armed pitcher, Wallace Bunker, a twenty-one-year-old right-hander who had posted a mediocre record during the season because of an injured elbow. In the game he could not throw a curve and did not have much of a fast ball. But he managed to keep the ball where the Dodgers could not damage it.

Before the final game, the Dodgers spoke cheerfully of winning four in a row and of the advantage they would own when they "got back to Los Angeles." But when they got back to Los Angeles, it was to hang up their ball suits for the season, because the

308

Orioles did not allow them any more runs at all, let alone another ball game.

The Dodgers had some reason to hope in the last game, however, for the Orioles, instead of bringing back one of their winners, gave another chance to right-handed Dave McNally, the only pitcher the Dodgers had been able to score any runs on. This time, however, Dave gave only four hits and no runs, to help the Dodgers establish a new record for consecutive scoreless innings in the World Series: thirty-three. Not since the World Series of 1905, when Christy Mathewson and Iron Man McGinnity helped the Giants beat the Philadelphia Athletics, had any club gone through three games in a row without scoring.

Don Drysdale, for the Dodgers, pitched one of his best games in losing number four. He too gave only four hits and struck out five, while walking only one. But one of the hits he granted was a home run by Frank Robinson. Soon after Robinson put the pitch in the stands, Willie Davis, the three-error man, made a truly incredible catch of a long drive by Baltimore's Boog Powell, a blow that would have given the Orioles still another run. But they needed only one and poor Willie's deed was soon forgotten.

The odds against four Baltimore victories in a row had been 20 to 1 at the start of the series. When it really happened, many a Baltimorean was made rich and all were made hysterical. But there was no champagne in the Oriole clubhouse. They had had some of that to celebrate winning the pennant, and nearly everybody had got sick on it. So they just threw towels around and shoved fully dressed people under the shower and squirted shaving cream out of pressure cans all over each other.

There were many who said, after this series, that Hank Bauer, that tough old Yankee, had won the series in Yankee style—coming up with the mighty wallop when it was needed, and providing the crafty pitching and tight fielding when they needed *that*. But it is doubtful if many old Yankees would agree. Win a series with a club batting average of .200? As Robin might say, Holy Babe Ruth!

Leading hitters:

BALTIMORE ORIOLES
D. Johnson and F. Robinson: .286
LOS ANGELES DODGERS
L. Johnson: .267

Winning pitchers:

BALTIMORE ORIOLES
Drabowsky: won 1, lost 0
Palmer: won 1, lost 0
Bunker: won 1, lost 0
McNally: won 1, lost 0